Creation to Resurrection

Creation to Resurrection

ISBN 0-9714539-2-6

First Printing March 2005
Second Printing December 2007
Third Printing October 2008
Fourth Printing December 2009
Fifth Printing December 2013

For additional copies visit your
local bookstore or contact:

The Blank Family
3230 Strasburg Road
Parkesburg, PA 19365

2673 Township Road 421
Sugarcreek, OH 44681

Contents

Preface

I AM NOT AN ARCHAEOLOGIST digging up artifacts which have not seen the light of day for many centuries. During my three score and twelve years, several Indian arrowheads are about the only very old items I have ever uncovered.

The profession of the tedious digging up around old historical sites, or going through fragile, yellowed papers in old, rarely visited archives, has produced much of the primary source of material for the writers of ancient history over the years.

However, the secondary information found in the pages that follow have all been dug up the easy way. What I have put on paper is a mix of what has been gleaned out of a multitude of Bible dictionaries and histories, along with the fascinating articles found in numerous encyclopedias and yearbooks.

All that I write about is secondhand. I have not dug up anything new out of the earth. Any history scholars looking for new and undiscovered historical facts will have to look elsewhere. This is not a book written by a scientist for other scientists. Much of what I learned was by looking up something and finding something altogether different on the way.

If I would have the ability to pass this on in a form only half as interesting as it was to me as I was reading it, my time and efforts spent in writing would be richly rewarded.

It may soon be evident to you that the pages in this book are not written on the level of the academic standards of professional historians. What follows is written with the eighth-grade limits of the one-room country schools of our plain people in mind. Much of what is written in books above that level is like a foreign language to most of us in these church groups.

Each of the chapters in this book is an essay in itself, so there may be some overlaps in some places. They are being sent forth with the hope and prayers that more of our young people will become interested in God's weaving of history with the Bible. Despite the greatness of the pharaohs, kings, and emperors of the past, their puny powers stepped aside when our overruling God guided history into the channels which only He could have foreseen.

To make a complete list of the treasury of sources available for further study for those becoming interested in the lessons of history would take too much space here.

For one instance; if you happen to find reading about ancient Egypt interesting, you will be able to find much more on that subject at your local library or bookstore. If your interest happens to become stimulated in learning more about the stars and planets in the night sky above us, or in God's marvels in the workings and processes of life within and around us, you will be able to find all kinds of fascinating and rewarding reading on these subjects at any library. Bringing home a few well-selected books from your local library will cost you nothing if you have them returned in time.

Such reading will be of much more lasting worth to your thinking than filling up your mind with only the made-up mystery and adventure stories without good moral teachings that abound in our days.

IT WOULD NOT BE RIGHT for me to miss mentioning those who deserve a special thanks for the help they have unselfishly given to this work.

I am sure the hopes and prayers of all who had a part in producing these pages are that anyone who may happen to read through them will be led to a deeper worship of the Almighty God above us—and to a better obedience to His Spirit within us. We know God's guiding Spirit takes up only as much room as we leave open for Him.

I feel regret whenever I think how often the patience of my wife, Annie, has been put to a test by my thoughtlessness when I was absorbed in my reading and writing. That the time at my desk has become a natural tranquilizer when I begin to get tense and uptight is no excuse. Without her support, my spare time writing projects would not have gotten off the ground. I am not worthy that God has led her, the easy-to-talk-to-and-live-with person that she is, into my life.

A special gratitude of thanks goes to Wilma Ford, who used her editing skills on my manuscript and her typing abilities to change my faulty handwriting to typed pages for the printer. I am wondering if she would have agreed to take on all this work if she had known beforehand the difficulties she would come across in rearranging my sentences and paragraphs into a more readable and understandable form.

The self-taught artist, Emma Stoltzfus, who also did the cover for our first book in this series, deserves a special thanks for using her talent to do the cover you see on the front of this book.

I give her father-in-law, Dan Stoltzfus, the credit for introducing our construction crew to the easy "cribbing" method for raising heavy weights when we were remodeling his barn some thirty years ago. During the years that have gone by since, we have raised and lowered many heavy and long beams elsewhere, and I am convinced this is how the pyramid blocks were put into place over 4,000 years ago.

I am grateful for the numerous reviewers of the manuscript who were more knowledgeable than I was on the different subjects I have written about. Thanks for the changes and corrections you have suggested. These reviewers, along with the proofreading abilities of the brother and sister team of Dennis and Marie Kline, have caught many of my embarrassing mistakes before they got to be permanently carved into a printed book.

Among these reviewers were some of my friends at the Evart Michigan Amish community whom I met only shortly before the book went to press.

I can also not thank Tom Reed of the West Chester University enough for his help and the time he spent with me while the book was shaping up. In his layout of the cover you will see a part of the fair-weather clouds of Utah that fascinated his eye for beauty. Sandee Young and her brother Jeff deserve a special thanks for locating an aerial view of the Egyptian pyramids I was looking for.

And I am grateful to the crew at Carlisle Printing for the excellent work they turn out. I can recommend their work to anyone who needs printing done. Rhoda Miller deserves special thanks for her work on the layout and design of the book, and I am grateful to Marcus Wengerd and Ervin Schlabach for their suggestions and help.

Last, but not least, I am grateful to the inventors of mechanical pencils, sticky notes, and binder clips, which, next to erasers, are the biggest helps to anyone handwriting a manuscript.

WHEN I WAS STILL of school age I always found it fascinating to read of the papyrus plants that helped to change the course of history by furnishing the raw material for the paper many of the ancient manuscripts were written upon. I think I even had daydreams of going to Egypt sometime to bring back several plants and grow them myself.

Of course, I was very much surprised when I learned during the writing of this book that the Joe-Pye Ponds, featuring exotic water garden plants right here in Lancaster County, was stocking these very same plants.

The plants I got grew fast, and I found out it is actually possible to make a parchment paper fit to write upon.

However, since then I do not recommend any writers making their own paper for their own books. Writing takes a lot of time, and if a writer would first have to hand-make all the paper needed, very little time would be left to get any writing done.

It has been said that very few writers completely escape the urge to destroy their nearly finished manuscripts and do something else that does not take as much time. I have come to know that feeling.

IF NOTHING WOULD HAVE interfered, I am sure much of the material in this book, plowing into the field of "where did it all begin?" and "where is our hope for the future?" might have made its way into some of the periodicals regularly printed by Pathway Publishers.

I now understand that this was not to be, and I don't believe the accusations and condemnations that were heaped upon the work which my friends there were doing to better our plain churches will ever be justified.

May God forgive those who would rather condemn than give God the honor for the good.

But then we have examples all throughout history that wherever something good exists, the enemy of our souls will be right there in his subtle way trying in one way or other to upset it.

May we always trust in our God who judges rightly

and will always take care of His own.

AFTER THE RESURRECTION and ascension of Jesus, His Spirit became the source of power for His believers, and the Christian Church came into existence.

The church had its birth in the city of Jerusalem, which in 70 A.D. was destroyed by a flood, just as Old Testament prophecy had said it would be (Daniel 9:26, Amos 8:8, and Nahum 1:8). This destruction by a flood, an unlikely ruin for a city on the top of a hill with no river or sea close by, came in the form of a flood of Roman soldiers who completely sacked the city, along with the temple mount, into a waste and desolation.

But by then the followers of the teachings of Jesus Christ had become scattered by persecution into every corner of the vast Roman Empire. The drama of the history of Christianity from that time until the present day is very interesting.

It survived terrible persecutions, but unfortunately over time became a state-supported church, which for a thousand years seemed to be more political than spiritual. It became reformed by the people who felt this was no longer a continuation of the church founded upon the teachings of the Redeemer of the world.

Later a group called the Anabaptists became convinced Christianity was still not reformed enough to include the necessity of living holy and consecrated lives. Some 160 years later, in 1693, this group unhappily became fractured into the liberals and conservatives.

Many far-reaching things took place on both sides during the 300 years that have gone by since, and not all that happened makes nice reading. The seemingly small decisions made by the congregations of both groups would pass the points of no return only a few generations later.

We want to learn from both their successes and their failures in keeping and passing on the scriptural faith of our persecuted forefathers. However, we have to wonder if they could still recognize our churches as a continuation of the faith many of them gave their lives for. There is already much in print on these happenings that can help us to leave a better church for those coming after us if the Lord tarries.

I HAVE NO WAY of knowing if God will grant me health long enough that I can turn my bulky files of history notes into another book or not, but in the meantime I urge my young readers to get better acquainted with the interesting stories of church and religious history that are already in print. This is a story which will be continued as time moves on and will not end here on earth until Judgment Day.

Our daily doings will guide the part that is still unwritten. May all of us become a more useful part of the circle of brothers and sisters in the family of Jesus Christ. This is the church founded on the teachings of our Savior, upon which He made the sure prophecy that no evil enemy will ever be able to destroy (Matthew 16:18).

I INVITE MY READERS to let me know of any errors or faulty thinking they may discover in this work. I am willing to take the blame for any and all mistakes.

If anything you do read in the following pages will somehow be a help to you, please give our God all the honor, because those who know me also know I would not be able to handle getting any credit for what appears in print in this book. I am a part of fallen humanity, which needs a Redeemer. I will be cutting off God's help to me if I keep back even the smallest bit of glory or honor for myself and do not turn it all over to Him.

I wish all of you out there that special gift from God about which I happened to read in a prayer in my young days. I have never forgotten it. "If we promise to use it only to your glory, dear God, will you grant to us the gift of clear and unconfused thinking?"

May God continue to shower His blessings upon us all in our pilgrim journey through this life. May His love and mercy lead us to a home where we will ever be with each other and with God.

Ben Blank
205 Churchtown Road
Narvon, PA 17555

August 3, 2004

EMMA STOLTZFUS

God's Wonderful Creation

God's Wonderful Creation

Can you explain the wonders?
  Do you have the answer?
As I look around me,
  All I see is greatness.
Greatness in the planning,
  Beyond all understanding,
Wonders without number.

The earth cannot remember
  Of its own creation.
The ocean has no thinking
  So it has no answer.
The mountains do not hear me,
  Mute they are to question;
I can then not ask them.

Shall I ask a human?
  You have mind and thinking.
You can reason clearly,
  You can think of bygones.
Far beyond discussion,
  There is just one answer:
This all a miracle of God is
  Endless in His power,
Truly Supernatural!

Chapter 1

Where Did We Come From? Where Are We Going?

WHY AM I HERE? Is what I see real, or is it only a dream? Does life from my birth to grave have any meaning or purpose? Will my awareness of what is happening around me outlast my life on earth?

Any human being, upon growing out of early childhood, wonders: When and how did it all begin?

THE MOST SATISFYING AND FULFILLING answers to these and many other profound questions come from a personal belief in the Almighty God. We can believe, with a sure confidence, that He called forth everything into existence. He is the Author of Creation.

In the beginning God created the heavens and the earth. We are created with the ability to believe that the universe and everything beyond is a masterpiece designed and built by a divine God. Believing this is an awe-inspiring experience and brings us a refreshing peace and restful assurance.

The belief in God as our Creator in our world of unbelief is like an invigorating breath of fresh air flowing into a stifling room that had been filled with the stench of an offensive odor. A faith in a loving Almighty God too wonderful to be seen with our human eyes can bring an inner peace to a searching, troubled soul.

GOD CREATED THE PLANET EARTH as a sanctuary of life; as a home for us humans. Although many animals have fascinating traits that seem almost human, it is our ability to think and act on such virtues as beauty, love, justice, and mercy that prove we are more than animals. There is something within our being that is far above all other creatures. We are created with a spark of God's divine intelligence. This source of spiritual warmth and light may be fanned to either grow increasingly, or be blown out. It is evident that man is the only species that is conscious of its own mortality and capable of discerning right and wrong.

The amazingly intricate, complex, and orderly works of God's Creation shows us that it was all intentionally and thoughtfully designed by a Creator of infinite and unbounded intelligence and power.

God's Creation goes far beyond our ability to ever explain; yet we can conclude that all this could not have happened by itself. The Supreme Being who did all this designing and creating is not small enough for us humans to comprehend or ever fully understand and explain.

No matter how much God's works are studied, man will never completely figure it all out. We know the existence of a well-made watch is proof enough of the existence of a skilled watchmaker, so it is really foolish to claim that the universe, infinitely greater and more complex than any watch, could have produced itself.

We don't need to try to prove that God exists. No skeptic or infidel has proved He does not exist, because that is impossible. No matter how hard they have tried, nonbelievers in God cannot disprove the existence of God.

The atheists and skeptics say they cannot believe in God because they cannot see Him. The Christian sees God in everything. "All that I have seen teaches me to trust the Creator for all I have not seen," said Abraham Lincoln.

Our knowledge has boundaries; God's does not. Our abilities are limited; God's power is not. Humans often have to say, "We don't know," or "We can't." This is not so with God.

"Tell me," said one philosopher, "where is God?" "Tell me first," said the other, "where is He not?"

The God we believe in is too good to be unkind and too wise to make a mistake. He is awesomely great—greater than all the architects and artists put together. Our God is the Almighty—of wonderful majesty, grandeur, and glory.

WHAT WE SEE HAD to have a beginning at some time. Creation happened only once and cannot be duplicated in a laboratory. If the Bible did not exist, it would be interesting and even necessary for learned men of science to tell us what they had come up with about the beginning of beginnings.

For a long time people who have closed their minds to learning anything about God have gone to great lengths in their search for a "fundamental theory that explains the beginning of everything."

You may be interested in a sample of one of these ridiculous theories, not good for much more than a chuckle or snicker. The following quote is from a textbook of science written by Herbert Spencer (1820-1903). He abandoned the Christian faith he had been taught in his young years after he became convinced science was more important than religious belief. He gained a wide reputation after he invented the term "evolution" in an attempt to explain a gradual development of life after it had "begun by accident."

He made the following statement, at that time considered the last word in scientific knowledge on life coming from lifeless matter. We will let you puzzle over this: "An integration of matter and concomitant dissipation of motion during which the matter passes from an indefinite, incoherent homogeneity to a definite, coherent heterogeneity, and during which the retained motion undergoes a parallel transformation."

Another one of their ever-changing theories of how the universe began without taking the Bible into account is the well-known theory of "the big bang." Put into a few words, this theory is a belief that in a split second everything in the universe started outward from a single pinhead-sized point. This theory says that everything came forth in one instant of time, eons of years ago, and is still expanding. Believers in this theory have to admit that a force and energy beyond anything they can imagine or understand brought forth the universe in one colossal flashing moment of time. They have tried to trace time back as far as possible to find a beginning. Of course, now they are starting to wonder what was happening *before* the big bang took place!

This theory is now being questioned, and although it was for a time hailed as the last word in explaining the birth of the universe, it is already considered to be outdated.

This theory was soon followed by the belief that the expansion would at some time or other reach its limits and, like a stretching rubber band, snap back to produce a violent and sudden collision, the magnitude of which would be beyond all human imagination. In other words, they think the certain, ultimate, and instantaneous end of all material things will be this grand finale—a second big bang. The next question, of course, is what will take place *after* that has happened.

We were not there, but God was. Let Him tell us about Creation!

How blessed and fulfilling is a simple faith like that of innocent children! They will believe without having to ask for all kinds of proof.

BIBLE-BELIEVING CHRISTIANS have known for many hundreds of years an idea that science is now trying to teach to us. The universe did suddenly burst into existence! The instant release of this vast amount of energy beyond all human comprehension (call it the big bang if you will!) was God's moment of Creation. The Bible has told us about this instant Creation for thousands of years!

We believe that by a fiat of the Almighty God, the beginning of the universe came about by an instantaneous Creation. God called into existence with His spoken Word everything that before had not existed. God spoke, and the universe that obeys His orderly laws of matter, motion, and gravity appeared; created in an instant out of nothing (Hebrews 11:3). On the day of Creation, the Almighty God put into effect the many natural and spiritual laws men cannot change. Light and life, which learned men of science call "The two most deeply unexplained, puzzling, and mysterious forces in the universe," were created and are fully understood only by our God of Creation. God may have included the attraction and repelling of magnetism, which in a small way is somewhat like the invisible pull of gravity, to make His natural laws even more complex for men to understand.

It appears that the belief of scientists in the second big bang is similar to our belief in the end of time. We believe this will happen at the Second Coming of our Lord Jesus Christ when "the heavens shall pass away with a great noise, and the elements shall melt with fervent heat, the earth also and the works that are therein shall be burned up" (II Peter 3:10). In its place will come "a new heaven and a new earth, for the first heaven and the first earth were passed away" (Revelation 21:1). "In the twinkling of an eye...the trumpet shall sound, and the dead shall be raised" (I Corinthians 15:52). On the last day of history, on Judgment Day, everyone will be judged "according to their works" (Revelation 20:13).

WE CHRISTIANS BELIEVE IN A GOD THAT IS ETERNAL. "From Eternity Past to Eternity Future, Thou art God," says one English translation of the Jewish hymn written in the Psalms, chapter 90.

Eternity is the length of our unchanging God's life. There has already been an eternity; another eternity will again come to pass. Our lives here on earth are but a small-allotted time between these two eternities.

Eternity cannot be measured in units of time, as we know it. There was no beginning to the eternity that was, and the eternity to come will have no end. This is something our finite minds with limited understanding are not able to comprehend. All we can say is that before Creation Day nothing existed except God, His creative power, and His divine intelligence.

On Creation Day the Spirit of God started the ticking of the clock of time. He also made it possible for time to be measured by the precise movements of the sun, moon, and stars. As we keep track with our clocks and calendars at the rate of 60 minutes to the hour and 24 hours to the day, time moves on. We are all riding along.

Each one of us has the same amount of minutes contained in every full day of our lives, no more and no less. Time on earth never runs backwards. We will never get back the time today that we wasted yesterday and we will never be able to go back into time to undo things we did earlier in our lives. We may look back and remember, but we are blocked from ever returning to those times.

We are constantly moving into what we call the future. What we will see and experience there is hidden from us, blocked from our view until that time arrives. There is a curtain drawn between the future and us. That curtain, a veil we cannot see through or around, will not be lifted until we are there.

When God's Word says that a thousand years to Him are as a day and a day is as a thousand years, He may be telling us there may be something elusive about time that humans will never be able to understand.

God created time and understands it. To us, that should be enough.

OUR LITTLE MINDS CAN GRASP only that with which we have had some experience, and so, in this life, we will never be fully able to comprehend God and His works. "For my thoughts are not your thoughts, neither are your ways my ways, saith the Lord. For as the heavens are higher than the earth, so are my ways higher than your ways, and my thoughts than your thoughts," says the Bible in Isaiah 55:8 and 9.

This remarkable verse was written long before scientists, with their precise present-day methods of research and measuring, discovered and proved the unbelievable vast distances God has created in the known universe.

At the time this verse was written, men generally believed the stars in the night skies above them to be only tiny dots of light inside an inverted dome above the earth. This would well have made God's thoughts and ways out of reach, but still not much above our own thoughts. The men of those times who studied the heavens above them declared that they knew how many stars there were in the universe. The count of stars in those days was a number believed to be exactly 1,026, no more and no less.

However, after the telescope was invented, man discovered that there were many more stars. As still bigger and more powerful telescopes were made, scientists learned that the universe extended outward much further than previously believed. To this day, there is no sure way for us humans to tell exactly how far the huge, almost empty space of the universe does extend. No scientist is even sure there is an end to God's vast Creation.

It seems strange indeed that so much of what was once believed to be true about God's Creation gets discarded and forgotten as soon as a newer theory makes its appearance. What is taught from the science textbooks of today is almost certain to be different from what will be taught in the schoolrooms of tomorrow. If past history is any guide, today's textbooks will soon be outdated and no longer considered scientific. What was infallible yesterday will be thrown out tomorrow. Some of what science is so sure of today may be only an amusing curiosity by tomorrow.

SCIENTIFIC DISCOVERIES MADE BY MEN since medieval days should not become barriers to our belief in God. Neither the universe nor the greatness of God is as small as may have at one time been supposed. When we learned that the stars above were virtually countless and of awesomely great proportions, with incredibly vast distances between them, we ought to have learned to increase our thinking about the not-to-be measured ways of Almighty God, who created all of the seen and unseen.

Both the very great and the very small give us proof of God's wonderful creative power. The infinite variety of plants, with their beautiful and highly complex structures, and the different kinds of animals living on earth with us bear witness to God's creativity (for which Mother Nature often gets the credit!). They are abundant evidence for the existence of a living God.

Since the world began, people living on earth should have known enough to worship and show a reverence and devotion to Almighty God, the Lord of all. But as can be expected in a creature with a fallen nature, that is not what always happened. Man so often uses his increasing knowledge of the universe to distract him from God's glory.

We should constantly grow in our awe-struck wonder of the Almighty God, who is able to do all the great and wonderful works of Creation.

GOD CREATED OUR FIRST HUMAN PARENTS with a purpose in mind. He wanted a part of His Creation to be friends with Him and to show a love to Him. He created the first man and woman with the power to be co-workers in His Creation. He created them with a life that would be reproduced in their offspring. Unlike the rest of His Creation, God also created them with a will that was theirs alone. God didn't interfere with the choices they made, but the consequences of the choices they made would surely follow. They had the choice to love and honor Him or to ignore Him and go their own selfish ways.

They deliberately disobeyed their Maker. Their self-will became their greatest enemy. They made God's world that He had called very good into something it was never intended to be. Only a generation later, envy, hate, and even murder would come to pass. By leaps and bounds, evil, or the absence of good, grew on the earth and, as we all know, has been with us ever since.

Before many generations passed, there were people worshiping the sun, moon, and stars. Some worshiped things they made with their own hands from wood, metal, or stone. They were awe-inspired by what they could see but not understand. They worshiped things created instead of the Creator (Romans 1:25).

Does this sound a little like us, obsessed with what we have done and the material things we have obtained? Could we have too much pride in what we think we know and what we have instead of giving God the thanks and the honor for it all?

MANY TRIBES OF PEOPLE began worshiping idols instead of the loving and living God. Others became atheists who denied the existence of an all-powerful God. On up to our time, these unbelievers are doing the unthinkable. They are making attempts to rule God out of His own Creation.

As the story goes, an atheist told a Christian that all Bibles would at some time be destroyed, for the time is coming when no one will need to have a belief in God, and nothing will be left to remind people of God. The Christian only smiled and said, "How are you going to get the stars down?"

The stars we see are silent witness to God's power and marvelous Creation. Step outside on a dark, clear night. Look up into the heavens. See what God has put on display for you. Ponder the vastness of the universe. Look down and consider how little space your own two feet take up.

Truly God has placed us in the midst of a wonderful and magnificent Creation! "The heavens declare the glory of God; and the firmament sheweth His handiwork" (Psalm 19:1).

You will understand why the Psalm writer exclaimed when he looked up at these very same stars some three thousand years ago, "What is man, that Thou art mindful of him, and the son of man, that Thou visitest him" (Psalm 8:4)?

How humbling it is to reflect how small we are compared to God and His Creation! We stand in wonder before God who sets before us thousands upon thousands of reminders of His mysteries. He gives us proofs of His love of creative order and beauty. The delights of nature show us a God who loves beauty and places it on exhibit for us. God must have loved variety, because He created so many different kinds of life!

NO PROOF, HOWEVER CLEAR, THAT GOD EXISTS would be evidence enough to convince those who make up their minds not to believe in Him. In the end, it is up to each of us to make our own decision to believe in God.

The "scientific" minds that had to invent something else to explain their unbelief are the source of many renowned scientific and political theories that do not take God into account. The theories of evolution by Charles Darwin and the godless communism of Karl Marx are several examples. Another skeptic was Bertrand Russell (1872-1970), who wrote a number of misleading books on why he is not a Christian and why he did not believe in God. Even though he won the 1950 Nobel Prize for his writings, he became a slave to his own lusts as a philanderer and adulterer. But even with his godless lifestyle he may have softened a little in his beliefs before he died. He did come to admit that the only hope of human survival is the concept of a God of love. He wrote to a friend just before he passed into eternity, "There must be something more important...although I don't believe there is." He had made up his mind that he did not want to believe, even though he saw evidence that he should believe in God.

Another well-known unbeliever, Sigmund Freud (1856-1939), has been called the "father of psychoanalysis," which is a method of dealing with emotional and mental disorders. This is a very complex science, with thousands of pages having been written trying to explain the analyzing of guilt feelings and perverted actions coming from childhood experiences of pleasure or pain, and to infer or guess what goes on in the apparatus of a patient's mind when reality and fantasy get mixed up. However, in his methods of trying to bring repressed memories to the surface, without also triggering unacceptable behavior, he made much more confusion than enlightenment when he did not include something like the beginning of a new and Godly nature mentioned in the Bible as being transformed "by the renewing of the mind" (Romans 12:2). This new birth of altogether different thinking and actions is also made understandable in 2 Timothy 1:7, "For God hath not given us the spirit of fear, but of power, and of love, and of a sound mind."

Freud was also greatly impressed by how Charles Darwin explained the evolution of life on earth without God, and was fascinated by the history of religion and mythology. In his last book, written when he was 84 years old, he went to great lengths to try to prove that God was only a myth invented by an Egyptian named Moses. It is indeed strange that in seeking to find the source of truth and peace of mind, he would spend so much time trying to explain away a God whom he did not even believe existed.

A well-known atheist, asked why he was so set in believing that the universe came into its own existence when there is so little evidence to support that belief, frankly confessed he had a strong material reason for not wanting God to exist. Had he led such a life that he did not want to think of a Creator who would also be the judge of the sinful life he had lived? Didn't he want to be reminded of changes he should make in his life, changes he didn't want to make?

ONE MAN, AT ONE TIME A CONFIRMED atheist, wrote of the experience that converted him to becoming a believer in God. One evening he was standing beside the bed of his small sleeping daughter.

While looking down into her innocent sleeping face, he was suddenly overwhelmed by his own thoughts. "This is surely a creature not created by chance," he thought. His thinking about an Almighty God was changed then and there.

There are actually two verses in the Bible that contain the four words, "There is no God." But we must also read the words immediately before these four words. The verses are not complete unless we also read: "*The fool hath said in his heart,* There is no God" (Psalm 14:1 and Psalm 53:1).

There is really only one reason why a human being will not admit there is a God: a refusal to humble oneself and confess we do not and never will understand all the wonderful works and mysteries of the Master Designer. God's ways are beyond our understanding of how, and deeper than our comprehension of why.

How blessed to know He is still in control! How reassuring to know that the future is in God's hands! Who but the Maker should be honored and worshiped as the Master!

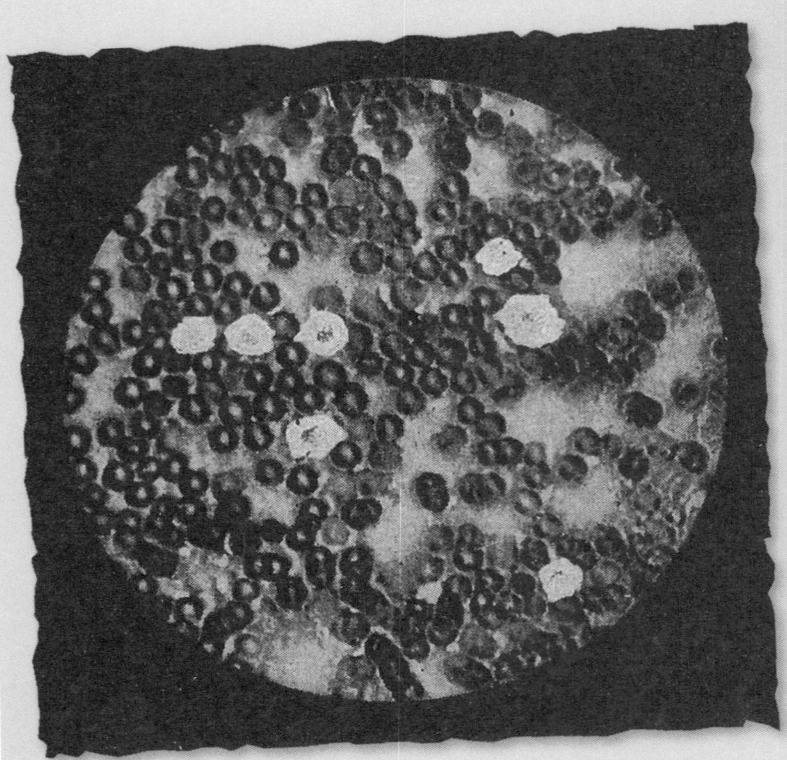

PHOTO CREDITS – BOOK OF POPULAR SCIENCE

The photo above shows a sample of human blood magnified about 1,500 times. If it were possible to enlarge a photo of an adult to this magnification he would be shown as being over a mile and a half high.

Shown are a few white corpuscles which are like policemen loyal to the body to which they are a part of. To keep us alive, they will efficiently and fiercely battle to their deaths against any invading enemy microbes. Most of these multitudes of different kinds of disease germs are able to reproduce from one germ to 20 million in only eight hours. These germs inside of us are really more of a threat to our bodies than accidents coming to us from outside. None of us would have lived very long after our birth without this immunity protection.

Also shown are the red corpuscles; those marvelous little bits of life that absorb oxygen as they pass through the lungs. They give up their life-giving cargo to the other body cells (the average adult body has a total of a million times a million of them) on every trip around the body.

The arteries of our bodies branch in ever smaller blood vessels until they are just large enough for these red cells to pass through, scraping the walls as they pass. The bloodstream, "flesh in solution" as it has been called, is kept flowing through the plumbing in our bodies by a hollow beating muscle fitted with one-way check valves.

Truly, we are fearfully and wonderfully made!

After the first crude telescope, enlarging about thirty times, was invented around about 1610, a view of the night skies was opened up that no one had ever seen before, or even imagined.

In this highly magnified photo of only a very small part of the night skies, several galaxies, or rotating clusters of stars can be seen. The other small dots of light are other stars in the galaxy of which our sun is a part of, or are galaxies much further out in the universe, some which may be as much as 600 million times a billion miles across at the center.

It has been estimated that there are at least a hundred billion galaxies, each one containing at least an average of a hundred billion stars. In spite of all this, the outer limits of the universe have not yet been found.

Like giant invisible cables, the attraction called gravity keeps the multitudes of stars, rotating around the center of gravity in their galaxies, from flying out into space, while the centrifugal force keeps them from crashing inward toward the center.

Each one of the stars was started on its vast and perfectly balanced sweeping orbit at Creation. Just because some of these orbits have been found to take eons of time to complete does not prove the universe to be billions of years old. To prove His greatness, God was able to start, and will be able to end, all of this without the larger orbits even having time enough to make a full circle.

It has also been discovered that all matter is formed of atoms. Each one in size is about as close to zero as you can get, but is still somewhat like a miniature galaxy of nearly all empty space. The tug of gravity, which all atoms have for each other, greatly diminishes as the distance between them is increased, but it is always still there.

Both the very large and the very small designed by our Almighty God are far beyond the human capacity of ever understanding all of it. It simply could not have happened by random chance.

Chapter 2

The Almighty God –Master Architect

IF THIS CHAPTER ON SOME of God's wonders were to be enlarged to contain as much information as is found in a hundred encyclopedia sets, it would still contain just a tiny part of the known and unknown of God's amazing Creation around us here on earth.

No one is able to fully explain the miracles of divine Creation. Life is too wonderful and complex to ever be fully understood. Look at the following selections about the wonders of life discovered by scientists learning about these mysteries that surround us:

•This summer, millions upon millions of fascinating and harmless fireflies will blink their friendly evening lights, exactly as billions upon billions of fireflies before this have done since the world began. Their cold lights come from an organic process that man has not yet been able to duplicate.

•The secretary bird feeds on small mice and on poisonous snakes. Their bodies digest this deadly snake venom as their daily food without any harm to their systems.

•The tides constantly churn up the oceans. If this churning would stop, the oceans would become too stagnant to support any sea life.

•How does a duck incubating eggs know she must hurry to get her breakfast and get back to sit on her eggs before they get cold?

•When disturbed, the bombardier beetle forces two kinds of acid fluids from its abdomen. They vaporize into a little cloud, explode in a "pop!" and scare enemies away.

•The bloodstreams of every living creature—human beings, animals, insects—and the sap streams of every living plant are an unexplainable mystery. We can think of all these "rivers of life" as highways with trucks running past walls made of living cells. Each cell has its own loading dock. At some places, doors open up to load these trucks with certain materials. At other places, they are unloaded. The DNA, working like a very complex computer in every living cell, regulates the loading and unloading taking place, as needed nutrients are distributed and wastes that have collected are carried away. Each one of us is only a small speck in God's vast universe, but each one of us has about 60 thousand miles of blood vessels in our body to distribute what our cells need to live, work, and reproduce. This length is enough to go around the world nearly two and a half times!

• The wellness of every living body, human or animal, depends on its immune system. There is a silent and unseen battle going on between antibodies manufactured by the blood and rapidly multiplying bacteria that produce toxic substances harmful to life. Human beings are equipped with almost a million different kinds of antibodies that seem to be trained to tell which particular kind of germ they are to attack. Depending on which side wins, the body will heal itself or it will die. You will never know how often your immune system has saved you from what otherwise would have been certain death. You would not have survived the first time you caught the common cold, or got a scratch on your finger.

• An electric eel can develop a flash of over 500 volts at two amperes. This is enough to kill its food or stun a man coming against it.

• Songbirds raised in captivity in soundproof cages will sing the songs of their own species when they are grown.

• The nests the birds are building this year are as perfect as those built thousands of years ago back in the Garden of Eden.

• Each one of the trillions upon trillions of snowflakes that have fallen since Creation are all a little different. In this same way, God uses a little different and unique pattern for every human being who ever lived. No two are exactly the same. What you are, exists nowhere else except in you.

• One of God's wonders has kept every one of us from becoming blind soon after birth. Our eyes, located behind virtually the only parts of our body not protected by skin, would soon have become destroyed by infection if God would not have built us with the unthinking reflex of blinking to clean them and coat them with germ-killing tears.

• Each of the million-times-a-million cells in our bodies (this number is a one with twelve zeros behind it) has something like its own chemical factory and control center that works with the other cells, enabling it to live, repair, and grow. Man has never made tractors that reproduce themselves or I-beams that repair themselves if they are held together long enough. He will never make a factory that turns grass into milk or grain into eggs.

• Until recent years all living cells were believed to be only very simple little bits of life. However, it has been discovered each typical cell in the human body is made up of ten million times a million atoms, of several dozen different elements, all arranged in such a complex way that life simply could not have happened by random chance. The control center in each cell that takes non-living substances to support its life is composed of very tightly-coiled, extremely-microscopic DNA strands, which are like very fine threads that would be approximately six feet long if they could be unrolled.

• If you enjoy doing numbers, you may be able to figure out how intricate our bodies really are with these fine DNA threads in each one of our many millions of body cells. Using the figures science has come up with, you may be interested in figuring how many people's DNA threads it would take to reach the nearest star which scientists have measured to be 4½ light years away. It has been determined that light travels at the speed of 186,282 miles a second.

• Every child is born with a small universe of 100 billion nerve cells called neurons in his or her brain. Our brain, the most complex structure known in God's entire universe, controls many thousands of body functions even when we are sleeping. We are not aware of most of this work of the body that is going on. Most of these systems, coordinated by neurons and connected by tiny electrical messengers that dart between the cells, are still a mystery to scientists who have spent nearly their entire life studying them. These neurons, interconnected by these little electrical impulses, make the human memory, which is like a huge filing system stored in the attic of the body, capable of retaining about 100 trillion bits of information, or about 500 times the information contained in a complete set of encyclopedias.

• The human brain could be compared to a computer, but it is programmed by something outside of itself called the mind. Right now as you are reading these lines, your neuron system is flitting the muscles of your eyes, and with the complex power of concentration you can picture what you are reading about. Anything, like the symmetrical and coordinated balance of ice skating, or an inventor imagining how a device he has never seen would work while he is using his hands at the same time, or even just driving a nail with a hammer, is like pulling an elaborate array of puppet strings at one time. In fact, if the workings of our body processes are included, it has been estimated the neuron system is capable of handling as many as 15,000 decisions a second.

• God has miraculously created our thinking and actions to be formed by habit patterns. The developing of both the good and helpful, or the bad and harmful actions and thinking, is made easier every time they are repeated. It works something like making folds in a piece of cardboard which are inclined to follow the creases made into it earlier.

• Our minds are too wonderful a gift from God to be abused by alcohol or street drugs. The trash that is permitted to enter our minds through our eyes and ears will also surely influence our thoughts and actions, and follows the law of: "garbage in – garbage out." But it is also evident that the human mind could not have been mindlessly created, and we can be sure that the same Power that brought it into being is also able to heal it.

• It is also a mystery how God will continue this process of thinking and awareness in the human bodies resurrected from the dust of the earth in the future, but we can be sure He will have a way. He did it once and we know He is able to do it again.

• While you are reading these lines, many billions of seeds will be sprouting somewhere in the world. Somebody or something has placed them in an environment where light, moisture, and temperature are just right to revive them from their dormant stage and trigger the beginning of their growth. Each seed was previously quickened into life and made viable by one pollen grain finding its way into the embryo part of a blossom that was incomplete until this union took place. This intricate pollen grain may have traveled miles on the winds or on a bee or other insect. The mysterious DNA in each cell of the seed regulates and keeps track of the seed's urge to live and grow.

• There are many thousands of processes regulated by the life within every seed. One process is that no matter how a sprouting seed is turned, the root stem will grow downward towards the moisture and nutrients in the soil, and the plant stem will grow upward towards the light. If just this one pattern of growth the Almighty programmed into each seed were to fail or be reversed, a sure and early death of the seed would be the result.

• The sun came up right on time this morning. Alarming headlines would appear on newspapers all over the world if the sun or moon were to rise only a little earlier or later tomorrow, or a little north or south of the scientific charts made up for their position. But we don't need to worry, because as long as the earth remains we can depend on God's sure promise that He will continue to run His universe in His exact and precise way (Genesis 8:22).

GOD'S BEAUTIFUL AND MARVELOUS CREATION is like looking through a small window into Heaven, especially when we think of His beauty, truth, and love. There are things that can be seen and felt, but God's Creation can never be fully explained. Only a closed mind will refuse to believe in God's greatness.

An entry was found in the journal of a deceased scientist who had spent a lifetime studying God's wonders. "There is a God, and He is good!"

The only way for us to learn how this interesting universe had its beginning would be for God to tell us about it. And He has done exactly this, very plainly, in the first chapter in the Bible.

"In the beginning God created the heaven and the earth (Verse 1). And God saw everything that He had made, and behold, it was very good. And the evening and the morning were the sixth day" (Verse 31).

PHOTO CREDIT – DAVID MUENCH

The photo above shows a part of one of the most spectacular gashes ripped into the earth. It can be seen that this was done by rapidly flowing floodwaters. Nothing else could have carved out such a formation.

Called the Grand Canyon of the Colorado River, this natural wonder is visited by over four million sightseers every year. In this immense gorge, the river flows through a cut about a mile lower than the rim of the canyon, which is from five to ten miles across. Depending on where the starting and ending points of the canyon are considered to be, it is from 200 to 300 miles long.

This area here and many other similar places on earth are extensively studied by scientists. The sediment carried downstream by the rapidly flowing Colorado River has been scientifically measured and has been estimated to average 500,000 tons per day. By then doing meticulous mathematical calculations on how many cubic miles of material has been apparently removed in the whole valley, it is supposedly proved how many millions of years in the remote past the river has been washing out the canyon.

The idea that the earth is millions of years old then comes from the theory that the processes of erosion, glacier movements, and volcanic eruptions have in the past always operated in the same manner as those in the present.

These figures are then also used by people who do not believe in Genesis to try to determine the ages of the different rock layers called strata.

These kinds of figures are also used to project into the future. For one example, it has been determined that the Mississippi River carries off something like 300,000 tons of sediment downstream each day. These figures are then used to calculate that if this keeps on going at this rate, the whole 1,147,000 square miles of the Mississippi Valley basin will be worn down to sea level in 4½ million years.

The pendulum now seems to be swinging the other way. New groups of Bible-believing scientists are now saying that it is clear that there was simply not enough water flowing at the bottom of this gorge to cut out this immense amount of material. Only a gigantic flood could have washed out the valleys and deposited the clay and debris found in the rock layers here and elsewhere throughout the world.

Only the waters in a proportion not known of before or after could have carved out the Grand Canyon. Only if something like a great natural dam holding back enormous lakes of water would have broken loose could something like the rushing and roaring waters have cut out a landscape such as the immense valley seen here.

Such rushing waters would also have made a sudden end to the massive amounts of plant and animal life and then covered it quickly enough to form fossils, oil, coal, and limestone rock.

And such flooding couldn't have lasted for thousands, or even hundreds, of years, or the whole earth would have become washed flat. There would be no more clearly distinct layers in the rock strata to be seen if it would not all have been done in a relatively short time by the sloshing back and forth of mighty waves of water.

The story of the mighty Flood and the falling and the rising again of the crust of the earth which caused all this erosion has been in our Bibles all this time.

The stories the rocks can tell were put there by the Almighty God so that they can be seen by all. This is a clear evidence that the Bible story of the Great Flood is not a myth and legend.

Keep on reading.

Chapter 3

The Big Gully Washer

The Power of Water

WE CAN ALL RECALL THE CLOUDS GROWING DARKER before a "gully washer" rain. After the violent downpour is over, we say we had a "cloudburst," with so many inches in our rain gauge in such a short length of time. Such a storm on a hot summer afternoon sometimes includes a short burst of icy hailstones falling from the clouds above us.

Often a rainbow appears after a storm is over and the sun begins to shine on the earth again. Despite gashes of erosion ripped into the earth here and there by the angry churning waters, the rains are God's way of cleaning and washing off His Creation. The clear skies above show not one dark stain of the black clouds that covered it not long before.

After a time, the earth will use God's power of life to heal itself. In a year or two the ravines cut out and the silt washed together will be grown over with new vegetation and become a permanent part of the landscape.

Calculating the amount of water falling from just a local flash flood is almost beyond belief. The rain released from the clouds in a four-inch downpour over an area of a twenty-mile radius would amount to over 360 million tons of water. And to think, all this water freely floated in clouds above us before the moisture droplets became converted to falling rain! We marvel at another one of the wonders of the works of God.

It is good that God created gravity to pull this water downward into the creeks and rivers to the levels of the oceans. Some will soak into the reservoirs of the earth, replenishing our wells and springs.

If the water did not sink or flow downward, we would need to haul away over 90 billion gallons of water from just this one local downpour. We would need to fill up and hook up over 9,000 trains; each train made up of one hundred 10,000-gallon railroad tank cars. We would still not have crossed the tracks one-and-a-half years later if we were to wait until these water-filled freight trains had all moved slowly by at the rate of ten cars a minute.

If this water didn't evaporate or soak in, we would need to pump it all away so that we wouldn't need to splash in four inches of water while working in our fields and gardens. Again, we would be pumping for a long time. To remove all the water from this four-inch rain that fell on a twenty-mile radius of land, at the average garden hose rate of five gallons a minute, we would be pumping for a long time. After 26 years we would have uncovered something like one square mile with almost 1,256 to go yet!

PROBABLY THE NEAREST ANYONE will ever be able to experience imagining anything like the torrential rains that the Bible says happened a long time ago, is at a project completed at Niagara Falls a number of years ago. This work was conceived to get sightseers to part with some of the dollars in their pockets.

A tunnel was cut out in the bedrock behind and under the roaring waters of the falls. Here the visitors can go down a 150-foot elevator and then walk forward for about another 150 feet inside the cavern.

They can see the back side of the great sheets of water pouring down into the churning bottom of the falls, which is only a few feet in front of them.

Although the tourists get drenched with spray unless they wear raincoats, they are safely behind a lattice of iron bars between them and a certain watery grave. Standing right beside the thundering roar of the water, with the shaking bedrock surrounding them, is a never-forgotten, awe-inspiring experience.

What would the earth look like after forty days and forty nights of a downpour something like this?

Stories about the Great Flood

I CAN JUST IMAGINE HEARING SOME READERS out there saying, "Oh, come on! Nobody is old-fashioned enough in our modern day and age to believe anything like a worldwide flood ever actually happened. We are enlightened enough to know this is all a myth—a legend of primitive and partly civilized people of long ago."

At least 270 different legends of a devastating flood have been found in the folklore stories of countries and tribes from all over the world.

A number have been read from ancient inscriptions on clay tablets found at different places. These tablets tell local stories of the gods they worshiped becoming angry enough to destroy their enemies with a flood of water.

These tales crop up not only in a few localities, but from lands all over the world. They come from China and Babylonia, from the islands of Hawaii, and from tribes of our American Indians.

One story from an ancient Mexican culture tells of a world very different from what we live in now that lasted for 1,716 years before a great flood destroyed it. As generations passed away, the details of this story may grow dimmer but never completely erase the memory of a great flood in the minds of the people of early history.

Some of these flood legends have been passed by word of mouth from one generation to the next. These have probably been changed a little with each retelling, and some evolved to become plenty far-fetched.

Most of these stories are completely absurd and many contain downright foolish details, but virtually all include one version or another of this one family who believed the divine warnings of a coming flood. They were then saved from destruction by getting aboard a huge barge or boat before the rains came.

That this story is found all over the world may verify the fact that the descendants of this one family dispersed all over the world at some time after the Flood was over.

WE ARE TOLD THE PRIMITIVE HEBREWS WERE a little different. They were a unique tribe that "developed" a philosophy of only one God in a world of pagan religions of every kind. The Hebrews were believed to have invented their story of the Great Flood because of a belief that their God is determined to punish the wrongdoings and idol worship of other nations.

In other words, the surrounding countries saw the religion of the Hebrews only as a way of trying to be superior to the people of other nations.

However, there is no doubt about it that the story in Genesis has a ring of truth that is found in none of the other flood stories. The story of the colossal Flood as told in the ancient writings of the Bible, unlike every one of the other folklore legends, has a true historical character.

It includes actual geographic locations and traceable family lines all contained in a clear and precise chronological time frame in history. This all helps to establish the reliability of the Genesis stories.

We Christians believe our Master and Savior Jesus Christ was and still is completely trustworthy. He would not have spoken of Noah and the Flood as a historical fact if it were only an imaginary myth and legend (Matthew 24:37 and 38; Luke 17:26 and 27). God's prophet Isaiah also considered the Great Flood an actual happening of history (Isaiah 54:9).

OUR GOD WHO FORMED THE HEAVENS and earth could easily have also spoken a finished ark into existence, but God wanted Noah and his family to do more than just stand idly by doing nothing. Some were needed to swing the axes and hammers. Other hands were needed to pick and cook the food for the workers.

Like the church of Jesus Christ to be built in a future era, God was the planner and architect, and the people, to be saved with God's help, would be the builders. The translation of the Bible you are reading may say that God told Noah and his family to *go* into the ark after it was ready, or you may be reading one of the translations where God is telling Noah to *come* into the ark. You will find the root word in the original Hebrew does have a double meaning. In one of the nuances of language translating, either "come" or "go" can be correct for this Hebrew word.

This also may indirectly tell us that God is everywhere. God is commanding the family of Noah to come and be with Him in the safety of the ark. He is like a kind and concerned father who wants his children in the house with him when he sees a storm coming. At the same time, God is also telling them to go away from the sinful people outside who will soon be perishing in their unrepented sins.

Here may be a time to close the pages of this book and lay it aside. Get out your Bible and very carefully and prayerfully read the Flood story all over again. Read it as if the scrolls of a complete Bible had just been discovered in a cave by the Dead Sea and you had never before heard any of its stories.

Noah

THE WORLD THAT NOAH lived in before the Flood had become very evil and wicked. His fellow human beings, made in God's image, began living like something worse than beasts. Their doings reflected their base and selfish natures. Their higher and nobler Godly natures and the good works they were capable of must have become nonexistent.

The world became filled with violence, bloody hate, and revenge. God's institution of sacred and pure marriage was totally disregarded. Even the sons of God, having a semblance of true religion, took as they wished any and all of the fair daughters of men. They did not respect or spare their womanhood. Living in lust was all that mattered to them.

How could innocent children brought into such a world ever have a good chance to live in close-knit and secure families and grow up to become people living Godly and holy lives?

God decided to destroy mankind from the face of the earth. Here God had a choice. Two of the countless things He brought into being at Creation were fire and water. Fire can reduce water into a floating vapor and water can extinguish fire. Both fire and water, needful and useful, are something people could never do without, but there is nothing as deadly or destructive as either of them when out of control.

God chose to destroy the first world with water. In the cleansed world following the Flood, God would need to again create two parents for another race of human beings that would be given an opportunity to make a new start and a fresh beginning. It would be a rebirth of the whole world.

If only one righteous family, however, could be found and saved, it would be possible yet to fulfill the promise of a Redeemer coming from the race of Adam and Eve. God found that family in Noah.

NOAH MAY HAVE HAD MANY REGRETS that the example of his walk with God (Genesis 6:9) and his words urging others to do works of righteousness converted no one beyond his immediate family. He may have felt like a failure.

But within his family something was done right, because his family was saved from such an evil world. Noah's family is an inspiration to families thousands of years later, and is evidence that close and Godly families are still possible as islands of righteousness and blessing, no matter how much evil and wickedness surrounds them.

If every family had done what Noah's family did, all would have been saved. We don't know how many other families in the first world were also told to build an ark. For all that we know, God may have given many other families the same opportunity to live in the cleansed world after the Flood.

WHAT HAPPENED AFTER NOAH AND HIS FAMILY were safely inside the ark should have convinced the unbelieving onlookers outside that there was something very miraculous and supernatural going on. A long line of animals, all in pairs, lined up and joined Noah and his family in the ark. Every kind of animal species on the earth was represented in this line slowly passing into the door built into the side of the ark. Some of the slow-moving animals may have started this trip toward the ark years before to be there on time.

Can we imagine the astonishment of the family of Noah when they saw animals that are hard to chase and catch, such as the two pigs, willingly coming in through the door? Imagine the amazement of the people outside watching animals such as lions and wolves laying down their cruel nature to walk behind or in front of the deer and the sheep.

In the ark, cats and dogs would need to learn peace with each other. Mice and rabbits would not need to look around in a continuous fear of their lives.

Everything would be like people living together in a peaceful church family. All would be thankful to be saved from the death and destruction soon to be raging outside.

HERE THE FLOOD STORY as told in the Bible is not exactly clear. It seems there may have been two oral Hebrew Flood stories circulating at the time Moses was writing them down on his parchment. Like both stories of two newspaper reporters writing about the same event, and like the two stories of the Creation of man—one in chapter one in Genesis and another in chapter two—both stories fully complement each other. Like the harmony of the four Gospel writers who did not sit down together to write about the life of Jesus, this orderly whole helps to prove this was not a single story that was made up.

Anyway, it seems the ark door may have been kept standing open for seven days after the animals and Noah and his family were all inside. This was an open invitation, a chance for those who had not even helped to build to go inside and be saved. But there was also the danger that Noah and his family could become impatient and make the fatal mistake of stepping outside for a while. There would be no coming back in after God closed the door. They would miss their safe journey from one world to the next.

Perhaps that long week was the greatest test of faith God put to Noah and his family.

Would we have stayed, sitting inside the ark with the door opened to the outside for this length of time, if what we believed in and worked for all those years showed not one sign of coming to pass? Could any of us have easily coped with the taunts and mockery we can well imagine came from those gathered just outside the door to watch what would happen next? Would we have started thinking there might not be anything after all to what God had told Pappy Noah many years ago?

While they were waiting, God's Spirit, which no human eyes can see, came and closed the door. The days of God's grace were now over. This locked door would never be opened again; either from the inside or the outside.

WE DON'T KNOW HOW DARK THE sky became before the rain started, but we do know a rain never comes suddenly out of a clear, blue sky. Anyway, during the next forty days and nights, a great and destructive havoc such as no one can imagine came upon the earth.

The waters rose and the ark and its cargo rose with it. The floodwaters came both from the deluge of rain and from the waters ascending upward from "the fountains of the great deep" (Genesis 7:11). This was not a local downpour in which the waters come gushing upwards out of the drains. Here the waters came rushing up from the river valleys everywhere.

Did God cause the waters of the oceans to rise by placing His almighty hands in the deep oceans or did He raise the floors of the ocean basins that He had lowered on the third day of Creation? Only He knows how He did this.

The upward-rising waters did no harm to all those safe within the ark floating on the Flood, but it put to death all life below and around them that depended on air in the lungs to live.

Any desperate shouting for help by those outside the door as the waters lifted the ark was useless. No one inside had the power to open the door and rescue the lives of friends, no matter how much they would have wanted to.

The boat that required all these years of hard work to build is often illustrated by artists as having a pointed prow in front to cut through the waters, but in the vast expanse of seas it would float on, there would be no shores anywhere towards which to sail.

The finished ark was more likely a structure built something like a large rectangular barge. It needed a roof to keep the rainwater from filling it up, which would have sunk it just as surely as any leak, large or small, would have done. Evidently this roof was raised one cubit (believed to be about 18 inches) all around the sides as a window to let light into the interior of the ark.

We now know what the outcome was, but the God-fearing family huddled in the ark didn't know at that time what all the unknown future had in store for them.

But they had the same assurance that we can rest in throughout all of our lifetimes. We know God always takes care of His own, no matter how unsettling the storm that is raging outside.

THE ARK DOOR THAT GOD CLOSED WAS never opened again. God guided the ark to a level place on the heights of the mountains of Ararat so that when the waters went down it would not tip over.

The Bible tells us the rest of the story—the coming out of the ark by removing the roof—immediately building an altar to worship God—the rainbow and God's promise to never again drown the whole earth with water—God's unfailing promise of the orderly continuation of day and night and the seasons as long as the earth will remain—His blessings upon Noah and upon the families of all three of his sons.

Effects of the Great Flood

We can be sure that Noah and his family, safe inside the ark, were not aware of all the changes happening to the earth below them, which God was destroying to make room for a new beginning.

They may have wondered how their perished neighbors so brazenly could have said it was never possible that a flood would happen, but could they have imagined that some of their own future descendants would not believe that this Flood ever happened?

Many years have now come and gone since the Flood. Since then, some of the descendants of Noah's family saved from the Flood by the Almighty God have begun to question that He even existed. Instead of believing that God made everything from nothing, they are claiming that nothing made everything. Spending much of the time and energy God gave them, they are coming up with new and clearly untrue theories, trying to explain Creation and the source of life without the Master Designer. They are trying to rule God out of His own Creation.

These theories are not based on the Bible, because to many people it is only a book which is "too unscientific and therefore impossible" to base any of their beliefs. These made-up theories explaining the works of Creation and the Great Flood ignore the Almighty God who sometimes chooses to work in natural ways, and at other times in the supernatural and miraculous.

One of the theories invented in their imaginations states that the first forms of life began at the bottoms of the deep oceans. Given millions of slow, natural processes, the lower forms of life evolved into the higher forms of life.

The time-worn explanation which the atheistic study of the natural world offers to defy the truth of the Bible is that the natural processes of "the struggle for existence" and "the survival of the fittest" eventually resulted in something like a superior animal called man, who then populated the earth.

In such a world, we could not be created in the likeness or image of God. We would be animals without conscience or morals. We would be distant cousins of all other life on earth: from germs to whales. We would be related to the giant redwood trees and even to the moss growing around their roots. We would happen to be here by pure luck and chance, not by the design of Master Intelligence. There would be no place for a God of love and mercy.

Despite the vast amount of evidence against the theory of evolution, which these few atheists and unbelievers invented only several generations ago, the idea spread like seeds scattered far and wide, and grew in the minds of young people all over the world. The seeds, sowed by the enemy of God when it seemed everyone was sleeping, sprouted and soon had deep roots.

In the space of a few decades, virtually all encyclopedias and natural history books, along with science textbooks, would present evolution, first as theory, then later as fact for which no further proof was needed. The teachings of evolution would, as the saying goes, be gulped down—hook, line, and sinker.

Of course, persons tend to believe what they were taught when they were still young and easily influenced. Even young people from Christian families in our beloved country, which was established on firm Biblical principles, had this error of evolution impressed upon their tender minds.

Drifting with the current, and without doing much real thinking, many young people started accepting this teaching. What is disturbing is that many young people began to trust what was in their textbooks more than what they read in their Bibles with their parents at home.

Changes to the Earth As a Result of the Great Flood

WHAT HAPPENED TO THE FACE OF THE EARTH during the one year and ten days Noah and his family lived in the ark would make the whole world look many millions of years older than it really was. Complex things happened when God was making utter ruin of the first world upon which the new would be built.

This biggest gully washer ever would lay down an intricate arrangement of many layers of strata and fossils. This washed-together sediment is dug into, pondered over, and studied by modern-day scientists.

In most cases, the simplest forms of marine life on the ocean floors were covered up first, followed by at least some of the fishes and the more complex sea creatures that met their deaths by accident. The bodies of the drowned land animals would mostly be in the top layers.

Anyone who is not a believer in absolute Bible truth might easily imagine this arrangement definitely proving the evolution of life from lower to higher forms, and then make up a theory stating that all this took millions of years. However, to complicate all this, the layers of strata order are sometimes found in a reversed order, having been washed together by the churning floodwaters.

This has so far puzzled evolution-believing scientists when such "upside-down" strata are discovered. So far, no "millions of years" theory has satisfactorily explained how this could have happened. Among some of the other findings that defeat the theory that these fossil-laden layers are millions of years old, is the fact that the pollen of a tree called the bristle cone pine has been found in every layer, from the very top to the bottom, which is supposed to contain only very simple life forms. It seems the Flood evidently came at the time of the year when this tree was shedding its pollen.

Another headache to the evolution theory is the virtual absence of any materials and metal dust in the supposedly millions-of-years-old rocks that could be traced to powdery fine falling meteors. If the ages of the geological layers found in the earth would reach as far back in time as nearly all of today's science books are teaching, all the layers of sediment would be loaded with fine particles from space from fine meteors which even today are being daily dusted upon the earth. The first moon explorers were surprised that this dust on the surface of the moon was only several inches thick.

It is now also possible for scientists to measure the very small increase of saltiness of the ocean waters. It has been shown that the rate is just right for it to have begun several thousand instead of many millions of years ago.

THE GEOLOGICAL FORMATIONS in rocks and landscapes all over the world may appear to some people as if they were formed during many lengthy ages of slow geological change, but to others what is found shows plainly enough that all of it is washed-together flood debris.

Yet now some scientists say that if there were no records of a great flood in the past, such as we have in the book of Genesis, they would need to invent a flood theory to account for the amazing discoveries being made. No other explanation accounts for all these layers of washed-together flood sediment that are uncovered.

Much of the thinking in the science of geology is slowly being changed. Many scientists will now admit that what is being found could be traced to a worldwide deluge of water, falling as the crust of the earth was racked and shaken by volcanic action and earthquakes.

It is a foregone conclusion that the report of a believing scientist and an unbeliever are going to be different. Even if they both see the same evidence and use the same amount of time to make the same laboratory tests, the opinions they come to from their two different lines of reasoning will not be the same. If both were to write a textbook, there would surely be differences.

No one will ever be able to completely figure out all the tracks that the Great Flood has left for us to see. God wanted to leave permanent markers in the earth to be seen by future generations, so that it will be easier for all of us to believe in His judgment upon the first wicked and evil world and in His future judgment to come upon our world, which is also becoming more wicked and evil.

The geology seen formed in the rocks of the earth can be a powerful testimony to the truths found in the Bible.

God's wonderful works of Creation, all the more overwhelming as scientists discover more intricate and complex designs, will never be fully understood. These layers of strata, showing the marks of the destruction done by the Great Flood will also never be completely figured out. Because they are the work of the Almighty God, what we know will always be incomplete and imperfect.

"Such knowledge is too wonderful for me; it is high, I cannot attain unto it" (Psalm 139:6).

THE KNOWLEDGE OF SCIENCE AND RELIGIOUS BELIEFS can live side by side. All Bible-believing Christians can be filled with wonder and led to a worshipful reverence of the Creator by appreciating the marvels of Creation that scientists continually discover for us.

There is probably nothing more interesting to school-aged children than to examine and study the marvels and beauties of the wonders of nature that God has put on display for us.

The difference in the species of plants and animals does not tell us that life evolved from one form to another. Like a carpenter builds different kinds of houses, and like the similar but different machines built by a machinist, it tells us that God made many varieties of life.

We can be sure that the technology of science, which should be pointing people to the amazing designs and architecture of the Almighty God, should not be given prestige and worshiped like the God who knows all things and can do everything.

There is something seriously wrong with any study of science examining the works of God that does not also promote a belief in the living God.

EVEN WITH ALL THIS BACKGROUND, our young people are still reading in their textbooks that the scientific evidence for such a great flood is completely lacking. They have been told that all this is nothing but legend. They read that the geological formations and fossils studied by using only exact scientific methods have never once proved a worldwide deluge of water.

Other scientists coming along today are not so sure. Some think it is possible there just might be a little something behind all these so-called folk tales. Nearly always, there are some factual happenings behind even the most distorted and handed-down folklore.

In attempts to track down the kernel of truth contained in such a remarkable number of stories with faint similarities throughout, new efforts are being made to find if the traces of such a flood really do exist. Could something really have happened centuries ago that may have hatched these many flood stories? Can any scientific evidence found show signs that there may have been a global havoc laying waste, and that devastation of this magnitude actually occurred in a past age?

Since a number of detailed studies requiring much time and experience have been made, some secular textbooks mention that a few seriously scientific archaeologists and geologists have uncovered unmistakable flood evidence that cannot be ignored.

Some places on earth do show that there may have been onrushes of very large volumes of water "which nobody seems to be able to explain."

As a result, it has almost grudgingly been admitted that "it is possible there may have been a number of limited area floods in the past."

ONE EXAMPLE OF EVIDENCE IS that the water level of the Mediterranean Sea may at one time have risen to flow overland into the Black Sea. The traces left by this unbelievable movement of such a wholesale mass of water are still being investigated by the study of sediment deposited in the bottom of the Black Sea. It has been hoped that an analysis of the debris may determine from what lands these floodwaters came. Much time and energy is being spent trying to reconstruct this flood.

We see, then, that some researchers admit something very unusual may have happened long ago that did change the landscape. However, we are still told "exactly what took place has so far not been fully determined."

Nevertheless, nonbelievers still continue to discredit the history of the Flood as told by the Bible as just another one of the 270 flood legends from all over the world.

The only credit given to the Bible story in many secular textbooks is that "the Bible account has been identified as having its roots in the legends of the ancient Hebrew people." It is not considered scientific enough to qualify as a true story.

It is ironic that 269 fanciful legends and imaginary myths of a flood that evolved over years into absurdities hatched by fertile imaginations should be studied as something like truth, while the true worldwide Flood story in the Bible is discounted as a "legend not being worthy enough to take much stock in."

Let us note here that there are a few folklore stories of Creation and the Great Flood, coming from different places in the world, that have parts strikingly similar to what we read in the first chapters of our Bibles. However, none have yet been found that make as much sense as the Bible record. If the Flood were only local, Noah wouldn't have needed an ark. God would have only needed to ask Noah to migrate outside of the Flood area.

We have to wonder why we wouldn't all just go back to the Bible in the first place and use it as a source book to learn what really did happen. After all, the Bible is the only true and trustworthy source of what really happened when God destroyed the first world because it had become wicked beyond any hope for repentance.

The Fossil Record of the Great Flood

ALTHOUGH WE DON'T KNOW EXACTLY HOW THE FIRST WORLD that Noah knew for 600 years looked like, there are many things, especially the unaccountable number of fossils found all over the world, which may give us some very good clues. What has already been found gives us much to wonder and think about as we study the power of the Almighty God. Although the Bible was meant to be a book on religion and faith, and not of science, nothing yet found disproves what the Bible has already told us.

To begin with, if a living plant or any large or small animal dies and decomposes, or is eaten by worms or scavenger animals while it is still lying on the ground, it cannot become a fossil. It has to be quickly and tightly covered over with earth as soon as it dies. This preserves it, something like the way we preserve food for ourselves by canning it, or like preserving forage for our livestock by ensiling it to keep out all the air.

To become fossilized or petrified requires that the normal organic cells of these buried and preserved bodies of animal life and unrotted vegetation are replaced with substances of stone by the action of mineral-laden water seeping through it. This complete process of fossilization has been proved to take even less than a hundred years.

There is hardly anything that meets all these unique requirements except a sudden flash flood. A slow and gradual process over many millions of years could not have formed any fossils. It would take something exactly like the Great Flood to form the massive "fossil graveyards" found all over the world. These heaps of washed-together fossils are at some places found in layers many hundreds of feet in depth. An army of detectives are going through these fossils to find clues to support the theory of millions of years of evolution, but in these fossil beds is the remarkable evidence of sudden death and destruction. Some of these layers contain fish and reptiles. Some animals are entombed right beside the fossilized bodies of their natural enemies. Only a sudden drowning flood that washed together and buried their remains could have deposited such evidence.

To support the theory of evolution, fossils would need to be found for thousands of generations of plant and animal life, showing a gradual change from one distinct species to another fully developed species capable of reproducing its own kind (Genesis 1:20-25). The evidence supporting evolution is simply missing in the fossil record. Fossils found are 100% perfect and complete, showing no evidence of gradual change. For example, no fossil has been found showing anything but perfect scales or perfect feathers. No creatures have been found which were something between a fish and a bird. This is a stubborn fact which does not conform to the great lengths which men have gone to explain Creation without a Creator.

The fact that these fossils are there proves the history of something like a one-year-and-ten-day splashing back and forth of floodwaters, and at the same time refutes and disproves a geology that would have taken long ages of millions of years to form.

The usual way to put a date on a fossil is to say that it was found in a stratified layer of earth that was laid down so many millions of years ago. When the question comes up as to how the age of this certain formation was determined, the reasoning goes around in circles saying that because the fossils found in it are so many millions of years old, it stands to reason that the geological age of this layer is then also so many millions of years old.

What is ironic is that the only "sure proof" for the millions-of-years theory is the fossil record, the same "sure proof" our God has left for us so that we can see a great flood did happen!

To be sure, we know the God who formed the landscapes and mountains of earth at Creation *could* just as well have placed all these layers of sediment—layers containing fossils, seashells, and the bones of fish and animals, fully developed and ready for geologists to uncover at a later time. But why would He have done this? After all, the God we worship saw fit at Creation to make something of much greater magnitude than fossils lodging in the rocks of earth. He made our first parents as fully developed adults, and the very first animal and plant life was created fully developed and ready to reproduce its own kind.

In our days, every ship captain keeps a daily logbook of his ship. God was the captain of the ark that floated on a vast sea without shores. The chapters in our Bible telling us of the Great Flood are God's logbook in condensed form. He sees fit to let us know what happened by giving us a condensed version in our Bibles.

All the evidence that the entire earth was at one time under water makes it easy for us to believe that fossils came from the action of the mighty forces that raised and lowered the continents under the water during the Great Flood. The disasters that underwater earthquakes, called tsunamis, have done in our times can give us a small idea what could have happened when waters covered the whole earth.

There is no geological formation anywhere that cannot be traced to the work of the back and forth surging of massive waves caused by the violent up and down heaving of the ocean floor, and undersea volcanic mountains. These underwater waves sloshing back and forth account for the sand and gravel beds we find today. The rounded stones found in huge quantities all over could only have been formed by a violent tumbling against each other.

These huge, moving underwater tidal waves created by this undersea volcanic and earthquake action easily explains why the Himalayan Mountain range, the highest range of mountains on earth today, contains seashells and fossils of ocean life. This range of mountains, along with the crust of the earth all over, was pushed higher and the ocean basins were lowered just before everything quieted down when the Great Flood was over.

In this holocaust of waters, as the Rocky Mountains were being pushed upwards into the form we know today, the sudden releasing of a huge lake of trapped water, when the bottoms of the oceans were lowering, could have ripped out in a short time all of what is now the Grand Canyon.

THE RECORDS LEFT IN THE ROCKS AND LANDSCAPES show us that some of this was happening all over the world. The geography of the earth before the Great Flood was vastly different from what it became after the Great Flood.

Today we can still see the slanted rock formations along the sides of the cuts made in the mountains by the builders of our interstate highway systems. When the layers of the rocks in the earth were being pushed upward, the crust of the earth crinkled and wrinkled and buckled, the way a piece of wet paper does as it dries out. The land areas being flattened down and then pushed up during the Great Flood formed the continents of the earth as we know them today.

As the flood waters retreated the different landscapes all over the world would be formed. Among the thousands of interesting natural features would be the Rocky Mountains and the Great Plains. The limestone soils of what would at sometime be Lancaster County, Pennsylvania, would be laid down, and sooner or later be grown over with forests. In what is now the Great Badlands of South Dakota, a much smaller form of erosion would keep on happening almost every year since.

The historic basis found in ancient stories of the lost pre-Flood continent called Atlantis may explain what happened to a vast area of the first world that sunk and then did not get pushed up above the surface of the Atlantic Ocean to the level it had been before. The top of this fabled land may be the Azores, a group of islands with volcanic mountains almost a thousand miles off the western shores of Europe. Something very similar could have formed the many islands in the Pacific Ocean.

Only a great flood and the convulsions of the crust of the earth beneath the waters would scientifically explain the finding of the bones of marine life and the teeth of sharks hundreds of miles inland in what is now very dry and sandy desert. The petrified remains of twisted tree trunks, some lying down and some standing upright through as many as twelve different layers of so-called millions of years of geological strata have been found, so whatever happened must have happened fast with no long, long periods of time in between. Some of these layers of rock contain thousands of pieces in jumbled heaps of anything from oyster shells to the bones of mice and elephants.

Each wave of the mighty floodwaters would leave what future geologists would interpret as "another geological era." These unbelievably large masses of water being splashed to and fro did in a year and ten days what would have taken the ordinary processes of nature many millions of years to do. Many books today talk lightly about millions and hundreds of millions of years ago, without backing their figures with anything more scientific than what are called "educated guesses."

Even the carbon-14 dating methods being used have been discovered to be very inaccurate for anything over several thousand years old. Many materials known to be recent are, when tested, erroneously calculated to be very ancient—to the embarrassment of the laboratory personnel.

A cataclysm like we read of in the Bible can simply and understandably explain the finding of rocks not related to the area—rocks which must have been washed in from many hundreds of miles away.

Explaining the Ice Ages

MANY ATTEMPTS HAVE BEEN made to scientifically explain what looks as if the ice now at the North and South Poles may at some long-ago time have extended over large areas far away from the poles. Many science textbooks try to explain all this as having happened in a long-ago age when the earth cooled and moving ice glaciers scarred out thousands of deep depressions in the earth. These became freshwater lakes. At other places, large gravel beds are found which are explained as fine pieces of rock dropped when these moving and scraping ice packs melted down when the earth warmed again.

But wait a minute. All this could also have happened during the Great Flood. All this ice could have come from hailstorms as gigantic as the rainstorms that raged for forty days and forty nights all over the world.

You may have read about the tundra, which is a vast treeless plain of frozen earth in the northlands where hardly anything grows. You may also have read about the huge, now extinct elephants called mammoths that have been found buried by the hundreds of thousands in the tundra. Large herds of these frozen animals with shaggy fur and long tusks curving upwards have been found with grass in their mouths and undigested vegetation still in their stomachs. Even now, their flesh is in a good enough condition to be used as dog food when it is thawed out.

What happened no one will ever know, but whatever it was happened very fast. Something happened much faster than a global cooling coming over long periods of time. These animals may have been caught in a huge hailstorm that suddenly came upon them. After they sank into the mud, which is now frozen the year round, the ice preserved them like a huge frozen food locker for these thousands of years that have come and gone since the violent storms of the Great Flood.

A SUBJECT IN VIRTUALLY ALL NATURAL SCIENCE textbooks is that of the large lizard-like reptiles called dinosaurs. Can we believe the theories we are told about these prehistoric creatures and still believe in Bible truth? There are no dinosaurs in today's zoos and nobody knows of having ever seen one. Some of the skeleton reconstructions and dinosaur illustrations seen today are only imaginary, based on several teeth or bones that were found. A small jawbone found suggests that the animal was plant-eating; when a large one is found, it is believed the animal fought with and ate other animals.

Many fossilized eggs of these monster lizards or large crocodiles have been found. Thousands of large footprints found in the mud have since hardened into rock. Many naturalists studying these tracks have come to the conclusion that these lizards' tails were long and heavy and that they walked around using only the hind legs.

However, who knows? If they were stomping the mud while they were running and half swimming when the muddy floodwaters were rising, they would have left tracks exactly like this. (What is also interesting is that human footprints have been found in these very same layers.)

Here again, God could easily have created the earth with all this tracking and bones and eggs already in the rocks, or the creatures called dinosaurs may have been animals that could not survive in the altogether different world after the Flood. Sooner or later they would fail to reproduce in the changed climate and habitat after the Flood and they would gradually die out. Some Bible scholars suggest the snake was changed from something like a large four-legged lizard to the slithering creature we know of today.

Bible References to Strange Creatures

IT MAY COME AS A SURPRISE TO MANY that the Bible mentions the names of several large animals and sea creatures. Working in different languages, Bible translators over the years often didn't really know what to call them.

The book of Job mentions several of these creatures. Although this book of the Bible is placed just before the Book of the Psalms of the Hebrew people, it is believed to be the earliest book of the Bible to be written.

There are several different creatures mentioned in the book of Job that must have had some Bible translators stumped, because the Hebrew names behemoth, leviathan, and tannin are written down untranslated. Other translations render these words as hippopotamus, crocodile, and sea serpents, while other translations call them whales, or simply monsters.

In a paragraph added to the end of the book of Job in the Greek Septuagint translation of the Old Testament, we learn that Job was a God-fearing grandson of Esau; born five generations after Abraham. Here he is identified as the Jobab of Genesis 36:33. The land of Uz, where he lived, may still have had a vestige of the worship of the true God such as the king of Salem had in Abraham's time (Genesis 14:18).

Anyway, this makes it possible that Job lived closer to the time of the Great Flood (mentioned in Job 22:15 and 16) than even Moses did. He may have known animals that are now extinct.

The Bible also mentions unicorns and dragons at a number of places, so they may not be as mythical as some people think. They may be some of the number of animal species that are now extinct. Many kinds of animals that are not seen today have been found, painted a long time ago on ancient pottery or on the side walls of sheltered caves in which human families, known as cave people, may have lived either before or after the Flood. We have no way of finding out how many kinds of God's creatures may have lived in ancient times but are still unknown to us.

There are many more creatures than the dodo birds and the passenger pigeons that are no longer in existence. For instance, it is known that at least forty species of birds and thirty-five species of mammals have vanished in the last 200 years in the United States alone.

How the Great Flood Changed the World

MANY PEOPLE WONDER WHERE ALL THE WATER that covered the highest mountains on earth came from, and just as good a question is: Where did all the water go after the Flood was over?

We know our Almighty God could have created all this extra water, and then in His miraculous way, made it disappear and dry up into nothing again during the one year and ten days the family of Noah was shut in the ark.

But what God did do is right there in print in the Bible: "And the waters prevailed exceedingly upon the earth, and all the *high hills* that were under the whole heaven were covered" (Genesis 7:19).

When the level of the water over the high hills was then increased only 15 cubits more (about 23 feet higher), all the mountains of the earth were covered. It may be that the surface of the pre-Flood earth was much flatter than it is today with our highest mountain peak at 29,028 feet and the lowest point in today's oceans being a trench about 35,800 feet deep. (It has been figured out that if all the land surface of the earth were to be evened out, all of it would be under 8,000 feet of water.)

When the Bible says that the tops of the mountains were seen (Genesis 8:5), it is telling us that the ocean floors were again being lowered and the surface of the earth, as we know it today, was being raised. Even though God used wind to dry off the soggy earth, He didn't need to increase or decrease the total amount of water He had created when the earth was made.

A hymn sung by the Hebrew people many hundreds of years later would contain a number of lines relating to the rise and fall of these floodwaters (Psalm 104:5-10). It is also almost incredible that a believing ancient Egyptian pharaoh would compose an even earlier Psalm mentioning this Great Flood which had occurred sometime like a thousand years before his time. (Story in chapter 5 in this book.)

THERE ARE HINTS IN THE BIBLE that the pre-Flood world Noah knew was vastly different from the world he stepped out on when he left the ark. Apparently major landscape and climate changes occurred. Two of the four rivers that had flowed out of the Garden of Eden (Genesis 2:10-14) are no longer in existence, and from the verses in Genesis 2:5-6 and 10, we gather that the whole earth before the Flood was something like a tropical forest. The air was dense and damp from being watered daily by a dense mist.

Fossils of palm trees and banana trees have been found in Alaska and Greenland, and in the other lands close to the polar regions. The fossils dug up in some of the earth's deserts and Arctic regions show that most of the earth may have at one time supported an even more luxuriant and abundant vegetation than the tropical rain forests of today. The areas in the northlands where at one time the great mammoths grazed in lush growth is only one example.

The fossils of plants and the man-made tools found in the great two-and-a-half-million-square-mile African desert, the Sahara, shows that it was at one time covered with a vegetation such as only the tropics have today. The fossils show that the climate and the plant and animal life, very unlike today, may have been almost uniform over at least the greater part of the earth. There would have been no desert or Arctic regions.

From what we read in Genesis 2:6, we can imagine the entire first world to have been like an earth surrounded by a canopy of water vapor, a great greenhouse, keeping the climate of the earth a steaming jungle with a moisture-laden atmosphere. This may explain the source of at least some of the falling rains, as this canopy of moisture-laden air broke up to uncover the clear blue skies we can see today when our rains are over. This would also explain why no rainbows arched in the sky until after the Great Flood was over.

Many of our creation-believing scientists, who also believe that the Great Flood actually happened, have theories of how God may have used natural causes to trigger these sudden weather and climate changes all over the world. There is even evidence that the courses of the ocean currents and the prevailing winds were at some time changed.

If God changed the tilt of the axis of the earth (like a spinning top leans to one way and then the other), this could have upset a balance that set off the Great Flood. This could also have started the patterns of the summer heat and the winter cold to be as regular as the rhythms of night and day (Genesis 8:22).

Another theory is that a giant meteorite may have hit the spinning earth, or a falling star from outer space may have knocked many natural processes out of kilter.

We are not sure. We do not need to try to figure out how God did it. It is enough for us to believe that it happened.

THIS PRE-FLOOD WORLD OF RAPIDLY GROWING AND luxuriant vegetation on land and the large amount of marine life and large fishes in the seas may also explain the vast underground coal and oil reserves that power our modern industrial and fast-moving mechanical world of the last several hundred years. These materials heat our homes and supply the power that keeps the many billions of pistons jumping up and down in our gasoline and diesel engines all over the world in our time.

People who study natural sciences tell us that coal is the tomb of plant life and petroleum is the graveyard of marine life and undersea vegetation. God could have instantly created all this material found in larger or smaller quantities nearly all over the world, but the Great Flood also could have put into motion every one of the processes needed to make coal and oil, without needing millions of years to do it.

If coal was formed by abundant vegetation (as scientists believe it was because of the unmistakable imprints of plant life found throughout every vein of coal), it had to happen suddenly before the vegetation decayed. Decomposed vegetation would not produce any coal.

The millions of acres of tall timber and the dense and heavy growths on the pre-Flood landscape could have formed coal. These enormous masses of plant residue would have been washed together into great piles at different places. Only a flood of water could have caused a sudden and wholesale destruction and then buried it immediately before decay set in.

The enormous pressure needed to rapidly convert all this into coal would come from the weight of the sediment and wet mud on top of it, and the volcanic action packing and heating it from below. The process used to convert wood into the charcoal for our barbecue grills works similar to the way coal was formed.

The large underground petroleum reserves also show evidence that enormous quantities of large marine life and fishes were trapped together and then covered up and heated before all decayed. This could have been made possible if massive whales and other large sea creatures (Genesis 1:21 and 26) splashing in the oceans were suddenly killed by underwater volcanic shocks, then being swept together. These masses of marine bodies were entombed by mud and sediment before decay set in. The pressure and heat of the volcanic action below it would turn it into the oil deposits, which are pumped out of the earth in our modern day and age. The desert sands of the Middle East with this oil underneath would become some of the most valuable real estate on the earth.

Laboratory demonstrations have shown that millions of years are not needed to make coal and oil formations. Substances very much like coal and oil have been made in only a few months' time by using the right organic materials under heat and pressure. All of this would have been provided naturally during the Great Flood. In fact, at the rate of oil seepage out of the rock walls surrounding the underground oil reservoirs, they would all be drained empty by now if they would have been formed millions of years ago.

THERE IS EVIDENCE THAT LIMESTONE IS COMPOSED OF SEASHELLS crushed very fine, and in some cases may be tightly packed very tiny marine life. These deposits found throughout the entire world could also have been formed under the waters of the Great Flood.

It is a fallacy that it takes millions of years to make hardened rock. Our ready-mix companies and our concrete contractors, by using the right ingredients mixed with water are making a material that hardens into a form of rock overnight.

WHILE ALL THIS DESTRUCTION WAS GOING ON, God was lovingly watching over the family that would soon be stepping off the ark onto a cleansed world they could not imagine when they entered the ark a year and ten days earlier.

God must have loved this family that He saved them and took care of them as He did. Oh, how grieved He must have been that nothing short of the suffering of His human form would save them and their descendants from something in the future much worse than a quick death in a flood!

Noah Doesn't Leave the Ark until Told to

ALTHOUGH NOAH HAD BEEN GIVEN some unmistakable signs that the land of the earth was drying off, he didn't take it upon himself to decide when to leave the ark. He waited patiently, and let God set the time for his exit.

With our loving God above us, and His Spirit within us as much as we give Him room, it is never necessary for any of us to ever despair and lose hope, or question the reason for our existence. Look within and be depressed—look to God and be at rest.

God's time is the best time. With the living hope that is only a prayer away, human beings will never need to take it upon themselves when to make the exit from this world.

None of us will want to miss out on both the duties and the joys God still has in store for us as long as He needs us in this life. Between our trials, which are God's blessings in disguise, what may be the best part of our lives is still waiting for us.

Only God knows when our work is finished. Only He knows when the best time is here for Him to take us home to be with Him forever. As long as He permits us to live, He has the answers to our problems and a purpose for our lives.

Let us leave the length of our lives in God's hands. God needs our work here on this earth until the hour comes that He will bid us to leave.

After the Great Flood

NOAH AND HIS FAMILY WERE THE ONLY HUMANS WHO HAD LIVED IN two totally different worlds: the before and after worlds of the Flood.

Noah's grandfather, Methuselah, who lived to be 969 years old, was the oldest man who ever lived. He died in the same year as the Flood. It is not known if he died just before the rains came, or if he had become one of the ungodly who perished because he trifled away his chance to enter the ark when God gave him the opportunity.

Noah lived in the time of Enos, one of Adam's grandsons, who died at the age of 905 years, when Noah was 556 years old. After the Flood, Noah lived up to the time of Abraham's father, Terah. Noah took leave of this temporal world for the eternal when Terah was 68 years old, only two years before Abraham was born. Noah's life came that close to bridging the years from Adam and Eve to Abraham.

What a number of dramatic events Noah had in his lifetime to think over in his sunset years!

Abraham's time was almost exactly halfway between Creation and Jesus Christ. We can see that the generations from Creation to the time of Abraham were very few, so the accurate passing on of the scriptural history about Creation and the Great Flood from one generation to the next is very credible. When the earth was young, people lived very long lives, perhaps because the earth was a pure and yet unpolluted natural environment. Life-threatening diseases may have been absent in this pristine and unspoiled world. If God planned to increase the population of the world in a relatively short time, these long lives would extend the childbearing age of humans by several hundred years.

NOAH COULD VERY WELL HAVE remembered his father Lamech telling of the talks he had with Adam, the first man on earth. Adam would have been the seven-times great-grandfather of Lamech, and going by the genealogy and chronology in the fifth chapter in Genesis, Noah's father was 56 years old when the somber day came that Adam died. Although he had originally been created to live eternally, the weary body of Adam was at last returned to the dust of the earth God used to form him 930 years earlier.

Oh, the interesting stories Adam may have related while he was still living! The father of Noah could well have spent many cool evenings of his young days outside of Adam's tent listening to the stories of bliss and unmarred happiness back in the Garden of Eden.

These very same stories Adam told (probably with a faraway look in his eyes) would find their way into the Bible, a book we all have in our homes. These true happenings would be strikingly different from the later invented myths of a world emerging from an unknown beginning.

What regret Adam would feel all over again as he spoke of those days in the Garden of Eden. What remorse he and his wife Eve went through when they fell from the state of pure innocence and peace God created for them. We can be sure Adam never finished his story without telling of the hope they had in God's promise of mercy that would come in the form of a Messiah (our Redeemer), born of the human race, who would destroy the power of the fallen and rebellious angel, Lucifer, who was the author of the deceit of our first parents.

NOAH HIMSELF COULD HAVE LISTENED TO ENOS, his five-times great-grandfather, a grandson of Adam, retell the stories of the dawn of the world's Creation. How we wish we could have been there when Noah later retold and passed on these stories (and probably many more) to his descendants.

We need to wish no longer. We can read a remarkably condensed version in easily understood words of the same stories Noah would have related to his descendants—in the first chapters of our Holy Bible. In the Bible we read a true, close-to-the-source, God-inspired account, because Noah didn't take leave of this temporal world for the eternal until Terah, Abraham's father, was 68 years old—only two years before Abraham was born.

Abraham was a man God saw teaching his family and household after him to "keep the way of the Lord" (Genesis 18:19). This family would accurately pass on the Genesis stories of the Creation and the Great Flood until Moses would preserve them on paper.

The concept of an Almighty God of both mercy and justice was not invented by the family of Abraham. It was the pure religion passed on from one generation to the next.

Noah lived on after the Flood for another 350 years. This is a long time. It is longer than living from 1660, when Thieleman van Braght composed the *Martyrs Mirror*, until now. It is longer than the time that most white people have lived in America.

Some of what Noah lived to see after the Flood would most certainly have grieved this man in his sunset years. Noah, who had walked with God, had done all that God commanded him to do. He had been a just man and perfect in his generation, and found grace in the eyes of the Lord (Genesis 6). Afterwards, however, he would also have reason to be disappointed in himself. This "preacher of righteousness" (II Peter 2:5), the man who built an ark to keep himself and his family alive, was still not beyond the reach of doing sinful actions. It would be evident that he was not the prophesied Savior of mankind because he was not sinless.

Noah got drunk. While in this condition he would say and do things he would be ashamed of later. Although it will never be clear to us exactly what happened, we do know Noah let his family down, and that two of Noah's sons, through their modest and respectful actions, got their blessings renewed. Another son, who made an improper joke of what should have been kept quietly sacred, would later bring something that was not good upon one of his own sons.

What this was is also not clear, so we will never know. However, it is a sobering thought to know that through our actions we can pass the blessing of good or the curse of evil to those going this way after we are gone.

IT WOULD BE INTERESTING IF THE BIBLE told us a little more about those three girls who, in honorable marriage, became wives of the three sons of Noah.

What helped them make the choice of joining the ridiculed family of a man odd enough to spend so much of his time building a huge boat on dry land? Had God made them homely looking so that they would be passed by and spared being tempted into sin by lusting men and boys out looking only for girls fair of face and figure?

Were these three girls' characters of such high moral ideals that they would not let themselves be enticed into doing the sinning everyone else was doing? Or had they been sinners who had now repented? With the birth of a new and divine nature, they would turn over a new leaf for the rest of their lives. If this was the case, they were believers in God's grace that saves repentant sinners and gives them another chance. If they were not orphans at the time of the Flood, they knew their own parents would soon be perishing in the watery depths of the Flood they believed would soon be coming upon the earth.

Whatever the circumstances, they made difficult choices, with very far-reaching consequences. These three girls, along with their mother-in-law, would become the mothers of many thousands of millions.

Their names are not given, so we may think of them as representing many millions of unnamed virtuous girls ever since that time. They became the forebears of everyone, including you and me, who has lived on earth from then on until the present day.

And their choice made possible an unbroken royal lineage from Adam and Eve to Jesus Christ.

Let us not permit anyone to tell us that anything we find written in Genesis is a myth and a legend. If we throw out the beginning of the Bible, what will we have left on which to base the truth of the rest of the Bible? God guarded His truth until it was safely contained in the written Scriptures. There the truth shall endure even though heaven and earth pass away.

What happened in Genesis is an inspiration to this family called the Christian Church, a family of believers in Jesus Christ, as the promise that "the gates of hell shall not prevail against it" (Matthew 16:18).

EGYPT–LEHNERT & LANDROCK

ENCYCLOPEDIA BRITTANICA – 1966

The chap you see on the left is sitting on the flat top of the Great Pyramid. This is the pyramid in the foreground in the aerial view above of the Giza pyramids of Egypt.

This largest tomb ever was built before the time of Abraham in the Bible for a pharaoh named Cheops. The pyramid standing next to it was built for his son, the pharaoh Chephren.

Well over 4,000 years old, no other structure ever built by man will stand in silent stateliness during as many human generations, or for as many centuries of history between Creation to Judgment Day than these tombs built for the bodies and treasures of the pharaohs, worshiped as god-kings.

A legend circulating for a time in ancient Egypt said that after sleeping in death for 36,000 years, a pharaoh's body would be resurrected to life again.

What is ironic is that their bodies and the great wealth supposedly sealed in with them were not found when the plugged passageways leading to the burial chambers were discovered and opened up deep within the pyramids. Because the later pharaohs had their temple priests rip practically all the gleaming white marble facing off the pyramid sides to use for temple building elsewhere, it is easy to believe they also desecrated the bodies and carried off the enormous riches buried with them.

But who knows? Considering the depravity of human nature, it is possible that, as a clever cover-up for their robbery, the hidden entrances and interior passageways became plugged and sealed by the plotting priests themselves, without any burials even having taken place.

Chapter 4

The Largest Tomb Ever

IN THE WRITINGS OF SOME ANCIENT SECULAR historians, we find many exaggerated statements.

Much of this may be due to their recording of dates, numbers, and amounts in a way different from the methods we think such information ought to be recorded in our day. Then also, at some places the figures may have been miscopied or very large figures may have been exaggerated as a boast.

One ancient chronicler wrote that the great library at Alexandria in Egypt contained 700,000 handwritten scrolls. This is very doubtful. Allowing only three inches of shelf space for each scroll would require something over thirty-three miles of shelving.

When another Egyptian historian writes about one of their cities containing an area equal to ten square miles with a highly fortified wall around all of it, we are left wondering how accurate his figures really are. That would be a lot of wall. He may be overstating his measurements a little bit, or he may have merely been making a wild guess.

Even the number of years that the ancient Egyptian histories say their pharaohs ruled cannot be depended upon as being altogether accurate. If the figures were all correct and didn't overlap each other, the dates of Egyptian history would add up to going back beyond the time of the Great Flood.

WE MIGHT THEREFORE QUESTION an ancient account if it told us that a group of Egyptian people quarried something like two and a half million blocks of stone, each one weighing an average of two and a half tons. Such a story would sound a little far-fetched. Where could such a large number of blocks have been used?

If the writer were to continue and say that every stone block was dressed to an accurate dimension and smoothly finished, using only primitive copper and bronze handheld chisels, and saws powered only by human muscle, we would begin to discredit the whole story.

But then, if the story were topped off by telling us these blocks were heaped into a nearly perfect level and square structure with the peak almost 500 feet in the air, and that this was all done with human muscle power, without the use of any modern transits, power saws, and mechanical construction machinery of any kind whatsoever, we would be ready to dismiss the whole story as nothing more than a big storybook fairy tale!

THE PYRAMIDS OF EGYPT, fascinating and well known, prove such works do exist. Still standing since being built before the dawn of written history, there were more years from the beginning of pyramid building to the beginning of the Christian era than there are years between the days when Jesus walked on earth and our present day. We may grasp how ancient the pyramids really are if we take the entire sweep of time from the pyramids to our present, and understand that when the halfway point was reached, Jesus had not yet been born on earth.

These clusters of pyramids are the only man-made structures built during the dim recesses of time that still exist in our day. These ancient pharaohs wanted their monuments built to last forever (a longgggg time!), and it is altogether possible that these pyramids may endure until God decides that the time allotted for humanity on earth is over, and that final day of history takes place.

THESE PYRAMIDS WERE BUILT FIRM AND SOLID. Because of their tightly fitted joints, they were not shaken apart and have withstood violent earthquakes. The one that devastated the nearby city of Cairo in the year 1301 A.D. did no damage to the pyramids. No structures like the pyramids have ever since been built by man.

There are at least seventy known Egyptian pyramids in and around the Giza area on the west bank of the Nile River. Some of the lesser pyramids were never finished. Smaller ones may still be undiscovered beneath the windswept desert sands. Some of the earliest ones, made of sun-dried brick, have deteriorated into not much more than piles of clay.

Three of the pyramids are much larger in size than any of the others. Of these three, the largest is called the Great Pyramid. It was built as a tomb for a pharaoh named Khufu and his queen. In an ancient Greek history of the pyramids, this pharaoh's name is written as Cheops.

No words or pictures can ever prepare a traveler for the first sight of these massive mountains of stone. If you stand directly in front of a pyramid, the whole sky to one side looks like it is filled with stone blocks. These structures, built for the purpose of containing the mortal remains of early Egyptian pharaohs until the great and glorious Resurrection Morning, are simply overwhelming and mind-boggling.

Cheops wanted a tomb worthy of his dignity. He wanted to be buried in a structure at which the whole world would marvel. If the size of a man's tomb indicated his greatness, this Cheops of about 4,000 years ago would be the greatest human being who ever lived.

The next to largest pyramid, originally only ten feet shorter in overall height than the Great Pyramid, was built for the body and treasures of Chephren, a son of Cheops.

The third largest was for Cheops' grandson, also a pharaoh, named Mycerinus.

When built, the Great Pyramid was about 490 feet high. It is now about 31 feet lower, since vandals rolled off the capstone and the next 12 courses.

Building Cheops' Pyramid

THE BASE OF CHEOPS' PYRAMID IS ABOUT 756 feet square and covers about 13½ acres. The method used in ancient times worked as well as any method in modern days, for the pyramid is almost as square, level, and oriented to the points of the compass as man today could have made it. No one is sure what reference points the builders used to find the true north.

The outcrop of rock upon which they built the pyramid was not cut level before the first layer of bottom blocks was laid. Because this bedrock upon which the first course was laid is much higher in the middle than at the sides, it would have been almost impossible to get the base perfectly square by the usual method of measuring across the diagonals. How this was done is still a mystery, and how the builders leveled the base course also remains an unanswered question.

When modern-day engineers checked the level of the first course, they found that one corner was higher by less than a half inch. Many transits used by builders today have a tolerance for error greater than this half inch in the approximately one-fifth mile between the diagonals of this pyramid.

The straightness of the base course is off by only a small fraction of an inch. We must admit the builders of 4,000 years ago took the time to do things right!

There are 209 courses of varied thickness in the Great Pyramid. The height of these courses varies from a little under 2' to a little over 4'8". These blocks are assembled with near perfect precision. The stones fit together so accurately that nothing thicker than a postcard can be inserted between the stone joints, which were put into place without mortar.

The original marble facing, polished to a luster smooth enough to reflect the gleam of the sun, made the pyramid look like one gleaming white block of stone. The facing is now nearly gone except for several places around the base, which was buried by the drifting sands.

This stone facing, also with joints fitting to a hundredth of an inch tolerance, was ripped off by later generations of temple builders. To build the temples, the ruins of which are still standing close by, it was easier to loot the marble off the pyramids than quarry it elsewhere and then smooth it off. The pyramid sides today are very irregular because vandals pried out a number of stones in their early attempts to find the entrance leading to the interior passageways of the pyramid.

IF THE TWO MILLION AND THREE HUNDRED THOUSAND BLOCKS of stone used in the building of the Great Pyramid were laid out in one row against each other, they would be lined up for the incredible distance of over 2,300 miles. If the blocks were cut up into cubes measuring a foot on each side, the line of blocks placed side by side would reach about two-thirds of the way around the earth's equator.

The total weight of the Great Pyramid is estimated at well over six million tons. If this weight of stone was loaded on a row of modern tandem-axle dump trucks, each 25 feet long and hauling 20 tons, the row of 300,000 trucks parked bumper to bumper would extend for a distance of nearly 1,450 miles.

Parked on the Pennsylvania Turnpike starting at Philadelphia, this line of trucks would continue over the mountains of western Pennsylvania to Route 70, through northern West Virginia, Ohio, Indiana, Illinois, and Iowa, with the final truck being parked somewhere in Nebraska.

If a stone quarry were to load and send off one hundred truckloads a day at ten an hour for three hundred ten-hour working days a year, they would keep loading trucks for at least ten years in order to complete the order needed for Cheops' Great Pyramid. The total tons for an order then needed to build the next two pyramids would be even greater.

The work done on the tomb of Cheops and his queen was simply incredible. Just chipping the six surfaces of each of these 2,300,000 blocks to accurate dimensions would be the same as smoothing a stone roadway twenty feet wide for 1,700 miles, which is the approximate distance between the cities of Philadelphia, Pennsylvania, to Denver, Colorado.

Nothing built by man before the 1800s had exceeded the height of the Great Pyramid and the volume of material used was exceeded only by the Great Wall of China.

AFTER THE FUNERALS WERE OVER and the bodies of Cheops and his wife were laid to rest in the deep interior of the pyramid, a little extra work was required before the job was finished. Fitting and polishing the twenty acres of marble exterior that hid the entranceway completed the lifetime project of the deceased pharaoh lying inside with his piles of accumulated treasure.

The legends of Cheops' oppression and disregard for moral living may or may not be based on truth. We know nothing of importance that this vainglorious pharaoh did in his lifetime, except to plan for his tomb. It would be interesting to know if he himself ever lifted a little finger to help with the work.

The Tools of the Egyptians

EVEN THOUGH THE USE OF IRON was known before the days of the Great Flood (Genesis 4:22), it seems the art of utilizing iron ore had become lost. No iron tools have been found among the pyramids, so they were built before the Egyptian civilization rediscovered how to make and shape tools of iron.

Although many copper and bronze chisels, along with wooden mallets, have been dug up, no tool as simple as a hand pick has yet been found. The Egyptian tools included muscle-powered bowstring drills and handheld pullback saws. (These saws and drills, believe it or not, were cordless!)

The Egyptians understood the principle of a weighted string for a plumb line, and a stretched string for a straight line. They used wedges and palm tree fiber ropes, but there have been no paintings found from the time of pyramid building of pulleys and block and tackle.

Although rollers may have been used under the blocks as they were pulled and pushed into place, nothing has been found with wheels from the time when the pyramids were built. The first paintings of wheeled chariots were made a little before the time the Israelites lived in Egypt. Like the Indians in our country before the white man came, nobody had gotten around to inventing the wheel.

Egyptian Accomplishments

THE EGYPTIAN CIVILIZATION was far advanced in many areas. They were geniuses in mathematics and geometry. They had a very accurate figure for *pi*, which is the ratio of the diameter of a circle to its circumference. They could figure out square roots, and knew how to work out the areas of circles, triangles, and other geometric shapes. They could figure out the volumes of solids and calculate how many bricks or blocks of stone were needed for a construction job.

The Egyptians also had somehow developed a system to determine latitude and longitude—a system not duplicated by scientists until recent years. This may be the reason why the Great Pyramid stands almost exactly on the 30th degree of latitude, one-third of the distance from the equator to the North Pole.

A smooth, flat area discovered under the sands and debris on the pyramid's north side, may have been used as a huge sundial and calendar as the Egyptians watched, over a year's time, the lengthening and shortening of the shadow of the highest tip of the pyramid.

Our 24-hour day comes from the early Egyptian stargazers who divided the day and night into twelve equal parts. Their New Year began with the Nile River's annual rise, which occurred at the time of the year when the Dog Star, Sirius, rose in the Egyptian sky. This same star, still seen in our night sky, was worshiped as a deity in the ancient Egyptian religion because of its importance.

The early Egyptians extracted copper from copper ore in those primitive days. They would then melt this copper with tin to make bronze. In order to cut the stone blocks of the pyramids and chip out the chambers and passageways in the bedrock under the pyramids, the ancient Egyptians developed a method of highly tempering the otherwise soft bronze chisels to a hardness like carbide. How they did all this is still a puzzle to modern expert metallurgists. It does not matter how it is analyzed, the metals still do not reveal the repeated hammering methods or the heating and cooling processes they may have used in hardening the structure of the bronze.

Their craftsmanship was very fine. They had looms with a very fine weave. Linen cloth has been found with a warp of 160 threads to the inch and a weft of 120 threads to the inch. The channel stitch, which moderns believed was invented only several hundred years ago, was commonly used in ancient Egyptians' sewn materials, and like a surgeon of today, they knew how to sew up wounds.

Some of the intricate wooden artifacts found may not have been bent by heating the wood in hot water, but formed by training a twig into the proper shape while it was still growing.

Knowing about all this superior intelligence and these natural abilities of the early humans so soon after Creation makes us wonder where the theory of evolution ever came from. This intelligence surely proves that humans in our days are not more of a genius in having the ability to clearly reason and acquire and retain knowledge, and then making use of it, than the ancient people were. We do not have superior thinking. We only have the advantage of knowing about more of the inventions of the people living before us than they did.

It only makes it more important than ever to be using our God-given abilities for good and worthy purposes.

The Nile River

ALL SCHOOL BOYS AND GIRLS who have an interest in geography know the Nile as the mighty river that flows through the country of Egypt. Because of this river there is no other country on earth like the land of Egypt.

The river flows northward for 4,160 miles, making it the longest river in the world. It flows through a series of cataracts too dangerous to travel by boat. The waters flowing over the rapids and through the deep, rocky gorges downstream from the rapids level out while going through a 1,600-mile-long ribbon of flatland. Along this length it runs through a barren desert, which is virtually a sea of drifting sands. Here no waters flow into the Nile. This is where most of the Egyptian people live.

When we think that virtually all the water that kept the people of Egypt alive and grew their crops for thousands of years, including the years the Israelites lived in Egypt, was funneled through a river gorge at some places less than 250 yards wide, it seems incredible. The water little Moses floated on many hundreds of miles downstream about 3,500 years ago would have come through this gorge.

The long, flat lowland river valley, bordered on both sides by a wasteland of rocks and desert sands, is only about a mile or two wide at some places. At the northern end, the average width of the farmland is about twelve miles from one side to the other, and the land is sheltered from the strong desert winds by towering cliffs on both sides of the valley. It is possible for a person to stand with one foot on fertile soil and the other on one of the driest deserts on earth.

There are no forests in the valley. There are date palms and a few low knotty sycamores, wood hardly fit even for boat building. This explains why the early Egyptian boats were usually made of bundles of reeds and why very little wood is used in the construction of buildings.

This valley and the large triangular Nile Delta, where the Nile branches out over flat lowlands before it enters the Mediterranean Sea, makes for a total of about six million acres of farmland in the country of Egypt. This land is all watered by the river that at some time rushed through the gorges in the upper river valley, much coming from the large 26,200-square mile Lake Victoria in East Central Africa. The yearly summer torrential rains in these tropical headwaters of the Nile are the source of the annual overflow.

Except for the few people living in the oases—the few low, fertile watered green patches remotely located in the bleak desert—most of Egypt's people live in or alongside the fertile Nile River Valley. Many people traveling in the vast desert lands outside this valley died a painful death from thirst and heat when they lost their way and used up the water they had carried along.

The soil of the flat Nile lowland, where abundant crops grow, is some of the richest in the world. For hundreds and hundreds of years this soil has been deposited by the overflow in the unique yearly rhythm of the Nile River.

Because of the rapids, the early Egyptians never went south far enough to find out where the Nile waters came from, although one ancient traveler and writer said he saw the sun shining directly into the bottom of a well at noon at a certain time of the year. They superstitiously imagined the Nile waters gushed from somewhere in the underworld; the same place they believed the sun disappeared to every evening.

Almost every day in the year brings sunshine with it. Many years pass without a drop of rain. Because the Egyptians did not experience rainy days, the early Egyptian language did not even have a word for rain.

Even while the river overflows its banks during the three- or four-month flood season, the bright sun shines as hot as ever.

WHEN THE YEARLY OVERFLOW ENDS and the levels of the Nile waters are again within its banks, the fresh silt soon dries off. Only several weeks later, the muddy flatlands become carefully tended farmlands covered with lush green vegetation, and the "life-giving water of the Nile" once again becomes a source for fish, a staple food for the Egyptians.

The water retained in the man-made catch basins irrigates the fields that are harvested before the next flood season begins. Even during the river's low season, some water is occasionally lifted to provide irrigation. This extension of the growing season makes it possible to grow two crops of some varieties before the water floods the fields again.

This annual level of flooding was not always exactly the same. If it was higher than normal, the houses along the floodplain got washed away. In years of low water levels, drought and crop failures followed.

Since ancient times, the river has been the artery of transportation for the Egyptian people. The early Egyptians needed very few roads, because nearly everyone lived near the river.

Going up and down the river was very easy. The Nile flows north, and a boat or barge going north could float along with the gentle stream of the river current. With the prevailing winds nearly always blowing from the north, it was only necessary to spread a sail to travel upstream.

This smooth sailing upriver ended abruptly at the first cataract, a natural barrier that prevented the people in the countries to the south from entering Egypt. Here the river used to deluge rapidly through a 20-mile gorge, at some places less than 250 yards wide. Beyond these rapids, it was too dangerous to navigate, so most of these lands remained unknown to the early Egyptians.

The Aswan Dam, a huge billion-dollar structure, was completed in 1968. Built where the river passed through the gorge, the dam helps level out the highs and lows of the Nile over the flatlands along the river, which were flooded almost every summer from July to October. This seasonal flood of from three to six feet of brown and muddy water over the farmlands is now held in check by this 375-foot-high dam that forms a man-made lake of 2,000 square miles behind it.

A traditional story, handed down in Egypt, tells of a time long ago when the river missed its summer flooding for seven years in a row; something not remembered as happening before nor since. Anybody acquainted with the Bible will know that the true basis for this piece of history comes from the time when Joseph was the prime minister of Egypt.

Burial Customs of the Egyptians

THE PEOPLE IN EARLY EGYPT buried their dead in sandy pits, and then piled a mound of rocks over everything. A grave with straight sides could not be dug in this dry sand.

To be sure of having eternal happiness in the after-life, the Egyptians started burying material things and clay jars filled with food with the bodies of the deceased, thinking material things could be used at the resurrection.

Some farming tools would be buried with a farmer and some cooking utensils with a housewife. A person fond of hunting would be buried with a bow and some arrows at his side.

Due to the very dry Egyptian climate, much of what was buried in these parched sands has been preserved in as good a condition as when the items were buried several thousand years ago. Garden peas, discovered in the tombs after being stored there since the time of the Egyptian pharaohs, were planted after being found and grew when they were planted.

Hardly any other place on earth has air so dry it preserves the inscriptions on the plastered walls and the writings on papyrus parchments.

TO DO HONOR TO THEIR PHARAOHS, the mounds of stone above the graves became more elaborate and were fitted into the shape of a pyramid. The era of constantly building larger and more durable pyramids was on.

As the size of their tombs became larger, the store of riches buried with the pharaohs became larger. Deep within these artificial mountains, the mortal bodies of the deceased pharaohs lay in silence with their wealth at their sides.

They believed in a future Judgment Day when those who had lived on earth would be separated according to the good or evil they had done while they were among the living. They believed in a day of final reckoning and that death did not end the existence of a person who had lived a good life.

Can you guess who would judge those who passed on? These Egyptians at one time had a strange custom. At the funeral those who knew the deceased would recount the good or bad things they knew the person had done and would pray to their gods that they would reward or punish the deceased for his or her doings.

Many inscriptions have been found with words such as: "I have never cheated or stolen from anyone. I have always obeyed the laws of the land. I have always been kind to my family." The hope of these writers may have been to help those who knew them to judge in their favor when they passed on.

How glad we can be that the praise or condemnation of others does not send us to our fate or seal our destiny! At the end of our pilgrimage we will be judged by our Creator, who knows our every thought and intention. We will meet our loving and merciful God, who reaches out to us with forgiveness if we are willing to repent.

Religion and Politics of the Egyptians

ALTHOUGH THE RELIGIOUS BELIEFS of many of the first families on earth soon became grossly corrupted, the Egyptians, unlike unbelievers in our days, kept up the knowledge of a life after death and believed in a future resurrection of the dead.

As the beliefs of the ancient Egyptians evolved, they began to consider their pharaohs as divine gods having a supreme know-all. Very elaborate funerals were held when they passed on. The many hundreds of religious rituals, some very absurd to our way of thinking, were eventually dictated by men who made careers as professional temple priests.

These priests, who would do anything to stay on a "best friend" status with the pharaoh, became the behind-the-scenes power of the political government.

This uncontrolled lust for power over other humans makes the rule of oppressive dictators so common even in the governments of today. No human being is capable, or even has the right, of lording such an ultimate power and authority over others without some dire consequence following it, but the Egyptian pharaohs made a try at it.

However, to their credit, and in spite of their pharaoh-honoring religion, the energies and wealth of the land of Egypt at the time of the pyramids were used for building and not for war and destruction.

God's beautiful plan of families and communities of people being helpful to each other was replaced by the pagan system of people struggling to establish power and control over others. The subtle dictatorship of the Egyptian pharaohs became a system exactly opposite of the servants-to-each-other that Christianity brought in the fullness of time by Jesus Christ (Galatians 4:4).

Tomb-Robbing in Egypt

VERY EARLY IN EGYPTIAN HISTORY, veins of gold were discovered in the rocky deserts of southern Egypt, and gold mining became intensive.

This shiny and rare metal, not subject to rust or corrosion, was considered to be an eternal substance. This was exactly what they needed to place in their tombs: an enduring and incorruptible substance for the hereafter. Unlike the dark tarnish eventually forming on anything made of silver, polished gold would stay shiny. Unlike objects made of stone, gold did not shatter into a thousand pieces when hit with a hammer. Hammer blows would only spread it thinner. It held together until it was reduced to a very thin foil.

Because this unique and hard-to-find metal was easily hammered into any form, it became the material for the intricate artwork of skilled craftsmen. These gold items were buried with the other treasures of the pharaoh.

To safeguard these valuables, the largest pyramids were honeycombed with a network of traps, confusing mazes, dead-end passageways, and false burial rooms. They used every clever trick they could think of to foil grave robbers and keep them from finding the burial vault.

A hidden passageway, very difficult to find, led to the real grandiose burial crypt. After the funeral, this hidden tunnel was effectively sealed by a series of heavy stone blocks that fell into place when the props were knocked out from under them.

The pyramid was then completely covered with highly polished white casing stones. The entrance to the deep interior could not be detected.

NEVERTHELESS, EVERY ONE OF THE PYRAMIDS was robbed of the rich treasures buried with the pharaohs. As the tombs were filled with treasures, there was something there to steal, and the profession of grave-robbing became established. None of the ingenious ways the builders devised to frustrate tomb robbers worked. Modern archaeologists who explore the pyramids are still looking for undiscovered passageways, but so far every pyramid found has been picked clean.

How the grave robbers learned the secrets of passages and got away with all this wealth is not known. Were one or more temple priests untrustworthy? The thieves needed only to bribe one betraying priest to make a copy of the blueprint of the pyramid. Perhaps threat or torture forced a worker who knew the secrets to tell which stone blocks were the sealing plugs and to guide thieves to the treasure rooms deep within.

Knowing how depraved human nature is, it is not hard to believe that some of the workers gave in to the temptation to remove the riches of the pharaoh before the sealing plugs were even dropped into place. If so, the deceased pharaoh never lay surrounded by his riches for very long.

At any rate, the era of pyramid building, perhaps 500 years, was over. Realizing there was no way to keep seekers of wealth out of the pyramids that dominated the scenery of the Giza landscape, the Egyptians came to believe it was more important to keep their burial wealth secure than to display their greatness in the monuments towering high above the desert sands at the Giza burial grounds.

The Egyptian pharaohs began to look elsewhere for places suitable for their own burials and for the secure storage of the riches they thought they would need on Resurrection Day.

They decided on a desolate area completely hemmed in by high rocky cliffs in the Egyptian desert several hundred miles to the south. This location, now known as the Valley of the Kings, is not far from the western bank of the Nile River.

The pharaohs and temple priests were naïve enough to believe they had at last found a hiding place where the material wealth that they valued so highly in this life would be secure.

Later Interest in the Pyramids

BY THE TIME OF THE MIDDLE AGES, the ability to read ancient inscriptions found on the walls of Egyptian temples and empty tombs was completely lost, and it was a mystery why these pyramids looming on the desert horizon were even built.

A common belief during the Middle Ages was that the largest pyramids were built with the interior bins that Joseph's servants used to store the huge grain harvest of the seven fruitful years.

When a rumor prevailed in the 1100s that the mysterious pyramids contained vast stores of gold, there was a revival of interest in these ancient structures. One group, thirsty for gold, worked eight months trying to find the entrance leading to the tomb. They rolled stones off the top and pried out a number of stones from the sides before they gave up. A remark was made that "it is harder to destroy a pyramid than it would have been to build it!"

Very clumsy methods, such as using battering rams or setting off gunpowder to blow holes in the exterior wall, failed to open the pyramids. Several hundred years later, when the main entrance was discovered on the north side of the Great Pyramid and the plug blocks were removed, a passageway to the innards of the pyramid was finally found, but the ancient tomb robbers had already taken the gold.

If there had been a heavy golden lid on the stone coffin in the burial crypt, as there probably had been, even that was gone.

Dating the Pyramids

EXACTLY WHEN THE PYRAMIDS were built will never be known for sure. The dates figured out by Egyptian historians have varied so widely that none can be considered altogether credible. Dates anywhere from 3733 B.C. to 2100 B.C. have been suggested, so we won't add to that hopeless discussion.

During the past 150 years, the age of the pyramids has been figured out by the chronology of the widely varying Egyptian king lists that have been discovered. But even these can be very confusing. Going down many blind alleyways of these chronologies can indeed be baffling, and only helps to put a hopeless blur on the dates of ancient Egypt.

One group of historians confidently claims to be sure of some of the dates of Egyptian history, only to be challenged by another group. One inscription tells of a pharaoh who ruled for 94 years and another records a 67-year reign. Others believe it is too difficult to know which of the ancient texts are accurate, making all the entries very suspect. For instance, it has been discovered that one king list had five different names for the same king.

To fit in with Bible history, the building of the pyramids could not have taken place much more than a few hundred years after the builders of the unfinished Tower of Babel were scattered from Shinar all over the world. Scholars think Shinar was a part of Babylonia, which is now Iraq, a country making modern-day newspaper headlines.

Going by the large number of Egyptian ruling dynasties and pharaohs who reigned from the time of the building of the pyramids to the time of the Israelite exodus from Egypt, we must conclude that the pyramids were built at some time after the dispersal at Babel but before the time of Abraham in the Bible.

What the Bible Tells Us

WE WHO BELIEVE IN THE ALMIGHTY GOD OF CREATION as having inspired the writers of the Holy Scriptures also believe in its verbal accuracy and truth. Unlike so many others who write on these subjects, we are convinced that what the Bible says can confidently be stated as fact. We believe that one way to cut ourselves off from the blessings of God's Holy Word is to start doubting it as a source of truth.

We believe that the table of years from Adam to Noah in Genesis, Chapter 5, and the continuation of that chronology from Noah to Abraham in Genesis, Chapter 11, is true and correct. God provided that information on the family lineage leading to Jesus Christ because it is the most important lineage in history.

No other ancient religion can place the beginnings and historical happenings of its past into the exact years and exact location of its origin.

In our days, there are many people unconvinced of the divine inspiration of the Bible, and therefore these people do not give much importance to these biblical numbers and guides.

If any reader has already made up his or her mind that these Bible figures are not reliable, it is not to be expected that they will begin to believe the Bible just by what they will read in the pages of this book.

However, if an inscribed clay tablet or a papyrus scroll would ever be dug up and would give the very same dating information that we read in Genesis, there would be newspaper headlines all over the world shouting the discovery of the most spectacular event in the history of archaeology.

The Bible also suggests an answer and solves the problem of the great population of the earth before and so soon after the Great Flood. The longevity of humans, in many cases 900 or more years, may have been made possible by the virtual absence of many diseases we know of today. In the early days of the earth, this pristine health and well-being could have resulted in very large families.

There is a Jewish tradition that Adam and Eve had a family of 33 sons and 23 daughters while in their bearing age, so this may have been God's way to rapidly populate the earth in this relatively short time.

The increase in knowledge and know-how and the ambitious and incredible building projects, such as the pyramids, which were accomplished in the ten generations, or about 350 years, from the Great Flood to the birth of Abraham (Abram) may seem impossible.

However, this is also believable and can be understood. We need only to look around and see the incredible changes made in only a generation or two in our days.

IT IS THEREFORE VERY MUCH POSSIBLE that Abraham looked on these same pyramids, or "cradles of eternity" as they have been called, when he was staying in Egypt during the famine in his homeland of Canaan (Genesis 12:10).

Because the land of Goshen is believed to have been near Giza, the pyramids could have been a highly visible landmark during the years of Joseph's affliction in the land of Egypt and where, appointed as prime minister, he was in a position that granted him the rare advantage of being a go-between, meeting with both the lofty pharaoh and the common people.

The number of years between the building of the pyramids and the exodus of the Israelites from Egypt may have been more than the number of years between the Reformation of Martin Luther and the present time. It is possible that the Israelite slaves making straw-reinforced bricks under cruel taskmasters may have seen the work of the slaves of at least 500 years earlier when they saw the outlines of the pyramids on the horizon.

So far, only one ancient Egyptian inscription has been found mentioning Israel. This is the earliest known reference to the Israelites outside of the Bible.

However, not one of the events described in the Bible story of the plagues and of the Israelite slaves leaving Egypt has yet been found mentioned anywhere in the ancient Egyptian records. Unfortunately, this has led some historians to doubt the truth of the Bible. Why wouldn't the Egyptians mention such a sudden ruin of their country?

This is not surprising. Many thousands of historical inscriptions found on the walls of their temples and tombs never once mention a defeat, nor do they mention any people who were as unimportant to them as their slaves.

The writings of nearly every ancient nation, except that of the Hebrews, proudly boast of their victories and triumphs in war, but never their defeats. The histories of other nations scornfully brag of their victories against the Egyptians, but going by the Egyptian versions of the same wars we would think they were the victors. In one painting of a sea battle, most of the enemy ships are pictured as being overturned, while no harm is shown being suffered by the Egyptian fleet.

It is interesting to think that Joseph and Mary, fleeing for the safety of the baby Jesus to the land of Egypt, may have looked upon these very same pyramids which at that time were already very ancient. It is also indeed ironic that the life of Jesus was saved in the same land that had forced the early Hebrews into a cruel bondage. Had He been killed in His infancy, what would have happened to God's plan of redemption for the human race?

On the night before His crucifixion, Jesus changed the Passover, held yearly for approximately 1,500 times to commemorate the memory of the Jewish people's release from slavery. The Jewish Passover would become the Christian Communion service. Held throughout the world in many different ways as a formal thankfulness to God for making possible release from the slavery of sin, this service alone makes the story of the exodus from Egypt credible.

Anything making such a worldwide impact and enduring for all these many hundreds of years since the exodus could not be based only on myth and legend. We know its roots are grounded in the trustworthiness and verified truth of the Bible.

Who Built the Pyramids?

THE PYRAMIDS TODAY ARE A MONEYMAKING tourist attraction. Tourists coming from all over the world pay to go on camel rides and buy all kinds of pyramid souvenirs. There are guided tours available through the amazing intricate passageways.

Because of vandalism, and because, on occasion, those who tried to climb the pyramids tumbled to their deaths, the Egyptian government made it illegal to climb to the tops of the pyramids after the year 1983.

But who actually built these pyramids, now so popular with tourists? We find out that exactly who these industrious pyramid workers were is not really known, and endless debates have been made on this subject.

For a long time it was assumed that multitudes of slaves captured in the wars with enemy countries were forced to work by whip-lashing taskmasters. Weren't the Israelites as slaves compelled to make a quota of bricks for the Egyptian pharaoh that was almost impossible to come up with? But then the Israelites had not been captured in a war, so this theory that the pyramid workers were war captives may not apply.

Then also, if the pyramid laborers were all slaves from an enemy country, how could the secrets of the hidden interior passageways leading to the golden wealth be kept? Just one escaped slave could lead grave robbers to an immense amount of wealth after the burial of the pharaoh.

To make this theory of the pyramids being built by slaves credible, some history writers of several generations ago imagined that these pyramid-building slaves of several hundred years earlier than the Israelites would all have been killed after the work was completed. This would prevent the secret of the plugged-off passageways leading to the burial crypt from becoming known to grave robbers awaiting a chance to pounce on easy riches. Some histories would state theories such as this as being true facts.

Some writers of histories speculated that pyramid-building came to an end when Egypt became too weak to bring home the vast number of war captives needed for pyramid work.

HOWEVER, THE TEXTBOOKS OF HISTORY will always continue to be rewritten. History will never be completely precise. In one instance, except for the Bible account and because of the silence of the ancient Egyptian histories on the subject, very little is known of the historical connections of the Egyptians with the Israelites while they were making their home at, or near to, the Nile Delta.

The ancient Egyptian artifacts under the low and sometimes swampy Nile Delta await the development of an archaeological method of digging through many deep layers of silt before they can be brought to light.

Whenever a new archaeological discovery is made, new theories soon follow and much guesswork and fantastic imagination is sometimes added to complete the picture. Each discoverer is inclined to fiercely defend his or her new pet theory based on what they have found and probably spent a lot of time and effort on. It is understandable that they all wish their research to be worthy of recognition.

Much of what is written on ancient history is trying to prove a point different from what a previous generation of scholars thought they had all figured out. This is especially true of determining a set of dates which may differ hundreds of years from what had been "firmly established" by competent scholars earlier. However, it is now generally agreed that fairly precise dates for any of Egyptian history is not possible before the ancient accurate-record-keeping Persians conquered Egypt in 525 B.C.

Any dating of events before that time is subject to almost endless debate and variations, so it is hardly surprising to find that the estimates of different Egyptian historians on the pyramid dates have varied as much as 1,600 years.

MANY OTHER THEORIES BESIDES the exact dates in Egyptian ancient history and the guesswork about pyramid-building are being challenged. Many theories have been changed in recent years.
For instance, a number of Egyptian histories of today do not believe the immense amount of human muscle power required to build the pyramids even came from slave workers.

The Nile River Valley had barren deserts on each side. It had almost impassable rapids to the south, and a relatively short and swampy coastline with "the Great Sea" on the north. This made Egypt a relatively isolated country for many centuries.

They may not have tried to conquer other countries at the time of pyramid-building. The vast number of workers which were needed to quarry, shape, transport, smooth, and place one huge stone block after another at the fantastic estimated rate of one every two minutes may have simply been off-season farmers.

They may have worked during the three or four summer months when farming was at a standstill because of the flooded Nile River Valley. As an army drafted into service for their country, there may have been a compulsory law that every able-bodied man must spend some of his time on pyramid duty working for the pharaoh. This would be like paying his tax for the rent of the pharaoh-owned land that he farmed during the eight or nine months when the river was again flowing within its banks.

THERE IS STILL ANOTHER theory about the pyramids that is surfacing among some of the serious students of Egyptian history. This theory comes from the dedication that can be seen in human nature when it is motivated by a religious conviction.

This theory is that the ordinary people of the country of Egypt didn't need to be compelled to work for the pharaoh. They wanted to! Unlike nearly all slaves who spend much of their days of trial and toil thinking about ways of escaping, these pyramid workers wanted to be resurrected to a life after death with their pharaoh.

These skilled craftsmen and strong laborers of many talents were loyal enough to the pharaoh that they were committed to worshiping him as a god. To his faithful and devoted subjects he was not once considered as a cruel and oppressive tyrant. Multitudes of common people had a religious dedication to the pharaoh and they gave themselves as willing slaves to do any tedious work he asked them to do.

This school of opinion of the ancient Egyptians believes that their religion was corrupted enough that the common people were really brainwashed into being convinced that if they served the pharaoh, he would guarantee them a life with him in the hereafter.

In other words, working on the pyramids would give them something like assurance of salvation.

There is no doubt that the precise planning and organizing of manpower to do such an immense work took a kind of genius that can never be fully understood.

The political power for manipulating such an army of people, whether it was willing or forced labor, is amazing and is simply unbelievable. The skill or "brain power" behind the planning and managing of the building of the pyramids at the dawn of history is the envy of the great developers and architects of today. The genius of the designers and builders of these ancient times was incredible.

That all this work was being motivated by a religious conviction and obsession can be a little alarming when we think of it being misguided and done all for such a wrong and useless purpose.

On the positive side, this can be a challenge to us all in the churches of our day. It is just as possible for any or all of us to move out from the shallow level of serving only self to a deep level of commitment to working at what our Creator has put us here on earth to do. Our daily work, no matter how mundane or routine it has become, can be a service and honor to God.

How Were the Pyramids Built?

HOWEVER, EVEN GREATER THAN finding out about the workers is the biggest mystery of the pyramids: how they were built.

No relief sculpture or wall painting showing the actual building has yet been found. Every single word written or illustration drawn in medieval or modern-day histories of how the pyramids were built, including what you will read and see illustrated in this book if you stay with us, is so far nothing more than "educated guesswork" or imagination.

It is almost certain that animal power was not yet used at the time the pyramids were built, so every bit of energy needed for moving the stone blocks, except for possible river transportation, came from the muscles of humans.

Any modern engineer would hesitate to attempt duplicating anything like the three largest pyramids. Even with our huge modern cranes, efficient rock-cutting power saws, laser transits, and cell phones needed to keep in touch with the army of foremen directing the multitudes of workers, hardly any construction company would tackle building a structure matching the pyramids—even though these were put up by men who did not know the simple principles of rope and tackle. Even iron tools were still unknown.

No one knows for sure how the heavy stones were transported and then elevated to a height of several hundred feet, but the blocks are there to prove that it did get done.

Some of the astonished people of the Middle Ages who visited the pyramids would come up with some bizarre and unscientific guessing of how the pyramids were built.

Many were sure that the ancient Egyptians possessed some supernatural power to help them do the mighty work.

To some of them, the unreadable Egyptian picture writings, found all over, were the hidden secrets of a forbidden knowledge that a mysterious extinct civilization of long ago had practiced. But however much they studied them, no one could read these ancient hieroglyphs, as they were called, which only made them more curious than ever. Perhaps some visitors from another planet in outer space had come to help them!

Others, taking a cue from Genesis 6:4, believed that in the days of prehistory, there lived a race of people large enough to put the pyramids together like children playing with toy blocks. However, the empty stone coffin in the burial chamber of the Great Pyramid is only seven feet long, so at least the pharaoh that the pyramid was built for must have been of usual size.

Of course, the theories coming up in the last several hundred years of how the blocks may have been elevated to their proper place are more scientific. Even so, hardly any of the explanations coming forth have been accepted as being credible by all the experts in ancient Egyptian history.

The artists for the history books printed a hundred or so years ago nearly always depicted immense ramps built of wood scaffolding with multitudes of sweating slaves pulling the blocks upward on wooden sleds, or with wooden or stone rollers directly between the ramp and the blocks. The idea for this method of building probably came from the discovery of one single wall painting showing 172 men dragging a sledge with a huge stone statue on it.

Then somebody must have thought of the scarcity of wood in Egypt, so after a time this theory of huge wooden ramps was laid to rest. There are hardly any recent books on the building of the pyramids showing wooden ramps.

The illustrations were replaced with drawings showing ramps built of heaped up sand. Some showed the bottom end of the packed sand ramp extending to a barge anchored at the edge of the Nile River several miles from the pyramid area.

Other artists showed these packed sand ramps built as an upward spiral around the increasing height of the pyramid. It seems these sand ramp theories may have come from the packed sand found in areas around several ancient Egyptian structures. It was guessed that the faint outlines of sand may be what is still left of the sand ramps built as a roadway to drag the heavy stone blocks to the top.

But where was this immense amount of sand hauled to after the pyramid was finished? It seemed no one knew for sure.

At one time the bright answer to this puzzle was that the ramps were not even sand, but may have been built of a salt that would dissolve when the builders rerouted the waters of the nearby river to wash it away after it served its purpose.

Other historians guessed that the ramps might have been built of sun-dried bricks later used for building houses in the nearby city after the pyramid was completed.

WE WILL NOW INTRODUCE THE GREEK TRAVELER and writer named Herodotus who visited the land of Egypt for several months around the year 455 B.C.

He was curious about what the Egyptians believed in. In fact, because of his writings on his views of the religion of ancient Egypt we probably know more about their beliefs than what we can gather from the Egyptian inscriptions themselves.

Herodotus was fascinated when he saw the pyramids. He must have asked all kinds of questions and wrote down what he learned. He said he was told that 100,000 men worked on the Great Pyramid for twenty years during the reign of the pharaoh Cheops.

Because another writer, Pliny the Elder, writing about 600 years later wrote that 360,000 men worked on the pyramid for twenty years, we have no way of knowing which account is accurate. We also don't know how accurate the information given to these historians really was. We are closer in time to the years that Pliny was writing, which was about 77 A.D., than he was to the time the pyramids were being built.

All that we know of the writings of Herodotus come from fragments of his work that have been quoted by later history writers. The complete manuscript copy of his writings may have been lost when the library at Alexandria was destroyed, when the Romans conquered Egypt in the first century before the birth of Christ.

In his writings, he often refers to "knowledge that I am not in a position to reveal," which may have been his way of saying he was not given the information that he asked for, or that he simply did not know!

Many historians of today do not take much stock in what Herodotus wrote about the building of the pyramids. He writes about iron tools that were used by the builders of the pyramids, when it is almost certain that the use of iron was still unknown back in that remote period of time.

He also writes of the machines the Egyptians used which were formed of short wooden planks that raised the pyramid stone blocks one step at a time. "Either they had as many machines as there were steps in the pyramid, or possibly they had a single machine, which being easily moved was transferred from tier to tier as the stone block was being elevated," he wrote.

Herodotus completely loses his credibility as a historian because of his writing about tools of iron and the use of machines. He has been called a misleading writer, telling his readers untruths about pyramid-building. The Egyptians he asked about their method of building 1,500 years earlier may have gotten their handed-down legends twisted up a little bit.

Everybody knows the ancient Egyptians never had any machines. The wheel and the pulley with rope

Herodotus May Have Been Right After All!

MUCH OF THE CREDIBILITY of what the Greek historian Herodotus wrote about his visit to the ancient land of Egypt has been questioned by the Egyptian historians of the last several hundred years. Especially so is his very brief account that he was told that the pyramid blocks were lifted to their places, over 1,500 years before his time, by using "machines made only of short pieces of wood."

As there are no ancient wall paintings known that illustrate the building of the pyramids, most historians continued to imagine the blocks were dragged upwards on sleds pulled by a multitude of men on ramps made of either sand or immense wood scaffolding. Herodotus couldn't have known what he was talking about.

But if Herodotus was right, every bit of the energy needed to raise the six million tons of stone blocks *upward* in the Great Pyramid came from the counter balance *downward* provided by the weight of the men working on it.

Shown in the first illustration on the opposite page are the wooden pieces needed to move a stone block upards from the ground level to the very top; almost 500 feet up; and then sideways to the opposite diagonal of the course already laid, which would be almost one-fifth mile away at the lowest course. Nothing else except these short pieces of wood and the muscle power of a handful of men working at each block would be needed.

The next illustrations, not necessarily in exact scale, show a way the pyramid blocks could have been lifted upwards only several inches at a time by rocking them up and down on short split-log blocking.

Not shown are the several men needed to place the log blocking into the proper places as the others worked on one side then the other to pull the stone down, gaining a little each time it was rocked.

Also not shown are the wooden sleds that may have been placed under each block to protect it from chipping until it was placed.

There could also have been a track from the Nile River barges to the pyramid site which may have been a stone pavement laid down upon which wooden rollers, acting as roller bearings, would have been used under the blocks as they were pulled or pushed. This roadway could also have been a track of only two lines of logs. The block balanced on these two rails laid fairly close together could have been easily moved slowly forward by a continuous combination of an up and down and sideways rocking motion .

This sideways rocking motion would also be used on the top of each course to move the block backward toward the pyramid. (See illustrations #5 and #8.)

The split-log blocking could be reused at every other course or tier, just as Herodotus thought could have been done. For the horizontal travel after being lifted to the level of the platform course, the blocks, steered by setting the rollers at an angle, could also have been moved by only a handful of men. The block shown in the last diagram is positioned on rollers, ready for sideways travel.

To make the up and down rocking process easier for the larger stone pieces, such as the nine stone slabs, each weighing about 44 tons, which were built into the Great Pyramid as the ceiling of the burial chambers, the lifting cribs could have been made more narrow and thinner blocking could have been used. The stone block would then be supported closer to the center, but more rocking cycles would be needed for every inch of upward travel.

One stone block found 20 feet up in an Egyptian temple was 64 feet long and 13 feet wide. However, there is no reason why this rock, weighing perhaps 1,200 tons could not also have been slowly lifted into place by this method. For safety reasons, in case the lifting center crib would have accidentally upset, the blocking on two larger sets of cribbing, one near to each end, could have been constantly kept close to the bottom of the stone.

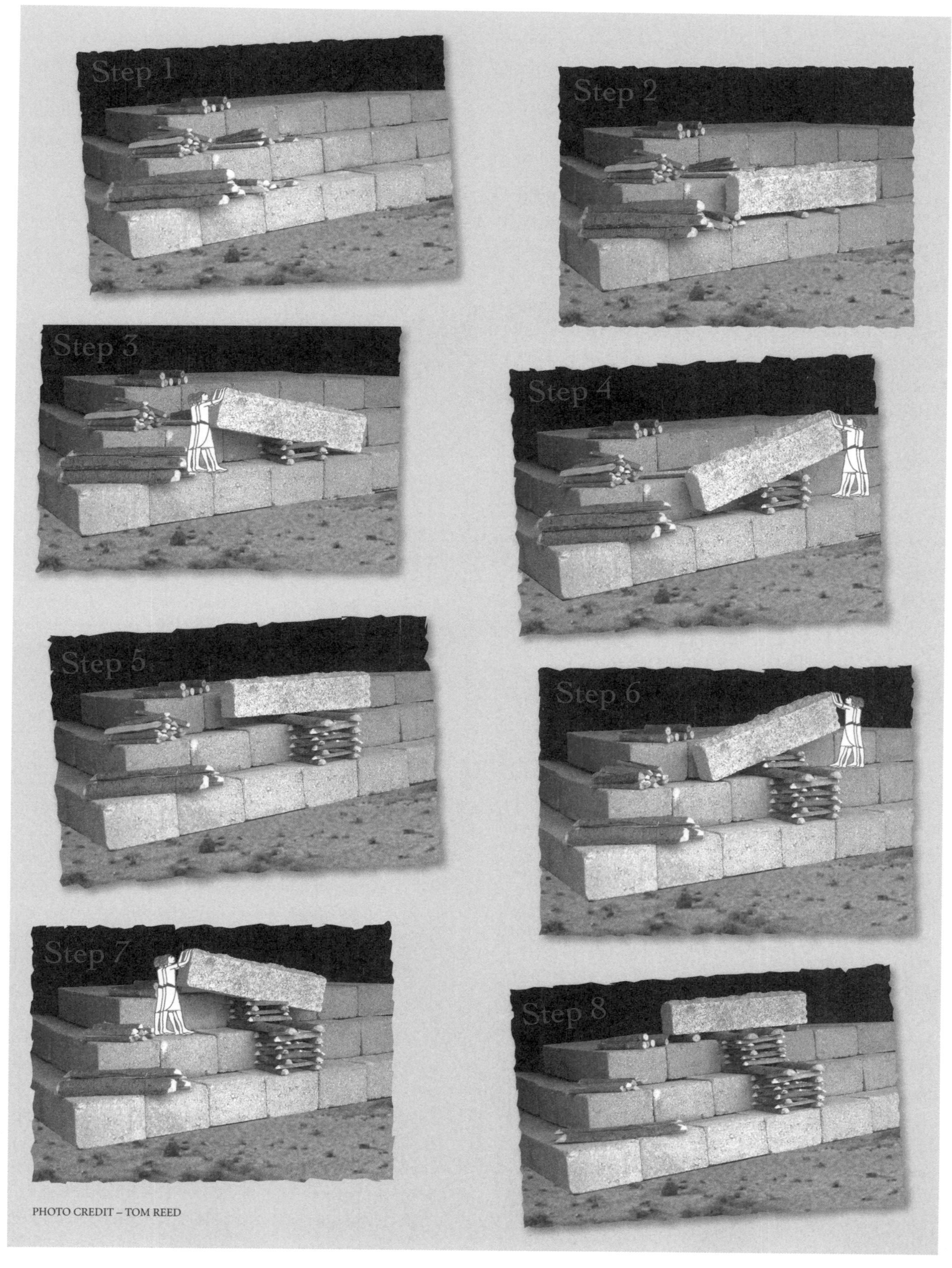

PHOTO CREDIT – TOM REED

going around had not even been invented yet. The only mechanical helps they knew about to make work easier were the lever, rollers, and the inclined plane or ramp.

PERHAPS THE MISUNDERSTANDING about Herodotus comes not from what he wrote, but from the translating of his writings. When he writes about the tools of iron that were used, the word may have meant tools of metal, or tools of bronze.

And everything becomes clear when the word "machines" is translated as "devices." There is a way to raise stone blocks or heavy beams or what have you with devices made only of short wooden beams or planks or short logs split in half exactly as he described.

Why this method, called "cribbing" by men of a generation or two ago, is virtually never mentioned in today's books on architecture or building is not known. One reason may be that since large jacks and forklifts are easily available, this method is too slow to consider using.

With this method of cribbing, used in building projects before power machinery became handy, several men could easily rock a heavy block or a long beam upward to any height for which they had blocking.

With the utter simplicity of this method, the heavy weight of the beam or block is slowly inched upward *by pushing one end of it down.* This device was also often used in reverse order to very gently lower a stone or beam of great weight.

TRYING TO DECIDE EXACTLY where these pyramid blocks were quarried has also brought out some interesting discussions over the years.

Some think they were cut out of the rock cliffs only a few miles away, while others claim there is no natural stone similar to that used in the pyramids closer than a place 570 miles up the Nile from Giza. Other experts say that on a ridge of cliffs about 700 miles south of Giza there is an outcrop of rock that resembles the pyramid stones. They point this out as a likely quarry used by the pyramid builders.

If the stone blocks were quarried at these places either 570 or 700 miles up the Nile, no likely places have yet been found along the river suitable as a harbor for the barges needed to transport the stone blocks.

THIS BRINGS US THE VERY real possibilities that the experts of today are fooled when they even think the pyramids were built with quarried natural stone.

Some of today's historians are convinced the pyramid blocks are not even natural stone, but may have been made from a form of poured concrete. If so, what the ingredients were and the methods used to process them to make this cement are lost.

There is also a possibility that there may have been a large deposit nearby of something like the Sacrete that we buy at today's hardware stores. When we add water and mix it together, we have something that passes as stone. When the deposit was exhausted, the pyramid-building would have come to an end.

It is also possible that the pyramid builders discovered a formula or method that we haven't figured out yet for making cement from the unlimited desert sands available close by. After all, making the modern version of Portland cement is a thriving industry in Egypt in our days. The manufacture of this cement is made possible because the abundant deposits of the raw materials needed to make it are found in the Egyptian deserts.

Let's pause a little and try to imagine what would happen if a civilization like ours became extinct and its ways of doing things were lost 4,000 years ago. Our archaeologists digging up a little here and a little there would hardly be able to explain and figure out where these people quarried, and smoothed out the stone-like material we call blacktop. They would be amazed at the large quantities they would find. It would probably take a long time and all kinds of theories to decide how this civilization got such a smooth finish on their paved roads.

THIS VERY LIKELY THEORY of the Egyptians using a poured concrete instead of cut stone would explain many things that have puzzled students of Egyptian history for hundreds of years. It would explain the close fit of the pyramid blocks, made much easier by using a number of reusable forms for making poured concrete blocks on-site, than smoothing the surface of a quarried stone block. The six very smooth surfaces of each of the 2,300,000 blocks used in the Great Pyramid, with each surface fitting to the one beside it to 1/50th inch tolerance, is made more possible and can more easily be understood.

This theory would explain the absence of large mounds of rejected, cracked, and broken pieces that would be found somwhere had the blocks been quarried and the sides chipped off to a very close fit. No quarry near the pyramids has been found that has the mountains of discarded stone chips nearby, which seems likely had the blocks been cut out of solid rock.

This may explain the absence of thousands upon thousands of worn-out chipping chisels that would be around somewhere had they been used extensively. It would explain the smooth finish on the pyramid blocks, with no crowbar, saw marks, and virtually no chipped edges or broken-off corners at the tightly fitted joints.

If the ancients did have a method of making a concrete that passes for quarried stone and had recorded this know-how on a papyrus scroll, that knowledge may have been lost when the great library at Alexandria in Egypt was destroyed.

If the pyramid blocks were really made of a poured concrete mix, their end product is something far superior to the cement formula we know of today. The concrete poured in our days sooner or later begins to deteriorate, and would likely never hold up for 4,000 years. However, if we consider the other achievements of this primitive civilization, we are not surprised. Perhaps we can still learn from them.

This theory of poured concrete is very credible. The millions of tons of cement used all over the world for building purposes during our times is called Portland cement because the finished concrete looks about like, and has the properties of, the stone quarried at Portland in England.

Portland cement, the modern material used in our time to make artificial stone, was invented in 1824. It may be more accurate to say it was only reinvented at that time!

RECOGNIZING THAT THE ANCIENT Egyptians may have had a method of making a mix that hardened into a superior material that looked like stone would solve another unanswered puzzle of understanding Egyptian culture.

Over the years, many thousands of narrow-necked bottles and vases have been found, which the early Egyptian archaeologists always thought were made of a fine-grained natural stone. Working through the long and narrow necks, it would have taken many hundreds of man-hours for a craftsman to carve and smooth out the insides of the bottles. Many are thin-walled and are polished inside and out with no chisel or drill marks showing.

Finding these bottles and the multitudes of polished stone beads, each one having a fine hole for the thread, made historians sure that these unhurried people of the Nile were not aware of the passing of time when they were doing something creative.

However, the archaeologists who always thought these bottles, vases, and beads were carved out of natural stone may have been mistaken. A number of Egyptian historians now believe the Egyptians may have known of a mix of fine desert sand and cement that we know nothing about. This material could have been used as clay that could be shaped on something like a potter's wheel before it hardened into a solid that has long been mistaken for natural stone.

We Need Not Look for Anything Better than Bible Truth

THOSE SOULS, SO PRECIOUS to God, living out their earthly pilgrimage in the valley along the Nile River three and four thousand years ago were doing all this work to honor their pharaoh like a worldly savior. Their religion had become corrupted from the knowledge the first families on earth had of the one and only Almighty God and the Savior He would send to earth in due time.

This gradual perversion of religion, slowly happening somewhere in the generations since Creation, was caused by weak links in the line of people who should have been accepting the torch of truth from their elders and parents and should have been passing it on to the succeeding generations.

With our Bibles, we have something much better and more inspiring to think about and live for than they had with absurd myths and untrue legends of many gods that became such a part of their daily lives.

The worship of the pharaoh and many other deities evolved into religious rituals that are almost ridiculous to our way of thinking. It is hard to understand why so much time is spent studying untrue myths and legends of the ancient people, which many people are saying is "nothing but a heap of rubbish."

Some of the worst things that came out of the worshiping of other gods were the pagan temple rituals that became a common part of the religious ceremonies. Many abominable and immoral acts of sin and lust, along with mysterious occult and demonic black art rites became acceptable, as long as they were done within the dark temple rooms.

We can well understand why the first of the Ten Commandments was to have no other gods except the one God of Creation. How reassuring to our minds and spirits is the simple faith such as the descendants of Joseph learned at the knee of this God-fearing hero of the Bible (Genesis 50:23).

WE CAN ALSO WELL UNDERSTAND why both Jacob and Joseph did not wish to be buried in Egypt. The last thing they did, when they felt their earthly end was near, was to tell their survivors to take their bodies out of Egypt and bury them in the land of their forefathers (Genesis 47:29-31, 49:28-33, 50:24-26 and Joshua 24:32). They did not wish to be buried in the pomp and splendor of their Egyptian neighbors.

God was to see that the burial of Moses took place in a region known only to God (Deuteronomy 34:5 and 6). This kept the Israelites from excessively honoring his dead remains. Having lived so long among the Egyptians, who worshiped their dead leaders, the Israelites might have built a shrine over the grave of Moses. This was something God didn't want to happen.

OUR CHRISTIAN BELIEFS COME from the Bible and not from a powerful pharaoh and his pagan temple priests. Our convictions of immortality, the endless existence of the soul, the real inner being of humans, are vastly different from that of the pagan Egyptians of long ago.

One interesting difference which may or may not be significant is that in Egyptian burials, always made on the west bank of the Nile, the deceased were also always placed facing the setting of the sun, believed to be in the direction toward the entrance of the land of the dead.

In most Christian graveyards, the deceased are usually turned toward the eastern rising sun, which symbolizes the breaking of eternal day.

In fact, it is known that the proper funeral rituals, invented by the temple priests, meant so much to the ancient Egyptians that they were reluctant to fight in a war abroad. They feared being killed in a foreign country because they were afraid they would not be buried in the proper way to insure their resurrection.

However, in spite of their errors, there is still much we can learn from the Egyptian ways of doing. Their belief in the resurrection of the dead and a life in the hereafter motivated them to use much of this life to prepare for the next. In a sense, this is what we should also be doing.

"No one returns again, who has gone hence," says one inscription found in a tomb. It has been said they had no more fear of death than the fear of walking in a familiar place in the dark. Their paintings depicting their ideas of eternity represent life on the other side going on as usual. One painting shows a husband walking after an oxen-pulled plow while his wife is scattering seeds in the fresh earth. Others show sailors reaching a port and farmers singing as they were reaping in the fields.

They were a people who found joy in life but never got beyond believing that life in the next world, when their eyes closed in death here and reopened on the other side, would be just like the one they left. But what can we say? None of us can ever imagine what being with God in His perfect glory will really be like.

I Will Fear No Evil

THERE SEEMS TO BE NOTHING that stops us more in our tracks than when we first learn that someone close to us has passed into eternity.

For varying lengths of time afterwards we experience a confused mix of emotions that we do not understand, which for a while leaves us virtually paralyzed and numb. This feeling called grief is an emotion that needs to be somehow expressed before we can experience a sense of relief. After grief is thawed out and expressed, we can begin to go on again with living, even though we will have a void in our heart that can never be forgotten.

That person, now gone, who has left such a very empty place in our lives, is really only a step ahead of us. Sooner or later in the future, every one of us will, as those who have gone before us, have our last experience on earth. For some of us it may come suddenly and unexpectedly, for others, it may take much time until our cancer or wheelchair days are over.

We cannot escape the fact that this experience ahead of us will be different from any other experience we have ever had. We learn of the deaths of people we knew, and some of us may have had the experience of a death in the family. But there comes a day when death will be closer than someone else in the neighborhood or someone else in the family. It will be our own death.

The last experience we will all have in this life is dying, which is going through the door opened for us to enter eternity. None of us will fail to keep that appointment set for us to meet our Maker before we begin the endless eternity in our future. God has an expiration date set for each one of us—when our today will be our last day on earth—our tomorrow will be in eternity.

No matter how much we spend for keeping our bodies alive and healthy, we still won't be able to avoid our hour of departure from this world. Even successful doctors and renowned faith healers who have helped others to health have had their turn to get a terminal sickness and pass on.

Like taking our hand out of a glove, death will free our body from our spirit. The glove will turn limp and quit moving. Where life ends, the body will lie until someone or something moves it elsewhere. But the body is no longer us. It is only like the pod or husk of the real kernel. "For in Him we live, and move, and have our being," says the Bible (Acts 17:28).

In an attempt to find out what the human spirit or soul really is, an experimenting doctor of several hundred years ago found out it is beyond being material matter. A person did not weigh one bit less after the minute of death when the soul had left the body.

Eternal life is the only part of our living humanity that can be kept from experiencing death. Everything living, except eternal life, which is a gift of the eternal, living God, is destined to end in death.

We know our bodies of clay in which our spirits are living are made of the same materials the dust of the earth is made of. "Dust thou art, and to dust thou shalt return," was spoken by the Creator to our first parents.

The preserved bodies of the self-glorifying pharaohs of ancient Egypt, which thousands of years ago were made of living cells and actual life substances, are still in their sleep of death. At some time sooner or later, their preserved shells will crumple to dust.

Their spirits, or souls, like ours, in a new body, incorruptible to decay, will someday stand before God, their Creator, to be judged. The inspiring poem "A Psalm of Life," by Henry W. Longfellow, which contains the lines "Dust thou art, to dust returneth; Was not spoken of the Soul," says so much in only a few words.

The real reason for all the spending of time and energies in the lives of the ancient Egyptians all came from the universal yearning in all human beings for an eternal life in the hereafter.

An eternal world for us beyond this short life is something that has been made possible for humanity by the resurrection of Jesus Christ from the dead.

GOD MAY HAVE PLACED LITTLE examples of death and the renewal of life in the wonderful world of nature around us to help us better grasp an understanding of the reality and mystery of coming to life again. The examples are like seeing only the shadow of something that has substance and is real. Death is not the final end.

The dead-looking seeds and bulbs we place in the earth in the springtime will, if they still have the embryo of life within, break open and grow into fragrant and colorful flowers and delicious and nutritious fruit. The dead-looking chrysalis in its crusty shell, having been at one time a creeping, leaf-eating caterpillar, will burst out of its prison. Out will come the creature that is no longer a worm, but one that God has changed into a flitting and colorful nectar-sipping butterfly.

God's mighty miracle of resurrection is a little like the sturdy oak sleeping in the acorn or the delicate little chick resting in the egg. It is the beautiful and fragrant flavor and delicious fruit still deeply encased in the heart of the bud.

God's rhythm of day and night and His yearly pattern of the seasons may have been created to help us get a small glimpse of the reality of life and death. The days that had a morning are followed by a night. The pleasing song of the evening vesper sparrow that breaks the silence of the sunset is just as beautiful as were the songs of those birds that joyfully sing at daybreak.

God can paint the sunset clouds with colors as beautiful as were the skies at daybreak.

The colorful blossoms of new life in the spring are rivaled by the colorful foliage in the fall of the year. The vivid hues of almost every shade seen all over the hills and mountains in autumn are really the colors of the leaves approaching their deaths. In a few weeks, they will be brown and dead. They will have let go of the tree branches that provided life-giving sap to them during the summer growing season. Their substances will return to the soil next to the tree roots from where their life-giving nutrients came from in spring.

The life within the dead-looking tree in the winter is getting ready to repeat the cycle again. The warm sun and springtime rains will awaken it to a new life, which will burst open and resurrect its leaf and blossom; a reminder to us of the power of God's resurrection.

OH, WE HAVE TO WONDER HOW it ever could be possible that there are actually people living on earth who do not want to believe in an Almighty Creator and the day of resurrection. They do not realize what they are missing in this life. What an inspiring tonic for our minds and spirits to think on these things!

We all know that only a divine miracle will make it possible that materials such as the ashes or compost that were the actual substances of living bodies of humans will ever again be resurrected to life.

However, what is even more miraculous is that God's wonder of resurrection has already taken place. We humans, who are living, thinking, and feeling creatures, are the first and greatest miracle of life. A life that is to be resurrected had to be first created, and that has already taken place. It is only by a divine miracle that you and I exist and are now alive; we are conscious of our surroundings. We can think, know, remember, and feel. We are humans, made in the image of our Creator, in miraculously working bodies. We are made of the very same materials found in the dust of the earth that God has wonderfully awakened to become an actual part of our living bodies.

THE PROPHET DANIEL in his last days here on earth wrote down the prophecies he received from God on the happenings to come and on the resurrection. "And many of them that sleep in the dust of the earth shall awake, some to everlasting life and some to shame and everlasting contempt" (Daniel 12:2).

But Daniel didn't understand. "O my Lord," he asked, "what shall be the end of these things?"

He was told "...Go thy way till the end be, for thou shalt rest and stand in thy lot at the end of the days" (Verses 8 and 13).

An eternity with a loving God is something to look forward to. We know we are not worthy, but He loves us enough to make it possible. Whenever we are able, let us show our gratefulness to Him for that love.

JESUS WANTED HIS FOLLOWERS to have a peace in their hearts and no fear of the unknown future. "Let not your heart be troubled," He said. "I go to prepare a place for you...that where I am, there you may be also" (John, Chapter 14). Because of His promise to be with us, we need to have no fear of evil; nothing needs to disturb the Godly peace in our minds as we walk through the valley of the shadow of death. (Psalm 23:4).

We do not need to fear the shadows. They are there only because of the light that exists behind them.

Our earthly end does not need to be much different than a sleepy child being asked to put away his or her playthings to take a refreshing nap. Let us not fear the day God comes to take us away. If we are prepared, He may be answering our prayers to show us His glory.

You may already have come across the story of the preschool-aged child who had been hurt in a serious accident. The story has made its rounds in several different versions.

This little girl may have heard from the whisperings around her bed that she might not have long to live.

She must have imagined her mother knew the answer to any question. "Mother, does it hurt to die?" she asked.

Breathing a silent prayer for the wisdom to give a proper and understandable answer, the mother turned her head to hide the tears running down her cheeks.

She found the strength to brace up. "Child, do you remember the evening when we walked across the bridge last summer to visit your uncle and aunt and your cousins on the other side of the river?"

"Yes, Mother, I remember," she replied.

"Do you remember how that evening the skies grew dark and the storm came up? The rain poured and the winds blew. The angry waters of the river kept getting higher. You were worried that before we would get home, the water could wash away the bridge. But your daddy held you close in his arms. Do you remember?"

"Yes, Mother, I remember," she said.

"Do you remember when you awoke it was the morning of the next day? The sun was shining; the storm was over; you were safe at home. Your daddy had carried you over the bridge when you had fallen asleep.

"My child, if it is God's will that you will not get well, that is what dying is like. You do not need to be afraid."

With this assurance in her heart, the child fell asleep.

PAUL JOHNSON

This black basalt stone was found by Napoleon's soldiers in 1799 while digging out a footer for a fort near Rosetta, on the coast of the Nile Delta in Egypt. A decree of an Egyptian king is carved on the stone in three languages.

After the stone, now displayed in the British Museum, was finished being deciphered twenty years later, a wealth of new information was opened up for historians of ancient Eygpt.

It seems the ancient Egyptians painted or carved something on nearly every available surface; a little like nearly every cardboard box or plastic or paper bag in our day seems to have some kind of print on it.

The knowledge of reading the complex form of Egyptian writing was lost and was silent and unread for at least 1,500 years. Not a single person in the whole world was able to read the marks made by the ancient Egyptians.

Many superstitious people believed the mysterious writings found in hundreds of thousands of tombs and temple inscriptions might be forbidden occult knowledge that only the ancient Egyptian magicians and sorcerers would have been able to read.

One of the three languages on this Rosetta Stone was in Greek, which gave language scholars a start in reading the other two languages. Although the ancient Egyptian inscriptions can now be read, we are still not exactly sure how the spoken language sounded. For example, we can still not tell if we are even rightly pronouncing the names of the Egyptian kings.

The deciphering of the Rosetta Stone was the key that helped Egyptian historians to reconstruct the interesting story of Pharoah Akhenaton and his queen Nefertiti.

The history of these two unusual Egyptian rulers who attempted an ill-fated turnaround in the religion of the Egyptian people is retold in the following chapter. They had somehow been led to believe that their subjects should be worshiping the God who created them, rather than the numerous false gods created in the minds of the heathen priests in their idol temples.

Pharoah Akhenaton even composed a hymn of praise to his Creator which is surprisingly similar to Psalm 104 found in our Bibles.

Chapter 5

Is It Possible for a Godly People to Influence a Heathen Nation?

THERE IS ONE PERIOD IN THE EARLY HISTORY OF ANCIENT Egypt that has fascinated all serious scholars of this unusual nation—a nation that is mentioned hundreds of times in our Holy Bible.

This is the interesting story of the Egyptian ruler named Akhenaton and his wife Nefertiti. The exact dating of this man and wife's reign varies widely, even among histories written by highly competent historians. However, most agree that this remarkable king and queen lived a little over a hundred years before the time of Moses.

Bible readers know well the story of the four hundred years the Israelites spent in Egypt. The Israelites may have lived under the reign of Pharaoh Akhenaton and Queen Nefertiti, arriving in Egypt several hundred years before this, due to the kindness of the pharaoh in Joseph's time (Genesis 47:5 and 6).

Direct evidence for many historical events will always remain elusive. There is a lot of scant evidence, and then new discoveries are made that directly contradict what has been discovered earlier. The result is that historians will never reconstruct exactly what happened long ago. Many things we wonder about will remain behind the curtain drawn between us and the past.

However, as far as we can learn from the inscriptions uncovered on the walls of the tombs and temples by archaeologists in recent years, the Egyptians at the dawn of written history were a people who worshiped hundreds of gods.

Religious Mistakes of Egyptians

EVEN THOUGH EGYPTIAN LEGENDS said that everything was created "all in one flash," their religion was soon sidetracked from the worship of only the one true God. The pure, clean faith and divine, sacred religion of the first humans after Creation became marred and imperfect as the religious thinking of each generation of families gradually became more polluted and corrupted.

As the population of the earth grew, most fathers and mothers were not interested enough, or did not realize the importance of passing on the real faith to the generations coming on. The lack of deep religious morals in previous generations may have contributed to more shallow religious living in each succeeding generation. Anyway, virtually all the tribes who migrated to the land of Egypt after the scattering of families from the unfinished Tower of Babel seemed to have soon lost all knowledge of the God of Creation.

In ignorance they believed one of their many gods had charge of the yearly overflow of the Nile River, upon which depended the years of famine or plenty in Egypt. Other deities they had images for and worshiped were supposed to rule the rising and setting of the sun.

The earliest Egyptian people were mostly a peaceful people. Their somewhat isolated land did not need much of their gross national income for war or defense. However, this rich country along the Nile River wasted much wealth and energy on religious beliefs in gods and pharaohs that warped their ideas about the life in the hereafter.

Many elaborate and costly temples for their variety of gods were built all over the land of Egypt. Multitudes of priests in these temples, living off the religious common folk, would spend their time performing the religious rituals they thought their gods required. Where we have our Bibles for our source of religious faith, the religious rituals of ancient Egypt were made up by the temple priests.

The early Egyptians were also a people who never seemed to tire of doing artwork. They painted and carved in minute detail on any available surface. Nearly all their walls and surfaces were covered with paintings or relief sculptures. Much of this art in the very dry climate of Egypt is still in good condition after several thousand years. From it we have learned much of the daily living of the ancient Egyptians.

However, we may be in error if we attach a religious significance upon every single item or painting brought to light.

THE RELIGION OF EARLY EGYPT honored their king or pharaoh as a divine god. The common folk were told pharaohs were gods in human form, sent to earth to make sure that what was best for the land of Egypt would be done. The pharaoh was accepted as something like the savior of the Egyptian people.

We have to wonder if this pharaoh worship, after the worship of the true God had been forgotten, was the corrupted promise of a Savior of the human race that God had given to Adam and Eve.

We are also left to wonder how the rulers, acclaimed as "living gods," but just as human as their lowly subjects, could in good conscience accept such honor and power. How could any human being keep from becoming self-centered and vain in a system that kept him in such high esteem?

How could the pharaohs, who thought of themselves so highly, still stay humble enough to rule with equality and justice? The pharaohs would even speak of themselves as "My Majesty" instead of using the word "I." Didn't the saying "absolute power corrupts absolutely" apply to the Egyptian pharaohs?

Because of the awesome power of the pharaohs, Egypt, unlike many other ancient countries, did not develop a written law or code such as our national constitution. It was unthinkable in ancient Egypt for anyone to protest the sudden whims of the pharaoh.

WE ARE NOT SURE HOW MANY CENTURIES passed into history under the total of at least thirty-one known dynasties (ruling families), during which time probably a total of a hundred and thirty or more Egyptian pharaohs ruled.

There is no starting date for Egyptian history. Each year their calendar was calculated according to how many years the present pharaoh had been on the throne, and it is now known that many reigns may have widely overlapped when Egypt was divided into the Upper and Lower Kingdoms. However, during the period from the time of the building of the pyramids until the time of the last independent rulers of Egypt only several hundred years before Christ was born, very few changes were made to religious beliefs and practices except for this one short time when Pharaoh Akhenaton and Queen Nefertiti ruled Egypt. This period of time when pagan gods were not worshiped has been called "the religious revolution of ancient Egypt."

Pharaoh Akhenaton described himself as "one who lives on truth" and his graceful queen's name—Nefertiti—means "the beautiful one has come."

Akhenaton was a pharaoh of the eighteenth dynasty of Egyptian kings, ruling the country for seventeen years. It seems the religious convictions of this very uncommon Queen Nefertiti may have had a great influence on her pharaoh husband when they made this short-lived attempt to reform the religion practiced in the land of Egypt. Her name and likeness appears more often in Egyptian artwork than does that of her husband.

It is also noteworthy that the artwork and sculpture that depict Queen Nefertiti does not show her wearing any jewelry, something very unusual for an Egyptian queen of those days. The desire to make an impression on others or to enhance her appearance with what she wore must have been absent in the mind of this queen. She must have been fully content with the physical looks that God gave to her.

THE RELIGION OF AKHENATON AND NEFERTITI rejected the worshiping of all idols and images. They had for some unknown reason become convinced that the graven images their forefathers worshiped had been invented and made by man—something had made them feel certain that people should be worshiping their Creator instead of paying homage to something that they themselves had created.

They abandoned the traditional and firmly established worship of many gods. Taking part in pagan religious practices was outlawed. The idol temples were closed and the images of gods and goddesses were destroyed.

Of course, the temple priests were no longer needed for religious worship purposes. With the rich royalties that the previous pharaohs had granted to them now cut off, the priests had to do something else.

But it seems they did not give up all of this as submissively as it first appeared, and we will hear more about these priests later on.

However, as far as is known of this sudden change of religion in Egypt, little or no violence or rebellion of the common people came with it. It seems they always accepted the pharaoh's authority and had no problems following all of their pharaoh's beliefs and what he told them.

They were probably ready for a simpler and more credible religion anyway. That the common people thought well of Akhenaton is noted in an inscription calling him "the good ruler who loved mankind."

THE NEW PHARAOH AND HIS QUEEN introduced the worship of one God only, and represented him as a kindly and benevolent God of light, very much like the true God of our Christian religion. They believed they were formed and created by the God they worshiped. They adopted "Living in Truth" as the slogan of their faith.

To be sure, this religion could never be identified as exactly like the beliefs of Noah, Abraham, Isaac, Jacob, and Joseph in all respects. Because this was before any of the Bible had been put to writing, it is understandable that the religion of the new pharaoh and his queen would have its flaws. Pharaoh Akhenaton had a new town built as the capital of Egypt. Everything was the most costly and the very best, something the humble tent-dwelling Bible patriarchs would never have thought of doing, even with all their riches.

These Egyptian religious reforms were not all 180-degree overnight changes, but there can be no mistake about it—their beliefs were very similar to the Israelites living in the land of Egypt at this very same time.

Although the God Akhenaton and Nefertiti worshiped was represented in the Egyptian wall paintings of this time as the sun shining overhead with the sunbeams reaching down to earth, this was not sun worship. They are shown as being under the protection of "Life-giving light rays" but this was still not a "sun cult" as some Egyptian historians of our time say it was.

Akhenaton and Nefertiti did not have images made of this God, because they must have realized He was much greater than they could portray in any art or sculpture.

This may have been a little like the cross in our days representing the religion of Christianity. The people of Egypt during this reign did not worship the sun any more than Christians of our day worship the cross. The paintings of this era which depict the Egyptians at prayer as the sun is rising do not prove they worshiped the sun. It is more believable that they had a practice of early morning prayer.

AKHENATON WAS A LITTLE different from what most of us now imagine an Egyptian pharaoh to be.

He was also a poet. An inscription has been discovered which is a hymn of praise composed by him to the true God, which he worshiped. Ancient

Egyptian inscriptions have also been found which may be musical notations for the tunes of their songs, but nobody today knows how to read them. There are paintings showing the Egyptian people with their mouths open in singing, but we have no idea how their songs sounded.

However, the words of this hymn are surprisingly similar to the Psalm number 104 found in our Old Testament. Many parts are so remarkably alike that it has been suggested that a Hebrew hymn writer of a much later era may have used this very ancient Egyptian hymn as a source for a song. After making a few changes, the Hebrew psalm found its way into the Psalm Book of the early Jewish people, which is essentially the prayer and hymn book of our Bibles.

Although all this about the origin of Psalm 104 is very credible, there is still much we do not know. All ancient peoples had some kind of song, so this psalm could have had its roots back into a time soon after Creation. The God-fearing families who were believers of the one true God may have sung the earliest version of this 35-verse hymn. A form of this song could well have been sung around the campfires outside their tents, before writing was invented to record the words of their songs and the daily events of early history.

KING AKHENATON AND QUEEN NEFERTITI had a family of six daughters, and if we go by the inscriptions and the very crude wall paintings of those days, they must have had a very close and loving relationship.

Unlike the very aloof and reticent Egyptian rulers before their time, the new king and queen evidently walked and rode freely around the town among the common folk. They were ordinary people living everyday lives. The royal family is shown in their daily doings as having a tender attachment for each other. One painting shows the pharaoh lightly kissing the cheek of one of his small daughters who had climbed upon his lap; another shows the king lightly holding the hand of his queen. Such scenes of feeling and scenes of the children of the royal family with their parents were rarely depicted in Egyptian art before this time. Being loving parents seemed to be more important to Akhenaton and Nefertiti than being the king and queen of Egypt.

One scene uncovered by modern archaeologists shows the family grieving at the death of the second of their daughters. This lightly carved relief sculpture shows Pharaoh Akhenaton reaching for the hand of the grief-stricken mother as they are weeping together at the bier of their daughter, only twelve years old.

Such scenes of grief were previously almost unknown in the somewhat exaggerated and distorted ancient Egyptian artwork of those times. This depiction of sorrow in the royal family was like the grief we read about in the Bible stories of Abraham (Genesis 23), Isaac (Genesis 24:67), Jacob (Genesis 37:33-35), and Joseph (Genesis 50: 1-3).

Their sorrow was by no means the grief of hopelessness for the deceased. It was the grief of the survivors of the departed facing the reality that they will have to go on with daily living in the absence of a loved one. As much as they were loved they were now missed. It was then as it is now. Only the fond memories of the departed are our keepsakes.

IT IS BELIEVED THAT THE third daughter of Akhenaton and Nefertiti was married to the youthful King Tutankhamen, or Tut, whose burial chambers made modern headlines when they were discovered by the archaeologist Howard Carter in 1922.

It is known that this King Tut and his wife, the princess, who was probably about three years older than he was, had two stillborn daughters before he died at the young age of twenty. This left the dynasty, or royal family of Akhenaton and Nefertiti, with no male heir to be placed on the Egyptian throne.

Interestingly enough, unlike so much of the ancient Egyptian art discovered in the tombs of other pharaohs, the tomb of the son-in-law King Tut contained very few wall paintings and art depicting the many different Egyptian gods. The temple priests who were recovering their political influence right around the time of King Tut's funeral may have placed the several pieces that were found there.

Because his gilded throne chair found in the burial chamber had a scene portraying light beams radiating from a single source from somewhere above, it is almost certain that King Tut had also been a firm believer in the religion of one true God during his short lifetime.

Despite all his riches and somewhat warped ideas of the life in the hereafter, it seems he had also accepted the religion that his wife's family had somewhere learned in the land of Egypt—the land that had a long history of being a pagan people worshiping many different gods.

UNFORTUNATELY, THE RELIGIOUS REFORM of Pharaoh Akhenaton was short-lived. It did not last much longer than his 17-year reign. It is believed that the political power that the infuriated and disgruntled pagan temple priests had organized finally prevailed. They were angry enough to turn away from even hearing about a religion in which their services were not needed.

Several years after Akhenaton died (or he may have been eliminated or banished, we do not know), the Egyptian people were led back to the worship of the many gods of their forefathers. It seems the temple priests, driven by political interests, finally destroyed the Egyptian people's acceptance of a single God who was, and still is, powerful enough to create and control all of Creation.

An army general named Horenheb, who must have been something like a military dictator, took over the Egyptian throne shortly after the short reign and death of Akhenaton's son-in-law, King Tut. An altogether new dynasty of Egyptian pharaohs was established. From this 19th dynasty came the pharaohs who several generations later would oppress the Israelites with an unmerciful slavery, which we read about in the book of Exodus.

Pharaoh Horenheb and his successors renounced "the religious revolution" of Akhenaton and Nefertiti. He got Egypt back to the old ways of the worship of many gods and goddesses. The changeover that was made was thorough and complete.

As far as is known, this change and this return to the traditional Egyptian pagan religion also happened without a major rebellion of the Egyptian common people. It seems the Egyptian people would always accept the rulings of whoever happened to be their pharaoh, without asking any questions.

The new city that overlooked the Nile River, which Akhenaton had built as his religious center and seat of government, possibly to get away from the pagan temples of his former capital, was torn down. The stone blocks were carried off and used in rebuilding temples for the worship of pagan gods. The place became deserted and what was left was soon covered with sand drifting in from the nearby desert.

The sculptures and wall paintings depicting Akhenaton and Nefertiti and the inscriptions about their religion were vandalized and only by chance has some of it been recovered. Much of it has been chiseled off the walls and there are marks of hammer blows on most of the artwork depicting their faces. It is difficult to find an undamaged wall painting or inscription about Akhenaton or Nefertiti under the drifted sands of this deserted city.

Although some of it did get missed, it seems the enemies of their reformed religion went all out to destroy all traces of the reign of Akhenaton and Nefertiti. His name is not even included in most of the lists of the Egyptian pharaohs. There is also evidence of the inscriptions honoring the next pharaoh, their teen-aged son-in-law, King Tut, as to having been scraped off the walls.

While searching for Egyptian history, modern archaeologists have found many embalmed bodies of the Egyptian pharaohs and their queens. To this day, however, nothing is known for certain as to when or where Akhenaton and Nefertiti died. The location of their tombs has completely vanished and there is no known record of a royal funeral and burial for them.

The next dynasties of Egyptian pharaohs wanted to hear nothing of this "heretic religion" anymore. They wanted to disgrace the memory of Akhenaton and Nefertiti and completely erase from Egyptian history any remembrance of their reign. Several years after Akhenaton's death, his religion was completely silenced and never heard of again until the site of his new capital city happened to be uncovered from under the drifted sands and explored by modern-day archaeologists.

The later pharaohs did such a good job of besmirching the name of Akhenaton as a disgraced blasphemer that no other Egyptian pharaoh would ever again dare to try to change the religion of the ancient Egyptian people. No pharaoh would want such a dishonor heaped upon his memory after he was dead and gone.

ALL THIS MAKES SENSE WHEN we read in our Bibles that "there arose up a new king over Egypt which knew not Joseph" (Exodus 1:8).

Even in our times, there are history book writers who speak unkindly of Akhenaton. He has been described as an "atheist" because he did not worship the traditional gods of Egypt and as a "heretic" because he did not believe in and keep up the practice of the long-established pagan customs of his Egyptian forefathers many generations before him. Some histories of ancient Egypt hatefully speak of "the rot and degradation of the reign of Akhenaton and Nefertiti." He has been called "the great scoundrel who showed contempt and scorn for the ancient wisdom of our land."

Akhenaton has been blamed for the beginning of the decline of Egyptian power among the nations, because he seemed to have been more occupied with his religion than he was in defending Egypt from the nations around it. He has been called "an odd religious fanatic, having a deranged mental state." In contempt for his belief in one true God, he has been called "a deluded rebel."

In other words, what happened here is what happened throughout history when a group of sincere people made a break from the mainstream to follow a path that is better and more Godly. It seems some kind of persecution will surely follow.

ANOTHER MYSTERY stimulating much debate among historians is as to where Akhenaton and Nefertiti got this idea of believing in one God only. The conclusions are many and varied, and, of course, nothing is certain. There is evidence that Akhenaton's religious queen mother, named Tiye, was the originator of these religious beliefs and influenced him.

In our days there are many historians who believe in the evolution of human beings from the lower animals. The theory that usually follows is that all religion and theological thought also progressed "from the lower to the higher." Mankind is believed to be advancing "from a primitive past to an enlightened future," a direct contradiction to the Bible, which so clearly describes the fall of man.

People who believe in this "process of religious development" are almost sure that in trying to trace "religious thought to its source" they find that Akhenaton was the very first of the ancient peoples to believe in one God only instead of in the numerous pagan gods.

They see him as "an enlightened leader who was one of the world's greatest religious figures," even though his ideas were scarcely appreciated or accepted in his time. Because they believe he was "the first human being in history to worship a single God," they say they are sure his "religious thought" was the beginning of monotheism, the doctrine that teaches that there is only one God. He has been credited with starting "an intellectual revolution which has spawned Christianity."

In trying to keep track of "the development of religions" they trace the beliefs of the Hebrews, the people to whom Jesus Christ was born, to "the genius of the pharaoh Akhenaton." They say his religion later influenced the Hebrew lawgiver and history writer, Moses, who was brought up in the Egyptian court a hundred or so years after the time of Akhenaton.

This line of reasoning would, of course, make none other than Akhenaton "the father of all monotheistic one-God religions" which would include the Christians, Jews, and Muslims. This gives the thinking of Akhenaton and Nefertiti credit for being the original basis and root of the Christian religion we believe in.

If we conclude that Moses first heard about the faith of his forefathers when he studied Egyptian history in their schools, we are ignoring the fact that he learned his faith in the short time of his early years on his mother's lap.

ANOTHER EXPLANATION about this short period of a one-God religion in Egypt makes more sense and is much more believable. This "theory" may be too "shockingly simple" for those who keep insisting on a complex "scientific interpretation based only on proofs that are believed to be infallible."

It makes sense to believe that Akhenaton and Nefertiti learned this religion from the Israelites living in Egypt during that time. These Israelites were descendants of Abraham. The Bible record says God blessed Abraham because "here was a man who will command his children and his household after him, and they shall keep the way of the Lord" (Genesis 18:19). Here was a tribe of people who through succeeding generations passed on the true stories of the Creation by the Almighty God. They told their children the true stories of the Garden of Eden and the Great Flood, and they made sure the next generations were taught what they had learned from their parents and grandparents.

We can be sure that the convictions and the high morals of this great number of God-fearing foreigners was noticed by their idol-worshiping Egyptian neighbors. A light cannot long be kept burning if it is hidden beneath a bushel. It is very credible that Akhenaton and Nefertiti came to the conclusion that this religion, lived in the daily lives of the Israelites, would be good for all the land of Egypt. They could have seen that here was a good faith being put to practice.

There is also this instance of a pharaoh several generations earlier, in Joseph's time, who was amazed at the Godly wisdom of the chaste and God-fearing "jailbird" standing before him. "Can we find such a man as this is; a man in whom the Spirit of God is?" he asked (Genesis 41:38).

That pharaoh noticed decent and respectable living when he saw it. He treated Joseph, his father, his brothers, and their families kindly. He gave them homes in the best part of Egypt when the land was in the grip of a severe seven-year famine.

It is possible that Akhenaton's hymn of praise to the God of light verifies that he knew of the Almighty God who spoke light into existence on the first day of Creation. It is very credible that the interesting story of Creation, passed down through each successive generation from the time of Adam and Eve to Noah and Abraham by word of mouth, and then to the Israelites living in Egypt, was the story believed by Akhenaton and Nefertiti.

"O the only God, like unto whom there is no other; Thou didst fashion the Earth according to Thy desire when Thou was alone," he wrote. He has several lines in his hymn that speak of the God of Creation, "who is the giver of life" and of the God "who enables men to live and breathe."

He may also somehow have become familiar with the history of the Great Flood and the scattering abroad of tribes and families at the unfinished Tower of Babel. Not yet written down, this history was told and retold by parents and grandparents to their young and interested hearers gathered around them. In one line of Akhenaton's hymn he speaks of "a flood upon the mountains," a line very similar to the sixth verse in Psalm 104, and in another he wrote of the God "who made different the tongue of one land from another."

These stories were so much more believable than those myths and legends of the pagan gods represented by absurd, grotesque, and terrible-looking images. It is certainly more credible to believe that the stories in Genesis come from a true source than it is to believe the skeptics of our time who think the Genesis stories in the Bible are only repeats of fictitious legends of ignorant groups of people at the dawn of history.

What is also different about the God that Akhenaton and Nefertiti worshiped was that He was (and still is) a God of love. The ancient Egyptians believed the pagan gods they worshiped bestowed their blessings exclusively on the Egyptian lands and people. The God which Akhenaton praised was a God of universal love to the people of all nations.

It is also known that Pharaoh Akhenaton had appointed a foreign Asiatic who was not a temple priest as his Grand Vizier, or the second most powerful figure in Egypt. This makes the Bible story of the non-Egyptian prime minister, Joseph, of several hundred years earlier, even more believable.

All this points to evidence that during the 400 years (Acts 7:6) that the Israelites lived in the land of Egypt, they were a good and Godly influence in that land. They must have been good "hometown" missionaries for the cause of the true God. Perhaps they were unaware that their religion and morals influenced the land of Egypt while they made homes there, even if only for a short time. They were a Godly presence among a heathen people. God works in mysterious ways His wonders to perform.

However, the good influence of the God-fearing Israelites in Egypt was only temporary. Several generations later a pharaoh who forced them into an almost unbearable slavery and ordered the killing of their baby boys came into power.

But God never forgets His own. God showed His miraculous power to the unbelieving and unmerciful pharaoh. His people, the salt of the earth and a light to the world, were set free. This freedom was an answer to their prayers for release.

The yearly celebration of the Passover by the Jewish people ever since then is proof enough that the Bible record of the Exodus is a true account. Anything like the Jewish Passover and its continuation in the worldwide Christian Communion service would not be in existence if it were based only on a legend.

THERE IS EVIDENCE IN THE BIBLE that the Israelites left a good influence on their Egyptian neighbors, even several generations after the reign of the pharaoh Akhenaton. Their beliefs must have been contagious in that a number of Egyptian citizens made the choice of leaving Egypt with them on Passover night (Exodus 12:38). The Bible says, "The Lord gave the Israelites favor in the sight of the Egyptians," so much that when they made requests of their neighbors for pay for the work they had done, the response was overwhelming enough to make them wealthy. The Hebrew words translated as "borrowing" or "lending" did not mean a promise to pay back again. It was asking for payment for what they had earned, as we would ask someone we worked for to give us what they thought our work was worth.

THE INFLUENCE OF THE ISRAELITES in the land of Egypt is a sobering thought to all Christians of our day, challenging us to go beyond merely saying we believe in the teachings of Jesus Christ. Think of what we could do if we practiced them and made them part and parcel of our daily living in this land where we have made our homes! Our lives may be the only translation of the Bible that the non-Christians of our day may ever read. Starting at the neighborhood level, God can use the influence of sincere Christians to make a difference in our world.

However, as we know, influence upon others works both ways. We would think a people whose parents and grandparents taught them of the one true God, and influenced their neighbors into such worship, would know better than to be later influenced into building and worshiping the same kind of pagan idols found in that pagan land.

But—we think it can't be true—only a short time after God released them from slavery, the Israelites made a god of gold and worshiped it (Exodus 32: 4). They even said this was the god whose power had brought them out of the land of slavery.

They fell into sins of lust, and were unthankful for God's daily blessings that kept them alive. They did not believe God could help them cleanse the Promised Land of idolatry. Given everything they needed, they still became discouraged and discontented.

The Israelites could have traveled from Egypt to the Promised Land in one year, but because of their sins they suffered defeats, along with trials and hardships, for forty years before they were permitted to enter their homeland. It has been said, that it took the Israelites only one night to get out of Egypt, but it took forty years to get Egypt out of the Israelites.

May our God help us that we do not worship the idols of gold and the gods of mammon, materialism, and pleasure in our land of prosperity.

May the Christians in our land live upright lives of blessing so that God will continue to bless America.

TUTANKAMEN
PHOTO CREDIT – F. L. KENETT

This wooden chair, covered with gold, was one of the rich artifacts found in the burial chambers of the Egyptian boy king named Tutankhamen. He died at about the age of nineteen, having become a pharaoh at the young age of nine; probably at the death of his father-in-law.

This piece of furniture may have been merely his easy chair, or it may have been his royal throne, and is now on display at a museum in Cairo. It dates back to probably a hundred or so years before Moses was born, give or take a generation or two. At the time of King Tut's reign, the Israelites, having been invited by Joseph, were living in the land of Egypt.

The crude scene painted on the back of the chair seems to show Tut's young queen taking care of her invalid husband. His wife, who would shortly be a childless widow, is giving his shoulders a rubdown. The chair shows signs of having its height increased as Tut was growing up.

This queen, Ankhesenamun, was one of the six daughters of the Egyptian pharaoh, Akhenaton and his queen, Nefertiti, who are known to have had close ties as a family. During their 17-year reign over Egypt, they unsuccessfully tried to get Egypt to drop its religion of worshiping many gods and adopt a form of the worship of one God only.

For their efforts in reviving a better religion for Egypt, the later pharaohs would call him "the pharaoh who turned heretic." The jobless priests of the idol temples were, in their revenge, successful in erasing the memory of Akhenaton and Nefertiti's reign from Egyptian history.

There are a multitude of unknowns in these turbulent times in the history of perhaps the most wealthy and powerful country in those days. Had Akhenaton and Nefertiti become inspired to worship the true God by the quiet influence of the Israelites living in their country? Was the young Tut only a puppet ruler when the worship of the true God was overthrown during his reign, and what was the cause of his untimely death? If he had abandoned the one-God worship of his wife's family, why is the symbol of this God of light still depicted on his royal chair from which he ruled the land of Egypt?

Chapter 6

Preparing for the Life After the Resurrection Day

AT THE DAWN OF HISTORY, the Egyptians were burying their kings deep within the interiors of the huge pyramids of Giza, close to modern-day Cairo. Although cleverly built to avoid having the burial chambers discovered, the tombs were always raided, the chambers discovered, and the valuables carried off. Professional grave robbers did much of this raiding, although some of the pillage may have been done by the subjects of later pharaohs who wanted to erase the memory of a rival dynasty that ruled before them.

After the pharaohs realized that the ingeniously hidden burial chambers, blocked by dead-end passageways in the pyramids, were not safe from discovery and plunder, they abandoned pyramid burial. They started preparing tombs for their burials in an isolated valley several hundred miles south of Giza. This area was a desolate, hot, and very dry hollow at the edge of the desert, a short distance west of the Nile River. In ancient times it could only be entered through a small natural opening hidden by a screen of piled-up rocks.

Later called the Valley of the Tombs of the Kings, this lonely and uninhabited place of sand and boulders, surrounded by cliffs hundreds of feet high, seemed to be the perfect place to hide the tombs of the pharaohs.

After a pharaoh died and the embalming of his body was complete, a funeral barge carrying the king would sail upriver on the Nile, loaded with material goods that the priests of the Egyptian religion believed the pharaoh would need in the next life.

Deep in the bedrock, or in the cliffs, the burial rooms were cut out. After the pharaoh's burial, the entrance was covered up with rocks and sand. Here it was believed the pharaoh's treasures would be kept intact until the Judgment Day, when the body of the king would be brought to life again.

Although grave robbers were put through torture and then executed if they were caught, every one of the royal burial rooms discovered had been illicitly entered and plundered. After thousands of years, there were no Egyptian tombs known that had anything of much value left. Only the bodies of the kings, or pharaohs as they were called, were left. These mummified bodies, some still having very lifelike features after several thousand years, were considered useless to the robbers, who were interested only in finding riches.

It seems the pharaohs had become so attached to their wealth and way of materialistic living here on earth that they hoped such living would continue in the next world. In error, they thought the next life, although unending, would be a life just like this one.

Howard Carter's Discovery

USING THE EXCUSE THAT THEY WERE NOT SEARCHING FOR RICHES, but rather working as scholars seeking a wider knowledge of ancient history, archaeologists started exploring the tombs in the Valley of the Kings. Modern scientists and historians admit that nearly everything known about ancient Egypt has been learned from digging through their cemeteries and graveyards.

The burial area in this large wasteland in the Egyptian desert had previously been carefully combed over by archaeologists at least a hundred times before Howard Carter began his exploration. Every one of the tombs found had already been stripped of their valuables by ancient grave robbers.

After spending six years and the amount of more than a half million dollars in today's money, Carter's finances had almost run out. He decided to spend only the rest of the summer of 1922 at the work. Then he would quit. These years of digging through many layers of sand and stone rubble made Carter and his workers lose ambition. They felt perhaps there was nothing of value underneath anymore.

However, one day the excitement ran high when a stone step was found cut into the bedrock. After many tons of debris had been carried away in baskets by Carter's helpers, sixteen steps downward were uncovered. They led to a sealed door.

Carter gave the order to pry the door open. Behind the door that had been closed and securely fastened after King Tut's funeral, Howard Carter found four rooms cut into the rock. Several thousand objects, priceless to the world of archaeology, were found there.

AMONG ALL THIS WEALTH WAS a solid golden coffin worth millions of dollars in today's money. Inside the coffin was the mummified body of King Tutankhamen, pharaoh of Egypt. This find still remains the richest discovery in the history of archaeology. Archaeologist Howard Carter's discovery of this tomb of King Tutankhamen was all the more remarkable because it was the only tomb of an Egyptian king ever found that had not been previously broken into and thoroughly looted by gold-greedy grave robbers. Only this one tomb, out of the sixty or more royal burials discovered under the rocks and drifting sands in the famous Valley of the Kings, was found virtually undisturbed since the pharaohs had been laid to rest. This was the only tomb of an ancient Egyptian pharaoh that the professional grave robbers of antiquity had missed. The mummified body of no other Egyptian king lay in silent majesty among his treasures of this world as long as King Tutankhamen.

The valuable objects in gold and silver and the art and jewelry items, along with the closed coffin of King Tut himself, were to be bathed in sunlight again. They had been hidden in the darkness for a period thought by many Egyptian historians to have been nearly thirty-three centuries.

The news of Carter's discovery made headlines on the front pages of newspapers all over the world. It wasn't long until thousands of news reporters and curious tourists were swarming all over the place. Carter complained of the hindrance the crowds were making in his work and a tight security was set up. Even then, it was not until seven years later that the work of carefully cataloging and cleaning every item was finished.

According to the inscriptions found by Carter after these years of tiresome searching and digging, this was the tomb of a very young Egyptian king called King Tut, for short. As was the Egyptian way to honor their kings, he was buried in great splendor.

He became king of Egypt at the age of nine, and died mysteriously only ten years later at the young age of about nineteen years old. He had been married to one of the daughters of Pharaoh Akhenaton and Queen Nefertiti, who are noted for their ill-fated attempt to revive the religion of the one God into the land of pagan Egypt. Akhenaton and Nefertiti had no sons, so this is probably why a son-in-law became the king.

After King Tutankhamen's burial, Egyptian workmen were chiseling out the tomb of a much more important pharaoh in the limestone rock just up the slope from King Tut's tomb. As the workman chiseled, the entrance to King Tut's tomb became completely hidden and covered over with many tons of stone fragments and large rocks falling from the cliffs above it. For this reason, it remained undiscovered for centuries.

However, some of the treasures Carter found just inside the entrance door were in a disorderly heap, and the door seal did show signs of having been sealed twice.

It has been speculated that an attempt to rob the grave was made soon after the burial occurred. It appears the grave robbers were caught in the act and the door resealed before much had been removed. The thieves would have been tortured and executed and the entrance again hidden by scattering a deep layer of rocks and boulders over it.

The debris from the workers making a new tomb and sand drifting in from the desert would have finished the cover-up.

CARTER AND HIS WORKERS were astonished and amazed at the incredible wealth they saw piled up in King Tut's burial vault. Besides the 2,400-pound golden coffin into which his lifeless body had been laid, the treasure rooms were heaped to the ceiling with thousands of assorted items. Anything from rare works of art to gold-covered furniture was included.

It has been said we can't take what we own with us, but it seems the Egyptian pharaohs at least tried. King Tut's tomb, strewn with all these priceless artifacts, proclaimed his greatness in the eyes of his Egyptian subjects. The valuables found in the resting place of this rather insignificant boy king make historians of ancient Egypt wonder what amounts of gold and jewelry were stolen by the grave robbers who found and hacked their way into the burial crypts of the really famous Egyptian kings.

The burial chambers of King Tut were supplied with every article, many in duplicate, that his subjects imagined their king might need for happiness in the next life. They wanted to make sure their king, who they believed to have been divinely chosen by their gods to rule the land of Egypt, would be stocked with all the material comforts he would need after his resurrection.

To make sure their king would have plenty of pastime after his resurrection from the dead, he was buried with four sets of a game board inscribed with thirty squares. Below each board was an elaborately carved drawer containing a number of differently shaped playing pieces made of white ivory and a dark ebony wood. However, nobody today knows how the game was played. There was no rule book.

The words on one alabaster cup were inscribed with good wishes for the deceased pharaoh: "May thou spend millions of years...with thine eyes beholding bliss and happiness."

The fancy sandals found in the burial chamber had the enemies of Egypt painted on the inner soles. When he would be using them in the next life he would be treading on his enemies with every step.

He must have been fond of hunting. Along with many other items found were a large number of bows and arrows and several luxury lightweight two-wheeled chariots, each built with two six-spoke wheels with leather tires. By this time wheels had been invented, something not yet known of about five, six, or seven hundred years earlier when the pyramids were being built (this is in line with the first chariots being mentioned in the Bible during the time of Joseph).

(Another pharaoh several generations after the time of King Tut would also be buried with his chariot. This was the pharaoh drowned in the Red Sea with his chariot and horses while on the chase after the Israelites who were leaving the land of Egypt.)

One interesting object found in King Tut's tomb was a heavy wooden gold-covered chair with a reed seat (pictured at the beginning of this chapter). This chair may have been his throne or his easy chair.

There is a painting on the chair back showing the pharaoh sitting on his throne looking tired and worn out. With a jar of ointment in one hand, his young queen is giving his shoulders a rubdown with the other hand. Was she, as a devoted wife, faithfully doing what she could to ease the sickness of her invalid husband?

ANOTHER SMALL DISCOVERY WOULD BE MADE in the tomb of the young king that would evoke more emotions than would any other of the almost

2,000 burial treasures discovered. When Howard Carter would later write of his work he mentioned there was nothing more moving to him and his men than the finding of a small handful of spring flowers on the coffin lid above the forehead of the deceased king.

Evidently when the funeral procession, the final earthly journey of King Tut, was moving from the anchored river barge to the gravesite, the lonely widow bent down and picked several common wildflowers that grew along the river's edge.

After the coffin lid was placed and the young widow in silent grief would leave this underground room forever, she gently placed the flowers on the lid as a small, poignant gesture of farewell to her husband.

They were found just as she had left them. After being undisturbed for over 3,000 years, they were very dry but they still retained a light shade of their original colors.

And we keep on wondering. Two small coffins containing stillborn daughters laid to rest were found close by the coffin of King Tut. We will probably never know why, when her time later came, this queen was not buried with the husband she loved and her two little children, gone on before her.

Where her burial took place, only God knows.

KING TUT'S WRINKLED but well preserved embalmed body was again restored to its resting place by Carter and his associates. However, the golden coffin and the other burial treasures were taken away and are seen by thousands of people every year in exhibit cases in a museum at Cairo in Egypt.

WELL OVER A MILLION DAYS have now come and gone since King Tut and those people who lived in his time have closed their eyes in death.

As is also a belief of Christianity, these Egyptians believed that death is not the end of everything. The grave is not an eternal prison for the soul. Death is not an eternal nothingness and an extinction of our existence. The Egyptians looked forward to a future resurrection of the dead—a day they are still awaiting.

If Resurrection Day will be as the ancient Egyptians were led to believe it is to be, the Egyptian pharaohs will be mightily disappointed when they awake from their sleep of death. The treasures they thought they would need for happiness in the life after this will all be gone!

ALONG WITH THEIR MISGUIDED AND WARPED ideas about life after death, the ancient Egyptians also had pagan ideas about the deity of their pharaohs. Their idea of a supreme being was unfortunately nothing higher than their pharaohs.

The love of honor and glory was the ruling principle of the political governments of ancient Egypt. Much of the labor and material wealth of Egypt was spent in building tombs for their kings and for the treasures that were buried with them. In our days we believe their energies and their gross national wealth could surely have been put to a better use than honoring a mortal man with such extravagance.

At the time of the pharaohs, Egypt was one of the richest and most powerful nations of the civilized world. The Egyptian people thought their pharaoh was a god who had temporarily come to earth to be the supreme ruler of this mighty and wealthy land. An inscription has been found honoring a deceased pharaoh as "the great and living god, my father, my reminder of eternity."

The pharaohs were dictators with absolute power. Any of their wishes and sudden whims were to be instantly carried out. The word of these kings, with their supposed ultimate authority, was to be unbroken law, and whatever they commanded was not to be questioned by anyone. As a god, the pharaoh would be too infallible to make a mistake, or if he did, he would not need to apologize or express a regret to anyone.

The level of their dignity was far above that of any other human being, just because they happened to be born in the line that destined them to become the pharaoh. Their "divine right to be king" elevated them to a status of being a god over other people. Everyone else was of a rank considered much lower than the pharaoh.

The belief of the government of our country that everyone is born equal was unknown in ancient Egypt.

The pharaoh who enslaved the Israelites and ordered the drowning of the baby boys, and the pharaoh we read about in the time of Moses and the ten plagues in Egypt were of the next, or 19th dynasty of Egyptian kings.

It is not exactly certain, but it is believed there were only a few, perhaps four or five, pharaohs between King Tut and the pharaoh of the Exodus of the Israelites of Egypt.

HERE IT MAY BE INTERESTING to mention a little of what is known of when the short reign of King Tutankhamen took place. Along with his father-in-law, Pharaoh Akhenaton, whom he succeeded, King Tut belonged to the 18th dynasty of kings in Egyptian history.

The nine or ten years of King Tut's rule were evidently a tumultuous time in Egypt. His father-in-law, Akhenaton, is often ignored and is not even mentioned in some of the lists of Egyptian kings because of his so-called "heretical" religion.

The young boy king may have been merely a puppet ruler after his father-in-law's death. The real rulers of Egypt at this time may have been the pagan temple priests and a powerful army general. Except for an elderly uncle who may have taken over the Egyptian throne for a very short time after King Tut's death, this army general called Horenheb became the next pharaoh in Egypt.

It is not hard to understand why Moses trembled and hesitated to go when God told him to ask the Egyptian pharaoh to let the Israelite slaves leave the land of Egypt.

We can also well understand why the proud pharaoh of the Exodus, who was convinced he himself was a god, would thunder his refusal to Moses when he was asked to permit the Israelites to go and worship their God in the wilderness outside of Egypt.

"Who is the Lord that I should obey His voice to let Israel go?" he shouted.

He would show these lowly slaves who their god was! He demanded the tasks of his already overworked slaves to be made even more unmerciful (Exodus, Chapter 5). It was a miracle from God that the pharaoh didn't order his guards to strike Moses and Aaron dead for being inept enough to even ask for a three-day freedom for the slaves.

We can also see why the brothers of Joseph cringed in great fear when roughly spoken to by the prime minister of the great Egyptian pharaoh.

Determining the Dates of Events of Long Ago

MANY STUDENTS OF EGYPTIAN HISTORY DATE THE DEATH of King Tut at about 1,338 years before the birth of Jesus Christ. Determining this date has met with many difficulties and is not altogether certain. Points of discussion come up over the years, and the exact date may be moved from several hundred years before or after this generally accepted date.

Historical authorities always find it very difficult to determine the exact dates of events of long ago. It stands to reason that there will never be a gravesite uncovered which will give the date marked, as say, 1,338 B.C. Our dating of years on the calendar and in history books as before (B.C.) or after the birth of Christ (A.D.) was not even used until several hundred years after Jesus Christ had walked on earth.

Exact dates were not important in the early days of written history. When a king started his reign, this date was used as a marker and starting point for events of his time.

Also, because so many of the population could not read or write, the records left to posterity are very scant. To give a little example closer to home, if people older than you are now had not kept records, or would have forgotten it in their minds, you would have no way whatsoever of ever finding out the exact day you were born.

The ancient people did not have accurate calendars as we have today, so the attempts to arrive at exact dates in ancient Egyptian history, and even of some Biblical events, are something very much like educated guesswork. Because of the difficulties in dating ancient happenings, and probably because God knows that it is not really important for us to know the exact dates anyway, it is impossible to always come up with any accurate side-by-side biblical and Egyptian chronology. In fact, the first known instance of a side-by-side chronology of the Bible and a secular nation is in Jeremiah 25:1.

The number of years of the rule of many Egyptian kings widely overlaps, making the dates much more recent than at first supposed. Trying to confirm dates in Egyptian history is very complicated, even by comparing the various Egyptian king lists that have been discovered. The clues found, usually the number of years a pharaoh ruled, or the age of the king when his oldest son was born, are often very vague and even contradictory.

Some of the genealogy and chronology in our Bibles is at some places difficult to interpret. The result is that the exact years, worked out by church historians and placed in our Bible references, sometimes also differ widely. We do not know why the genealogy of the first chapter of Matthew and the accounts of the kings of Judea in the Old Testament books of II Kings and the list in II Chronicles have some names missing and are not exactly alike; but it may be to tell us that the message of the Bible is of more importance than its system of arriving at exact dates. It is not that the Bible has errors when we discover that the words "beget" and "father of" may at some places mean "an ancestor or predecessor of" or "grandfather or great-grandfather of."

Even spellings of the various genealogies are sometimes different because some translators spelled the names out as they thought they were pronounced in the original language.

DESPITE THESE DIFFICULTIES, MANY HISTORIANS believe this King Tut may have lived somewhat after the time of Joseph in the Bible during the 400-year sojourn of the rapidly multiplying population of the Israelites in Egypt.

When King Tut was laid to rest, most of known history had not yet happened. Because writing with an alphabet was invented only several centuries before King Tut's time, virtually all the events we read about in world history took place while the body of Tutankhamen, in stillness and silence, lay waiting for Resurrection Day.

If the timing of most of these historians were at all accurate, the Israelites would not cross the Red Sea out of Egypt until several generations after the burial of King Tut. The children of Israel, who at that time were still on friendly terms with the Egyptian pharaoh, could at one time have been subjects of this youthful Egyptian pharaoh.

Except for the book of Genesis in the Bible, there were not many existing and true stories of world history written down before the time of King Tut's death. All the drama and history we read about in the Bible from Exodus to the book of Revelation had not even begun to unfold when the funeral was held for King Tut.

WE HAVE TO WONDER HOW such a system of idol and pharaoh worship and their perverted ideas of the life in the hereafter ever got started. How could the families who settled in the land of Egypt after scattering from the unfinished Tower of Babel ever forget the worship of their Creator?

How did the original faith of the first families of earth get corrupted so soon after our first parents became expelled from the innocence in the Garden of Eden? How did these corrupt beliefs of the afterlife and the bowing down to made-up gods, along with considering human rulers as gods, ever become a national religious system? How did the very perverted and distorted religious practices of giving excessive devotion to a mere human being instead of to God, and believing that material things would be needed for a happy afterlife ever come about?

God's Plan for Our Family Life After the Garden of Eden

THERE ARE TWO REASONS ONLY THAT COULD CAUSE the original true beliefs and spiritual values of the first humans to become apostatized.

The first is if some of the elders in a generation fail to pass their Godly beliefs to the next generation.

The second is if some of the younger generation reject and fail to accept and live up to the truths they were taught by believing parents. In passing from one generation to the next, this torch of truth can become extinguished. The fragile tie between people of different ages and groups, call it family bonding if you will, is only one generation away from becoming extinct.

If its importance is no longer considered important, it will become lost.

AFTER ADAM AND EVE DISOBEYED GOD IN THE Garden of Eden, they had to get out. As in Heaven, no evil was permitted there. But we must remember that not once did God curse the person of Adam and Eve. He still loved them too much for that. In the Bible account it appears as if they hesitated when God pointed the way out of the garden to them, because in the next verse we are told God had to drive them out.

What came next after God had driven them out of their place of innocence has a much deeper and wider meaning than an angry God telling them what kind of a curse they would live under for the rest of their lives. Here the first prophecy appears of Christ smashing the head of evil so that its poisonous fangs can cause no more death.

What is often believed was a curse of birthing pain upon Eve and a curse of sweating labor on Adam is not that at all. God would not curse anything as honorable as birth or honest labor.

God's purpose of family is wrapped in these verses. These verses could be called God's ordination charge upon our first parents. They are the very condensed instructions for functional and Godly family living, telling how to direct physical, mental, and emotional energies in the family.

The original Hebrew of these verses suggests that the pain and sorrow both Adam and Eve would go through could be nothing more or less than a travail of prayer. The "bringing forth of children" in the Hebrew includes not only bringing children into the world, but it also includes the rearing and training of children, so in a wider sense God is telling Adam and Eve that they will need to go through a travail of prayer for the nurture of their families.

God's plan of Adam and Eve living together as a holy and sacred marriage family unit, in a partnership with God, was God's wise way for preserving and passing on the Godly faith from one generation to the next. They did something right, as many of their descendants did build altars unto the Lord.

God wants this relationship to be like a triangle. The closer that Adam and Eve were to God, the closer in heart they would be to each other. Because these first gleams in many marriages do become cold and icy, this fondness for each other would be much more than affectionately gazing at the stars in each other's eyes. It would be standing by each other's side while they are both looking toward the future. It would be having a healthy respect for each other's likes and dislikes.

Being together as a closely bonded family would be so different in the flawed world outside of the Garden than it had been in the perfect conditions in the inside. One of the first things God did was to place Adam in the role of leadership, which in Christianity means to forget self while working for others. This is not always easy. God then spared Eve from making the most responsible decisions for the family. Surely this did not mean that either Adam or Eve would be asked to be as a mindless puppet or dominated slave of the other. The best thing a father can do for his children is to love their mother. Christ loved His Bride, the Church, so much He gave His life for it. If Adam were to Eve as Christ was to the Church, the desire, longing, and love of Eve would be for her husband. She would make such a home for Adam that he would not be happy elsewhere.

There is no guarantee that the children in a family will always appreciate and follow the teachings and examples of their parents. However, what the father is, does influence the children's first thinking about God, and what the mother is, does influence their thinking about the church to which they are taken with their parents.

In a still wider sense, it takes all the believers in a church family to realize the seriousness of parenting and bringing children into the world, and to support and influence the church of tomorrow by their prayers. There is an old African proverb that says it takes more than two parents to raise children—it takes the entire village. As children grow up, they need help so that they do not look in the wrong places for inner peace and happiness. Young people growing up in a church community need the feeling of God's security, so that a Godly faith can be kept up until God's clock will have wound down and time shall be no more.

PHOTO BY
LOUISE BEACHY

Young papyrus plants at Joe-Pye Ponds.

PHOTO BY
TOM REED

Mature papyrus plants at Longwood Gardens.

The plants shown above are papyrus plants (Latin botanical name—*Cyperus papyrus*), which used to grow abundantly in the marshes along the Nile River. The rush and flag plants mentioned in Job 8:11 are believed to be papyrus plants.

These plants growing along the riverbanks were like the reeds mentioned in the Bible (Isaiah 42:3 and Matthew 12:20). When windstorms came up they would be blown flat. When the wind was over, all except those broken or kinked would stand tall again.

The papyrus plants proved to be one of the most useful plants in ancient Egypt. It was used in a variety of ways. Clothes, rugs, and sails were made of dried papyrus reeds. The roots were edible and were a regular item of the Egyptian diet, and even a kind of chewing gum was made from the plant. The dried reeds were used as fuel.

The stems of the plants were used in making sandals, baskets, and rope. Rope made from the papyrus plant has been found in tombs dating back to the times of the pyramids. Small boats were made from reeds bundled together.

The basket with the little bed into which the baby Moses had been lovingly placed would have been made with papyrus stems woven tightly together and pitched. The thick growth of flags along the river, which partly hid the basket and kept it from floating downstream, would have been papyrus reeds.

But one of the most remarkable inventions in the ancient world was when someone discovered that a strong and flexible paper could be made from the plants. Papyrus paper began to replace the bulky scratched-upon and baked clay tablets.

Wall paintings have been found in Egypt showing the cutting and gathering of papyrus stems. They were peeled and sliced into thin layers and laid on a cloth with the pieces slightly overlapping lengthwise. Another layer was then laid crosswise on top. When they were slightly moistened and pounded together with a wooden mallet, the natural glue in the stems held the pieces together. When they dried, the paper was smoothed by rubbing a smooth shell over it.

Papyrus paper was very durable and flexible. Some rolls estimated to be over 3,000 years old have been unrolled and rolled up again without damage.

It is believed that the Egyptians may have been one of the first civilizations to invent the art of writing. This art fed the growth of civilization by preserving ideas for future generations. Due to the permanence of writing, the following generations did not have to go through the tedious process of learning everything all over again.

It is also believed that in Egypt more people could read and write than in almost any other ancient country known.

What is one of the most remarkable events in history, and shows God's guidance at work, was that the Israelite nation grew up in that country. The life of the baby Moses was then saved from a certain death to grow up to learn reading and writing in the court of the Egyptian pharaoh. He then went on to write down God's remarkable and condensed journal of mankind's first 2½ thousand years on earth.

Chapter 7

All a Part of God's Master Plan

WE ALL KNOW WELL THE STORY of the small baby boy found by an Egyptian princess along the banks of the crocodile-infested waters of the Nile River.

At this time, the Israelites were slaves in Egypt, and by order of the pharaoh all baby boys were to be thrown into the river and drowned. Pharaoh didn't want these little Hebrew boys to grow up, because they might then take part in a civil war and overthrow his power, for he was the most powerful man in what was probably the most powerful nation on earth.

And his edict had teeth. In Josephus' history of the Hebrews, he mentions that if a family did not obey in killing their newborn sons, the whole family was to be executed.

Unlike so many of the downright absurd myths born in the fertile imaginations of the pagan idol-worshiping people in ancient times, the stories in our Holy Bible are so true to life and believable. The accounts are all true happenings, and some of those happenings were miraculous!

In the aftermath of the totally unexpected events of our lives, we can rest assured that the gentle guiding hand of our God of love will somehow, at some time, bring out an ultimate good from all that does happen. God's goodness will always be more powerful than any evil that any amount of perverted men or the legions of the devil will ever be able to do.

IT WOULD BE INTERESTING TO KNOW more about this unusual princess who rescued Moses from the river. She was born to a family of privileged royalty, but her name is not found in the Bible record. We do not know if she was a teenager or was mature and past the prime of her life. We are not told of her status in life. Was she single, married, or widowed? She may have been single, and was becoming aware that the years were creeping up on her. Perhaps she was married, but she and her husband were childless and she was losing all hope that the mother love God had placed in her heart would ever be put to a worthy purpose. Would the tiny fingers of a child of her very own ever clasp tightly onto one of her fingers? Or she may have experienced the waves of grief only really understood by mothers who have had the chilling hand of death ruthlessly grasp a child they have loved out of their arms. Since we don't know, the little that was written about her will have to be sufficient.

God places a mother love, one aspect of His divine love, into the hearts of all normal girls and women. We do not know what she experienced in her past, but we know she had enough mother love in her heart that she wanted someone she could call her own to cuddle in her arms—arms that still felt so empty to her. Whatever the circumstances, she may have wondered if her deep longing to teach someone especially dear to her while sitting upon her now empty lap would ever become fulfilled and be a part of God's Master Plan.

Human nature, with its feelings and emotions, is basically the same the world over. It has not essentially changed and is still as human as God created it to be in the beginning.

It is not always easy to truly believe that God will shower the blessings upon us that He knows are for our very best when we say, "Thy will be done." None of us is qualified to tell God what type of blessings should be sent into our lives. God's blessings are always better than our selfish desires. If we gratefully accept both the bitter and the sweet that God sends into our lives, it will all help us to fulfill God's ultimate purpose for our life here on earth.

THIS DAUGHTER OF THE EGYPTIAN PHARAOH saw something very unusual floating among the high papyrus reeds at the river's edge. She asked that this little watertight basket be brought to her and opened up.

Here was a small baby, probably still sleeping, in the soft little bed inside the well-made basket. Only a short time before, this helpless babe had been lovingly wrapped in the blankets that could still have been damp from the falling tears of his natural birth mother.

Everyone born on this earth had someone responsible for him or her. This mother had taken her God-given responsibility seriously. Had she heard that the pharaoh's soldiers were checking out the rumors of a hidden Hebrew baby boy in her neighborhood and decided on a daring plan? She made the little reed basket, lovingly placed her precious child in it, and hid it at the river's edge, a good place to keep her baby from being discovered.

Would he sleep on and stay quiet until all danger was past? None of us ever had hours as anxious as hers were that morning. Just a little whimper when someone was going by would betray the presence of the hidden baby.

But suddenly the little basket is discovered! Now the hinges of history are hanging on what happens next. The baby's young sister, possibly still surviving only because she happened to be born as a girl, innocently runs up to the scene. And God is watching over it all.

With the little Hebrew baby boy in her arms, it would have been easy for this princess to do what her cruel pharaoh father had charged all his people to do (Exodus 1:22). Then the river would have been the watery grave for another one of the sons of the Israelites.

But can you believe this? At this exact time the little Hebrew babe woke up and started a pitiful wail. The motherly instincts of this princess took over. The tears of the innocent child cradled in her arms touched the tender mother heart in the breast of this Egyptian princess.

If she ever felt any ill feelings toward the Israelite slaves, foreign intruders in her country, it evaporated right there. Her mother love must have been a reflection of God's love and goodwill—the exact opposite of her father's hostility and intolerance. Only by having had good feelings toward the Israelite race could she have unreservedly adopted one of their children as her very own.

At some time the pharaoh father of the princess who found the baby was finally influenced to change his edict about the drowning of the boy babies. Keeping this up would have resulted in a whole generation of no men or boys among the Israelites. Perhaps this daughter of the pharaoh had a hand in getting her father's cruel ruling changed.

This Egyptian princess, not the natural parents, named the baby. She gave him the name of Moses. In Egyptian, this name means something like "has been born to me," and has the Hebrew meaning of "I drew him out (of the river)."

There must have been no doubt in her mind that she actually became a mother the day she first held this little Moses in her arms.

We can also be sure that this experience made other changes in the life of this princess. Whatever ambitions and goals she cherished before would from this day onward be changed and be more noble. Being a mother would surely make her a little less selfish. A godly mother love includes the virtue of seeking to be a good example.

ALL THIS MAY BE A LITTLE UNREAL and unbelievable to a weary and sleepy mother getting up in the middle of the night to attend the needs of a crying child, but here God used the crying of a little child to alter the course of history. This cry of a baby who was unaware he was under a death sentence was a little part of the fulfillment of God's Master Plan.

God was at work that day, answering a lot of prayers. The precious child of the Israelite slave couple was saved, the Egyptian princess had a child she could call her own, and God made a beginning in the chain of events that would answer the prayers for deliverance and freedom for the Israelite slaves.

And the prayers of the baby's natural birth father, Amram, were answered. Josephus writes that Amram was a man of prayer for his descendants and for his country.

To be sure, that fulfillment would be eighty years in the future. The baby would grow and would need forty years of learning experience in Egypt and another forty years of wilderness living before he would even be ready to act on the work for which he was placed on earth.

All the careful scheming and plotting of men could never have guided the happenings that resulted from the mother love God placed in the heart of the daughter of an arrogant Egyptian pharaoh—a very unlikely place. This was a part of a plan God had in mind to unfold in due time—no one on earth could have prevented any of it from happening.

בראשית ברא אלהים את השמים ואת הארץ: והארץ
היתה תהו ובהו וחשך על־פני תהום ורוח אלהים
מרחפת על־פני המים: ויאמר אלהים יהי אור ויהי
אור: וירא אלהים את־האור כי־טוב ויבדל אלהים בין
האור ובין החשך: ויקרא אלהים | לאור יום ולחשך
קרא לילה ויהי־ערב ויהי־בקר יום אחד:

Because translating was considered tampering with God's Holy Word and because the Jewish people thought it was exclusively for them, the Scriptures would remain in this form for well over 1,000 years.

The marks such as you are seeing above are the primary source of our religious faith, as well as that of millions upon millions of people since the world began. These lines are the first entry in God's journal. They tell us of His first day of Creation.

They are the first five verses of our Old Testament in the Hebrew language—the original language of Moses and the prophets. Except that most of the early Hebrew writing did not have spaces between the words, the ink marks Moses made over 3,400 years ago on a parchment scroll made of papyrus paper would have looked very much like the lines you see above.

Moses would dip his pen made of a papyrus reed into a bottle of ink, probably made of a soot and water mixture, every time he wrote a few words. He would use fine sand or a blotter to dry the ink every few lines.

Of course, the original parchment manuscript of this writing, which has a significance that is impossible to measure, has long since returned to dust, but the writings beginning with these lines, our Holy Bible, have been copied and recopied and translated and retranslated and put to print more than any other writing on earth.

The first two-and-a-half lines of the writing seen above explain even more than religious faith, inasmuch as the scientists of our day tell us that everything can be explained by time, space, matter, force, and motion. Here it takes only the first two verses of the Bible to do this.

A literal translation of the first two verses of God's journal from the Hebrew would read something like: In the beginning (time) created God the heavens (space) and the earth (matter). And the earth being without form and empty, and darkness was on the face of the deep. And the Spirit of God (force) moved gently (motion) on the face of the waters.

Go through the above very slowly and see if you can find the marks representing the Hebrew word for God, which occurs six times in the first five verses in the Bible. Remember that the Hebrew lines, unlike the German or English, read from the right to the left and the sentence structure is different at many places from the order which we are used to.

Chapter 8

Called to Write God's Journal

PROBABLY MOST OF YOU READERS out there are familiar with what became of little Moses, the Hebrew boy brought up in the court of a great Egyptian pharaoh. This story does not need to be repeated here.

God was thinking ahead. He would need a God-fearing family lineage somewhere here on earth. From this family, the world Savior would be born, a descendant of Adam and Eve. The Christ Child could not be born into an Egyptian, Greek, or Roman family who had never heard of the true God. Many generations earlier, the religions of these nations became sidetracked and given over to idolatry.

Because Abraham moved away from a pagan land and into a land God led him, God picked his descendants to be His chosen people. These imperfect people fell into sin as easily as other people, but they were still called "the chosen people," because God had to choose a people in which the lineage would lead to a God-fearing family to which Christ would be born.

LET US REVIEW THE TIME IN HISTORY when the Israelites were slaves in Egypt. God's charge to Moses to free these slaves came to Moses when he saw the bush that was burning but did not become consumed.

God used Moses' background of his years from age forty to eighty years old to teach him the ways of herding sheep and to learn the ways of living in the wilderness.

In his earlier background, from boyhood to the age of forty, he probably learned more than any other Hebrew before him had the chance to learn. Without a doubt, he studied reading and writing in school in Egypt. His adopted mother, a royal princess, would have seen to that. The Egyptian way of picture writing, invented not much more than several hundred years earlier, was much different from the Hebrew way of writing, which depended on an alphabet based on sounds. Because the writings of Moses were not in the Egyptian language, it is even possible that he had a part in developing the alphabet for the language of his people. No other Israelite of that time is known to have had the schooling required for such a work.

Because Jesus Himself talked about the writings of Moses at several different times, the theory of some modern-day Bible critics that the first five books of our Bible were written by a scribe much later —in the time of Daniel or Ezra—simply does not hold out. However, before this period, very few Hebrews were educated to read and write. The Bible itself says very little about scribes before this time, therefore the possibility exists that these books were very seldom recopied until the time of Daniel or Ezra.

Even if someone else later added the last chapter of the fifth book, and such verses as Numbers 12:3, they can still be called the five books written by Moses.

THESE FIVE BOOKS WRITTEN BY MOSES are the first of the sixty-six books bound together in the book we call the Holy Bible. Some forty different writers inspired by the Spirit of God wrote this book. Some were kings, while some were not much more than slaves. Some had a high degree of education; others had practically none.

These writers were like mail workers bringing letters from God to our mailboxes. If we don't take time to read the Bible, it is something like never taking the time to bring in our mail.

The five books Moses wrote and the book of Job are among the oldest writings in the world that are known to still have lots of copies in existence.

The Bible is a collection of books that can be read in about eighty hours. This is just long enough to contain God's Word in one book, but the treasures buried in these pages will never all be dug up. All other books will sooner or later be "milked dry" when we learn what the book is trying to teach us. Not so the Bible. Its wisdom will never be exhausted. No matter how often you read it through, you find new insights by reading it again.

The Bible teaches us the mysteries of life and death. Some of the books such as Revelation raise more questions than they have answers. The Bible contains the account of the Creation and the prophecies of the end of the world—the birth and death of the earth we are living on. It tells of the new Heaven and the new earth in the hereafter.

The timeless and unchanging teachings of the Bible tell us of the eternal right and wrong. We will never see anything titled, "A New List of the Most Recent Amendments to the Bible." We throw away yesterday's newspapers. Some books, relevant a hundred years ago, are now nothing but antiques. The Bible is forever.

The Bible, the handbook and textbook of Christianity, begins with the majestic words, "In the beginning God created the heaven and the earth," and ends with, "The grace of our Lord Jesus Christ be with you all. Amen." No other beginning or ending could be more fitting. Everything between the front and back covers of the Bible is held together by these words.

THE UNIVERSE AND EVERYTHING IN AND BEYOND IT did not just happen. It is too complex. All of Creation is planned, orderly, and working together in such a harmony that to even think that it all fell together by chance is a denial of the myriad proofs we see. A true scientist believes only what he or she can see. We can see so many miracles in God's Creation that we believe in miracles.

Everything built has to have an architect and builder who is greater and has more intelligence than what is being created or brought forth. The Bible tells us of this all-powerful and all-knowing God who had every detail of Creation planned in His mind.

Except for the forming of our first parents with His own hands and the life He imparted into them with His eternal breath, everything else came forth by His spoken Word.

Creation was a one-time happening, so something like this cannot be reconstructed in a laboratory. We are only asked to believe it. We say we cannot understand God, but can something you make understand you?

There were no reporters there when Creation happened, so the only eyewitness there was our own Triune God. If we had never heard of the Bible, we would probably wonder why this Creator seems to stay silent and not somewhere plainly put on record what happened at Creation, when no one else was around to see it being done. And in the same way as when children ask questions, the answers to those who wonder will need to be at the level of their understanding.

Well, that is exactly what our kind and helpful God did. He didn't want the humans He created guessing, so He inspired the Bible writers to dip their brush or quill pens into ink and write His story in a condensed form from the Creation week to the book of His divine Revelation on rolls of parchment.

This is like God's journal. God is a Spirit, so much of what we humans are asked to do to promote His glory has to be done in a tangible, or in an actual seen and felt way, using our God-given abilities and strengths—each of us in our own way.

These writings were God's journal of what He wanted us humans to know about Creation, the Great Flood, and the lineage of and events leading to Jesus Christ.

Here the question could come up about these Bible writers or secretaries writing down God's Word as was given to them by the Spirit of God. We could question why God's journal would not start out like a letter with, "In the beginning I created the heaven and the earth," and end with, "My grace be with you all. Your Friend, God." This can be better understood when we realize that what Moses and the prophets said and wrote had to be changed from what God in Spirit form had said into a form that humans could read. Not until Jesus was on earth could anyone speak with God's authority such as His actual words recorded by the Gospel writers that begin with, "For I came down from Heaven" (John 6:38); "I am the door" (John10:7); and "I am the resurrection and the life" (John 11:25). The words the Gospel writers heard came directly from God's human form who had come down to our level of humanity.

The truthful and understandable reporting of the four Gospel writings, by those who were there when it all happened, tell us of the Savior who lived and died, but more importantly that He died and lives!

If God, as He had planned to sometime be here on earth in His human form, would be here for one lifetime— exactly as all of us also are—then His resurrection from the dead would demonstrate on ahead the resurrection from the dead for all of us.

In the Bible, we read of God's plan for the Second Coming of Christ, which will happen on the Judgment and Resurrection Day, the youngest day in history. These prophecies are like the earlier prophecies about His birth into the world. Because some of these prophecies seemed to contradict each other, most of them could not be fully understood until after they happened.

In the same way, we will not fully know the eternity following our lives here on earth until we are there to experience it.

The people of long ago had untrue myths and legends made up by idol worshipers. They could either believe or reject these myths. Most people believed them.

The choice for us in our days is deciding to either accept the constantly changing guesses made about Creation by unbelievers, or to reject them and believe God's unchanging Bible as the absolute truth. Because the Bible has the voice of authority, this choice should be easy. The Bible is so much better and more inspiring than trying to figure out Creation without our Creator.

PROBABLY ONE OF THE GREATEST PROOFS that can lead us to trust Bible history as truth is that none of the other books throughout history, claiming to be of divine origin, has seen predictions of the happenings of the future so perfectly fulfilled as those in the Bible.

Even today there are at least 26 other books in the world existing as the handbook of a religion, such as the Koran of the Muslims and the writings of Gautama Buddha for the Buddhists, but every one of them lack prophecies which have become fulfilled.

People are always fascinated with trying to know what will happen in the future, but let any of us try to prophesy what will happen tomorrow, or even just later in this day! We can make guesses, but usually something else happens.

Because we can't see into the future, only God's inspiration can do prophesying. Bible prophecy has hundreds of instances of 100% accuracy in prophecy fulfilled, not only shortly after, but also many hundreds of years after the prophecy was made. Inspired prophecy is the correct foretelling of the plans our eternal God has designed for the future. It is history written of or spoken about ahead of time.

We need only consider the past record of some very unlikely Bible prophecies fulfilled to the letter to make us feel sure the Bible is completely trustworthy. God is totally faithful in keeping His promises. In Him, there is a complete absence of deceit. God cannot be wrong in prophecy because, as in Creation, if He declares something to be, so it will be. All the promises and predictions in the Bible are sure.

Not one single prophecy in the Bible has been proven false. Although some are yet to unfold, such as the prophecy of the end of the world, some of the greatest wonders contained in the Bible are the prophecies that became precisely fulfilled at a later time.

The book of Isaiah alone makes over a hundred prophecies about the Savior. Not a single one missed being fulfilled in the New Testament, even though they were written over 700 years before Christ was born.

When the prophecies of the sufferings of the Messiah were made in the Old Testament, everyone still thought He would arrive with a might that would make God's chosen people in Judea the rulers of the whole earth. No one ever imagined He would be rejected and put to a torturous death such as the prophet Isaiah predicted. At the time of Isaiah's prophecies, the cruel execution of political criminals by crucifixion had not even been invented yet. The only explanation for this accuracy is that the divine God who knew the future inspired the writings of these prophecies.

One of the objections that has been made by unbelievers in removing the Bible from our tax-supported schools has been: "I don't want my children to be reading the obscene and criminal details of such stories as King David's dark sins or such as Rebekah telling her son Jacob to lie and deceive his blind father, Isaac."

But this lobbying in our days is also really the fulfilling of a Bible prophecy made about 3,000 years ago. God's prophet Nathan told David that "because of this deed thou hast given great occasion to the enemies of the Lord to blaspheme" (2 Samuel 12).

NOW WE COME TO AN IRONY IN THE BIBLE. These are the passages that have bothered many Bible readers over the years. If the Bible is meant to teach the best standards of behavior and to contain the instructions for a renewal in our spiritual lives, why do we then read so much of otherwise God-fearing people who made miserable failures and a blundering mess of their lives? Shouldn't the Bible contain only stories of heroes of the faith?

Except for Jesus, the Bible is not about perfect people. Its pages are stained with the stories of the sins of some of the forebears of the Christ Child, such as Lot's wife, who was the grandmother of Moab, a forebear of Ruth; of Judah, a seeker of harlots and the seller of his own brother into slavery; King David, the adulterer and murderer of Uriah; and some of the kings of Judah who easily out-sinned many of the pagan kings of other nations in those times.

It was not because of their worthiness that they were destined and counted in the line leading to Jesus Christ. Because so many of these people who knew better lived in lives of sin, they were more responsible than those people of other nations, who like children in their innocence, did not know better. The sins of Jacob, Moses, David, and Peter, along with many others are written in the Bible for all to see. No one is spared.

Especially in the Old Testament we read of wars and murders. We read of adultery, deceit, and fraud practiced even by God's chosen people. With very few exceptions, the Bible in its down-to-earth way tells the life stories of many people without ever trying to hide their human failures and willful sins. These people would have blushed with shame and embarrassment to know God would permit their deeds and sordid details of their actions to be included in His Holy Word, and read by people hundreds of years later.

In these stories, the Bible also tells us the heartaches we do not want that often follow a sinful action. So often sin leaves a harvest of bitter tears and remorse in its wake, even though God has forgiven us.

Through much of his life, David had tragedies in his family that may well have had their roots in his poor example as the head of a family and the king of a nation. Jacob deceived his blind father, and years later his sons deceived him in a way that nearly put him into an early grave (Genesis 37:35) .

The Bible uses these stories to tell us of God's undeserved grace and mercy to the repentant. David's heartfelt repentance gave us Psalm 51, that great masterpiece coming from a true sorrow for past sins. It was followed by God giving David a clean heart and a renewal of the spirit within him, along with complete forgiveness. Jacob is blessed before he leaves the world. The prodigal, or wasteful son, is welcomed home as a part of the family and is not given the punishment he deserves for wasting the hard-earned money his father freely gave to him. Peter repeatedly tells his Master that he still loves Him and is commissioned to the duties of an apostle. Like the Creation, when God created something out of nothing, the Holy Spirit creates a new and clean heart for the repentant sinner.

We could say the Bible reads very much like a daily newspaper. Both the good and the bad that happen are recorded. The reason that the Bible has so many stories of people doing sinful things is because the Bible tells it exactly as it was. No one was saint enough to be spared.

On the Judgment Day, it will also be like that for all of us. Nothing will be hidden. Our lives will be exposed as they really were lived. On that day it will become known if we reached for God's lifeline of saving grace or if we rejected it because we still enjoyed wallowing in sin.

That is why Jesus so severely condemned the Pharisees. By trying to cover up their faults and sins, and putting up a false front of trying to appear better than they really were, they were simply following the way of our fallen human nature. We all know better than to try to excuse our willful sins by claiming "our human weaknesses" or by shifting the blame on others. We all know well enough that our sinful examples have often led others astray. Our actions were often the cause of sin in others.

There is a better way. God can heal. Can you imagine how bloody and black and blue we would look if all the injuries and scratches on our bodies had never healed since we were small?

"Confess your faults one to another, and pray one for another, that ye may be healed" (James 5:16).

God's grace erases the harm sin can do in a human life, and He gives us strength to bear the reaping in this life—the reaping He sees we need because of what we sowed. But His grace also enables us, in the future, to stay away from the sin that so easily has beset us in the past. This grace is much better than any human cleverness of trying to keep sin hidden. Surely God's healing after being cleansed is better than trying to keep up a good reputation by using only a false front.

IT IS A MIRACLE THAT THE BIBLE still exists. If it were not divine, it would have been destroyed and lost forever many centuries ago. The terrible persecutions directed against the Christians over the centuries also came with a full fury against their sacred writings. Many thousands of Christians perished during these persecutions, which were then followed by the scrolls they owned being piled together and burned.

One of the best proofs that the Bible is divinely inspired is the fact that the lives of millions upon millions of people have been forever changed for the better by studying the Bible. Nothing else gives us as much peace and comfort in this evil world we are living in as the promises of the Bible.

We do not need to fear the future. We need not be afraid to fully trust an unknown future into the hands of the God we know. A believer does not need extra proof outside of the Bible. What the Bible says is enough; we believe it.

Dwight Moody used to say that the Bible will keep you from sin, or sin will keep you from the Bible. When you open your Bible again, ask its Author to open your heart. The better you know Him, the more interesting His Bible will become to you. However, meditating on the Bible is a little like carrying water in a pail with a leaking bottom. We are human and cannot hold it all, but the bucket gets a little cleaner every time it is used.

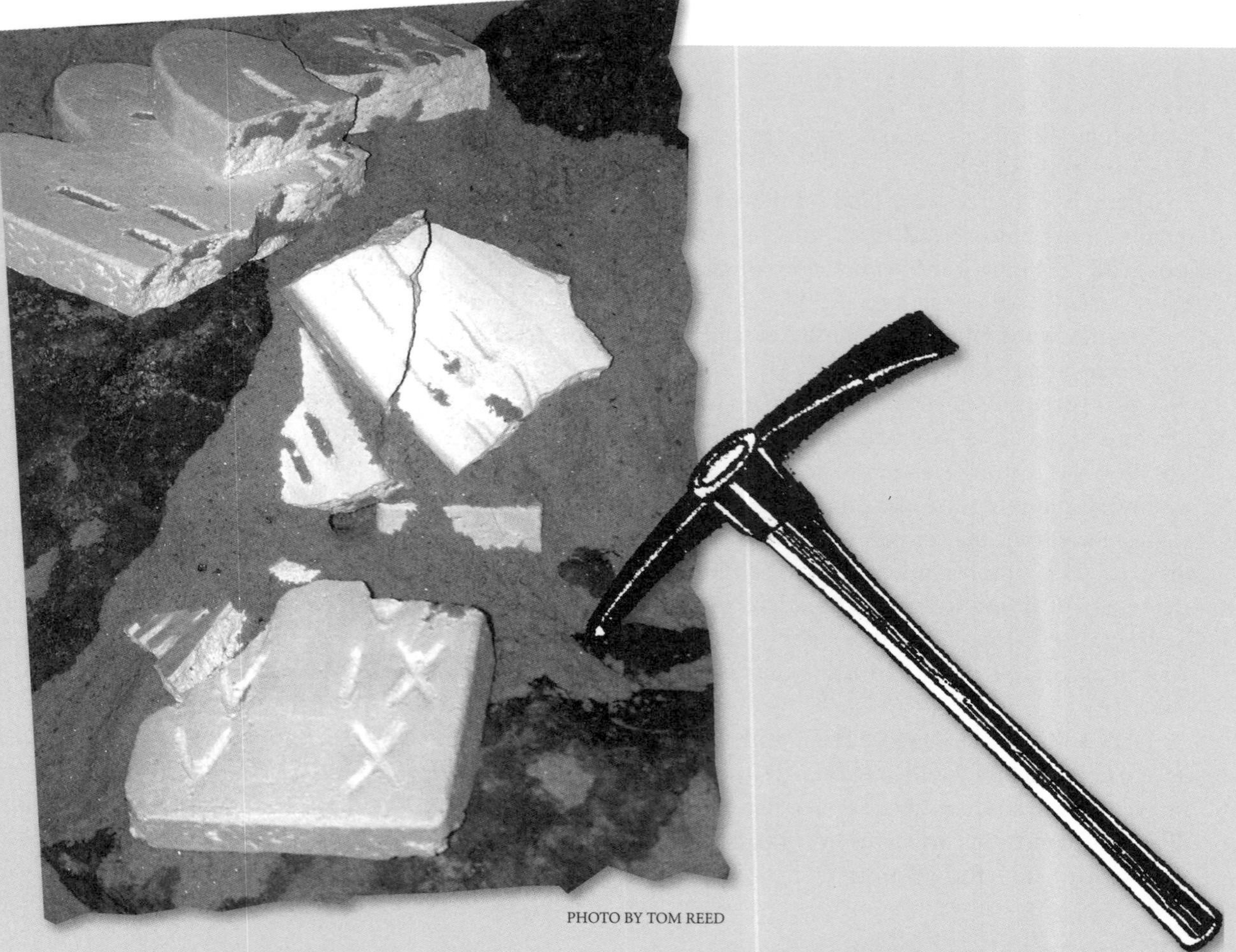

PHOTO BY TOM REED

The first two flat slabs of stone carved out by God Himself and inscribed with the Ten Commandments (Exodus 20) with His own fingers didn't last long (Exodus 24:12; 31:18; and Deuteronomy 9:10). They were shattered to pieces when Moses, angered at seeing the breaking of the commandments by the people he had taught them to only a short time before, threw them at his feet (Exodus 32:15-19).

God asked Moses to hew out a second set, which He again inscribed on both sides with His fingers. These two stone tables were then placed in the Ark of the Covenant, a wooden chest placed in the Holy of Holies room in the tabernacle (Exodus 34:1-14; Deuteronomy 10:1-5). This was something like a portable temple, taken along on their wanderings—a place where God dwelt among His people.

This ark, containing the two stones inscribed with the Ten Commandments was later placed in the Holy of Holies room built by King Solomon on Mount Moriah. This was the same place where Abraham went to offer his son Isaac, probably about a thousand years earlier.

This temple was destroyed by fire when the Babylonians captured Jerusalem. The ark, with the two inscribed stones, was lost, and to this day has never been proved to be found again.

The Holy of Holies in the rebuilt temple standing at the time of Jesus was empty and did not contain the ark with the tables of stone.

If the pick of some archaeologist would sometime uncover the shattered pieces of the first set of stone tablets in the earthquake debris or under the drifting sands at Mt. Sinai, or the second set, blackened but unburned somewhere in the ashes under the temple mount, the discovery would be the greatest ever in the history of archaeology. Newspapers all over the world would headline the confirmation of the Bible stories.

However, would we be better Christians if we would actually be able to see the original Ten Commandments in a museum case? Would these commandments of God be kept better in our lives if we were to have the opportunity to trace our fingers on the very same inscriptions carved out by God's fingers pressing over them?

Hardly. We already have a multitude of proofs that the Bible is trustworthy, and we do not need to look for something spectacular such as seeing the original Ten Commandments stones.

We are able to see what God's fingers have worked when we see the life He has created in even the least of His creatures, such as the lice made of dust material that the Egyptian occult sorcerers could not duplicate (Exodus 8:16-19). On a clear night we can actually see the works of God's fingers above us (Psalm 8:3).

What we need is the commandments written not with ink, but with the Spirit of the living God; not in tables of stone, but in the tables of our human hearts.
(2 Corinthians 3:3).

Chapter 9

What Mean Ye by This Service?

IF YOU WERE A LITTLE BOY OR GIRL IN ONE OF THE HEBREW FAMILIES just before they forever left the land of Egypt and its harsh slavery, you would have sensed something very different and strange was taking place.

Let us now imagine what the first Hebrew Passover celebration in Egypt was like, seen through the eyes of the small children in the Israelite families.

Your mother does not put leaven or yeast in the bread dough she gets ready this morning for your family bread supply for next week. At all other times, she adds a small bit of leaven to the bread dough, and it mysteriously makes a gradual change throughout the mix so that the bread is nice and fluffy after it is baked.

Your father and oldest brother come home from the long day at the brickyards this evening for the last time ever. They are as tired out as usual, and you see fresh marks of a cruel whip that has lashed their shoulders again. They are always driven just a little harder than their weary bodies can take.

Even more unusual this evening, you see your father take up in his arms one of your cute pet lambs he had put into a pen four days earlier. After taking up a knife to put the innocent lamb to death, he does another strange thing.

He catches the blood of the dying lamb in a basin and takes a handful of twigs from a hyssop bush growing in your courtyard. Dipping the twigs in the basin of blood, he splashes a red stain on the two side jambs and on the overhead lintel above the entrance door of your home.

You eat the bread your mother baked earlier. The bread, made without leaven, tastes like a dry cracker or wafer, yet contains every bit of the nutrients in regular bread. While you and your family eat the roasted lamb, your mother and father ask all the family around the table to make sure their sandals are tied on their feet and tell you all to put on your cloaks. It is as if all of you are going on a long journey. Your father takes into his hands the staff he always uses while tending his small flock of sheep. He does not carry a sword or spear because he does not have any.

A summons comes for your family to make a quick departure. You are ready. You are leaving Egypt.

AT THE STROKE OF MIDNIGHT ON THAT NIGHT, a frenzied cry from the house of the nearest Egyptian neighbor was heard: "Our oldest son is dead!" As is still the way in our days when a death occurs in a house, the first thing the Egyptian neighbors did was to rouse their neighbors for help.

But every one of the Egyptian families also had a death in the house! Even the oldest son of the pharaoh, the heir to the Egyptian throne, was dead. A great cry of lament, such as never before or after has been heard, loudly echoed throughout all the land of Egypt.

Who all would be dead, or what would be destroyed next if an eleventh plague were sent over the land of Egypt?

Pharaoh was taking no more chances. He sent word to the Israelites to get out of Egypt as fast as they could. "And bless me also!" he added. We are not sure what he meant by these words that may have been the equivalent of "Pray for me also!" Was he finally admitting that a God existed who was greater than he was, even though he was the majestic pharaoh who fancied he felt the awe everyone had while being in his presence?

Or, perhaps, as his actions shortly afterwards would imply, he couldn't admit defeat and was still ordering them to show high honor and respect by blessing him before they left. The wording in the Hebrew suggests that he was still demanding the credit and thanks from his lowly Israelite slaves for his permission to let them leave the country.

The oldest son in every Israelite family was still alive and well. He was able to thank God for his Godly father and mother whose obedience to the Passover ordinances had saved his life.

Every one of the Israelite families went out of their Egyptian homes for the last time that night. Their portals into freedom were stained with the life-blood of the innocent lambs that earlier in the week had been romping around with their other little lamb playmates.

This Exodus of the Israelites from Egypt is the only instance known in history that such a large number of slaves were freed without a bloody civil war being fought. God wanted to show His chosen people that His miraculous power was able to do the impossible of bringing around the hard-hearted pharaoh's permission to leave. The Israelites were freed without being disobedient and rebellious or violent to their masters.

Satan's plan would have been for the Israelites to stay in Egypt until they would have adopted the idolatry of the country they lived in, but God had other plans. What He had prophesied to Abraham over 500 years earlier had come to pass (Genesis 15:13 and 14).

This length of time the Israelities were in Egypt, can be understood that they were as slaves for 400 of the 430 years from Joseph to the Exodus (Exodus 12:40 and Acts 7:6).

We are not sure exactly into what time frame this Exodus of the Israelites fits into the chronology of early Egyptian history. However, it is possible that some of the older folks leaving Egypt remembered hearing their parents tell of seeing the funeral barges loaded with the coffin and the treasures of King Tutankhamen going by on the Nile River on their way to the burying grounds of the pharaohs.

But then, many historians of ancient Egypt in our time will not even admit that the Bible story of the Exodus is a true fact. They tell us that nothing has yet been found in any of the ancient Egyptian inscriptions of such an event.

This is understandable. Not one of the ancient Egyptian historians mentions an Egyptian defeat in a battle, even though we learn from the ancient histories of other lands that the Egyptians often were defeated. The stories of the ten plagues and the departure of their Israelite slaves would not be included in the annals of their history.

In the Bible, there are references in at least ninety different places of God bringing the children of Israel out of Egypt, so the doubts about this being a true story can be laid to rest.

Then also, the institution of the Passover, celebrating the end of the tears shed because of the cruel and bitter slavery in Egypt, is proof enough. This is the earliest religious ritual known that is still held in our time. This would hardly be possible if it was based only on myth and legend.

THIS PASSOVER CELEBRATION, with its unleavened bread and roasted lamb, was to be held by the Hebrews every year as a memorial "throughout your generations... forever" (Exodus 12:14, 17, 24, and 42).

A family ritual developed around this yearly practice. Children would ask their parents, "What mean ye by this service?" (Exodus 12:26). God knows that at no other time is the door as open into a child's heart as when they start asking questions. At no other time in their lives do parents have such an opportunity, by the way they answer these questions, to form and mold the pliable clay in these young hearts.

Probably every one of the Hebrews would remember when at some time or other in their childhood they were asked to open the little yearly Passover service around the family table with this question.

With the curtains drawn to keep out the world, the youngest family member able to talk would be prompted to ask, "Why is this night different from all the other nights in the year?"

The oldest person there, usually the father, but sometimes an older uncle or a grandparent also living in the house, would then answer the innocent child's question by telling them the story that all Hebrew children never got tired of hearing. All small children love to have stories of times long ago related or read to them and Hebrew children were no exception.

The young people always looked forward to these yearly fascinating and interesting stories of God's power guiding the history of their people. These stories were the introduction to their thinking about God for the rest of their lives. When God instituted the Passover celebration, He knew how necessary it is that young people learn of their Godly heritage from their elders. These stories, told in the Hebrew language, kept the memories of the background of their people alive in their minds as long as they lived.

This yearly Passover around the family table, followed by all helping to sing several hymns, could have been the greatest single source of keeping the Hebrews together as a separate and distinct people, even though they would be scattered among other nations throughout the world, on up to our times.

The close and strong family bonds that can be created around the kitchen table are still God's best way to pass on the faith.

We can imagine the true history of God's chosen people would be the same narrative, but probably told in a little different way each time by the different parents and grandparents. All the history was too long to tell every time, but if new and interesting lessons in living could be included every time it was retold, the story would not be as monotonous and tiring to the little children.

We can imagine some fathers would begin their history story with the Great Flood. Here in the valley of the two rivers, the Tigris and the Euphrates, downstream from the mountains of Ararat where Noah's ark came to rest, Noah and his descendants lived until they were scattered at what was later called Babylon.

The families who migrated to the Nile River valley began to worship the kings for which they built the pyramids for their tombs. The Great Pyramid may have been built while Noah was still living, 350 years after the Flood, but we have no way of knowing if he ever got to see it or not.

Some fathers may have begun their narrative with Abraham, who left his sun- and moon-worshiping cousins and uncles in the valley of the two rivers and settled in a land where he could worship his God away from the influence of a pagan religion. He settled in the land of Canaan, where there were still pockets of belief in the true God, such as practiced by Melchizedek, a priest and king of the city of Salem (Genesis 14:18-20). To these Israelite fathers, the story of Abraham would be considered the beginning of the history of God's chosen people. By beginning the history at this point, the story would be shorter and end before the hour became late and the youngest children too sleepy to listen in.

Other fathers may have started this history story with the Creation, where God created the heavens and the earth two thousand years earlier than the time of Abraham.

These fathers would also include the story of the first salvation, when only one family of devout believers was saved from the Flood and lived to begin repopulating the earth. During the first years the Passover was kept, it would not have been clear yet if Noah, or Joseph, or Moses was the promised Savior of the human race. The prophecies of the Messiah were still very vague and obscure at that time.

Nevertheless, the point to be brought out in the little history story around the family Passover meal was to refresh their memories of that night when the Death Angel was close, but passed harmlessly over them because of the sign of blood at their doorposts.

Of course, exactly what the lifeblood of an innocent, slain lamb signified, and had to do with being thankful for the release from a cruel slavery, would also not be clear at that time.

But the yearly Passover did bring to remembrance God's promise to send a Redeemer into the world through the Jewish race. They knew this Savior would be a descendant of Adam and Eve, who had lost their one-time opportunity to live forever in the Garden of Eden.

AT THE TIME OF THE FIRST PASSOVER, this story that the Hebrew parents and grandparents kept alive by telling to the younger family members, had not yet been written in a book. But God's long-range plan was to have all this put down in writing around the time that the Israelites became a nation of their own.

Moses did this at some time during the last forty years of his 120-year life (Exodus 17:14, 34:27 and Deuteronomy, Chapter 31). His five written scrolls of the history of the world and the laws God gave to the Israelites were placed in the tabernacle, which was something like a portable temple in a tent that was taken along as they wandered from one place to another.

Because nobody but a few of the tabernacle priests could read and write, these writings were brought out once every seven years and read to the people. This would renew the story in their minds, especially to the fathers, whose duties included passing on these stories and teaching their children around the family table, especially at Passover time (Deuteronomy 31:9-13).

Jesus Christ would change the Jewish Passover into the Christian Communion service some twelve or fourteen hundred years later. These lessons of life brought out at the Passover table are remembered by uncounted numbers of Christian Church families who still regularly gather around the Communion table in our times.

At almost any given time in our days this service is being held somewhere in the world by those who know that Jesus Christ is the Savior promised to the world.

This promise was given something like six thousand years ago by the Creator to the first created man and woman in the world. All human beings who have lived on earth since then, were they believers or not, can be traced to these two people. This makes God's offer to be led out of the slavery of sin open to everyone.

THIS STORY OF BEGINNINGS that most of the fathers may have used to open up the history of the Jewish people would start at the Creation week. It would include God placing the first man and wife in "the garden of delight," which has been translated from the Hebrew language as "the Garden of Eden." They were given a home in this little Heaven on earth and were told "to dress it and to keep it."

Some of the families around the Passover tables, hearing the histories begin with the Creation week, would be reminded of the overwhelming beauties and the almost infinite varieties of life that came into existence by God's spoken Word. After the three united forms of our God (the Almighty, His human form in Jesus Christ, and His Spirit which can be anywhere) said, "Let us make man in our image, after our likeness"—soul, body, and spirit—(Genesis 1:26 and 2:7), God made our first parents—the masterpieces of His Creation. They were the only part of God's Creation that was a result of the works of His hands and not spoken into existence.

Every human being since then, with our body, soul, and spirit, is a very small, separate, unique, exclusive, and individual copy of the Trinity.

What Adam and Eve did is the story of the golden opportunity given to all of us to stay away from sin as we slowly grow out of our youthful innocence and start to know better. All of us can recognize ourselves in the story of the fall of Adam and Eve. All of us can say that this is also our story. We need a Redeemer who will forgive us and give us a new resolve and strength to do better from now on.

MAN SPOILED THE "very good" that God had pronounced when looking over His finished Creation. The big investment and trust that God had made in creating the human race or bringing to life (place your name in the space provided here ____________) with the ability to choose good or bad, was now ruined. Because the first man and woman sinned, they were no longer holy like their Creator.

After they had made the choice of doing their own will instead of doing God's will, they were no longer fit to keep on living. They were the only ones of God's perfect Creation that were not in harmony with God's plans. They were a blot that should have, in justice and a righteous anger, been struck dead.

How would a God having both perfect justice and a perfect love and mercy now handle this problem? Would He now change His mind about sin and look the other way, or would there still be a way that would not violate His perfect justice and righteousness nor His perfect mercy and grace?

God is first of all a God of perfect love. The penalty of sin must be paid, but He would not abandon the human race. The Spirit of God made plans to come to earth clothed in His human form and die for the sins of repentant humanity.

All throughout the Old Testament, God gave mankind the promise of a Savior coming into the world who would pay the price of dying so that humans who wished they had not sinned would be forgiven and eternal death would not have to follow.

In this way, He would not set His perfect holiness nor His perfect justice aside. "For God so loved the world, that He gave His only begotten Son, that whosoever believeth in Him should not perish, but have everlasting life" (John 3:16).

IN THE LAST THIRTEEN CHAPTERS OF THE FIRST BOOK of Moses is the story of Joseph. This would probably be included at almost every Passover table. There would be no better story to teach forgiveness and chaste living to the young Hebrew teenagers.

This is a story of how to have victory over a temptation that would leave regret and remorse in its wake. When Joseph was tempted to sin, he overcame it in a way that still works in our day. He was much stronger than the woman who was daily trying to lead him astray, but he knew he was not stronger than the temptation of awakened passion if he stayed where he was.

"How can I do this great wickedness and sin against God?" he said as he fled from the scene of temptation. Because of this one victory over temptation, he was falsely accused and put into prison, but God was able to use all his trials as stepping-stones from slavery to becoming a co-ruler with the Egyptian pharaoh. Even the pagan pharaoh could see that the Spirit of God lived within Joseph (Genesis 41:38).

In this position, he had every opportunity to revenge his false accuser, but we do not hear of her again. Joseph could also have evened the score on his brothers who hated him and had sold him into slavery. But like being led out of temptation, the presence of God's Spirit within him enabled him to do what would have been humanly impossible to do.

He forgave them for the evil they had done to him. He considered it all as a part of a good plan God had to keep his brothers and their children from starving in the famine caused by a seven-year drought throughout Egypt and the surrounding lands (Genesis 50:14-21).

Joseph's trials were all a part of keeping the lineage leading to Jesus Christ alive until the fullness of time had come. His victory over temptation had far-reaching effects. It indirectly defeated the satanic efforts to prevent a Savior being born some two thousand years later.

And we can be sure Joseph didn't become envious and spiteful when he heard his father prophesy that the Savior would come through the lineage of his brother Judah, whose life had made a complete change of direction, rather than from him.

Joseph had already been richly blessed. He would only be too glad to see God's blessings overflow into the lives of his brothers. God has enough blessings for everyone.

AT THIS PASSOVER FAMILY TIME, it would be a good opportunity for the parents to recite the Ten Commandments and teach their children why they were so imporatnt. Here was the golden opportunity to explain the reason God had given His laws to His chosen people.

These were the ten brief and simple rules of living which every child could easily understand. They were the wise rules a holy and loving God has given to set mankind apart from living like wild beasts.

Of the Ten Commandments, the first four commandments could be condensed in the sentence "to love the Lord thy God," while the last six give us instructions on loving our neighbor as ourselves.

The Ten Commandments are the laws of respect to God and to our fellow humans going through this world with us. Many courtrooms of our land have a plaque on display inscribed with the Ten Commandments, the basis of law and order. They are not like a set of rules made by fallible humans that sooner or later get to be replaced by other lists because they become obsolete and out of date.

This list of commandments from God is revered, not only by Christians, but also by the Muslim and Jewish people. It has been said there are now about two million laws on the books to enforce the Ten Commandments.

The finger of the Almighty God Himself wrote the ten laws on two stone tablets. It has been suggested that the reason for two copies was that every contract has one copy for each party. Both copies were kept in the Ark of the Covenant, in the tabernacle, which was the place God dwelled among His people.

These Ten Commandments were not given to Adam and Eve because they were not ready for them yet. They would not have known what honoring their parents, or what stealing or committing adultery meant.

Moses taught these laws to the people and was angered when he found out they had broken them only shortly after he had taught them. Throwing the stone tablets at his feet, he shattered them to pieces only to have God require him to carve out another set.

It remains to be seen if in the future someone will unearth and discover the fragments of these stones carved by God Himself. These broken pieces could well be still lying somewhere under the drifting sands at the foot of the mountains where Moses received the Ten Commandments. However, to this day, Bible scholars cannot exactly agree which of the mountains in the Sinai Peninsula was the one beside which the Israelites had set up their camp.

What is known is that the keeping of these laws would insure having a society of peace and trust. However, men and women with their morally corrupt natures have been busy ever since breaking and shattering these commandments. Mankind needs a Redeemer to save him from the consequences of his own wrongdoing.

ERWIN BOHN

WYCLIFFE HISTORICAL GEOGRAPHY

One of the triumphs of modern archaeology has been learning to read the inscriptions found in the temples and tombs, and on the brick tablets and papyrus parchments of the civilizations of long ago.

What made these unknown languages even harder to figure out was that no one knew if the lines read toward the right, as in our German and English, or from right to left, such as in the Old Hebrew. Languages are different because some letterings were later discovered to read both ways, like a farmer plowing first to the right and then to the left. Some were to be read up and down.

What cracked the code for the vast number of inscriptions found, which told about the early life of the ancient Egyptians, was the chance finding of the Rosetta Stone in 1799. (Story in chapter 5).

Solving the puzzle of the wedge-shaped letters of the complicated cuneiform writing of the ancient Chaldeans and Sumerians was made possible by deciphering the inscriptions shown in the photo above, which told of the bold deeds of Darius the Great.

Carved in large lettering looking like "bird tracks made all over wet sand," the inscription appeared in three languages, two having later become extinct. King Darius wanted future generations of many different lands to know of his greatness. The relief sculpture shows Darius stepping on one of his enemies while he is passing judgment on nine other captured kings standing before him. They are tied together, with their hands tied behind their backs.

Cut into the stone face over 330 feet up on a steep rocky cliff, this 60 feet wide by 22 feet high panel includes ten columns with 1,200 lines of text in the languages of the ancient people of Babylonia, Assyria, and Persia, living in the Tigris and Euphrates valleys in the land of Mesopotamia.

Unlocking the keys to these mysterious inscriptions also found in several hundreds of thousands of clay tablets, was not easy. In the middle 1800s a young man, Sir Henry Rawlinson, was to devote several decades of his life to this task.

Even with the aid of a telescope, he found the transcribing of the two unknown languages into his notebook almost impossible. He then recorded much of it by standing on the top rung of a ladder he had set up on the 18" ledge that remained at the bottom of the panel at several places. After nearly slipping to his death, he hired a daring native boy, who had no fear of the heights over the deep chasm below, to balance himself on a rope swing. Working together, they made impressions of the carvings on wet paper pulp which could be studied when they had dried.

The photo of the coin on the lower right has the likeness of the curly head of Alexander the Great on it. Instead of hoarding it in hidden vaults, Alexander got much of the vast amounts of gold and silver booty from his battles minted into coins stamped with portraits of himself.

This money created a prosperity throughout his empire. It eliminated the necessity of weighing out a certain amount of gold or silver to pay a debt or to buy and sell.

But more importantly to the vain Alexander, his likeness became known to the millions of people who lived under his rule after his victories.

The mountain with Darius the Great's inscription from a distance. The carvings are near to the top in the right center.

An Alexander the Great Coin.

Chapter 10

God Will Put the Kingdoms of the World in the Dust

THE NATION OF ISRAEL BEGAN the night the Hebrews left Egypt. The slavery God permitted to be placed upon them probably kept them from accepting the pagan Egyptian religion of their harsh overseers. Their slavery may have been a blessing in disguise. At least for a time, it brought them closer to God and helped to keep them together as a united people.

At Egypt's border, God opened up a miraculous dry path through the Red Sea. This path, with walls of water on both sides, did not stay open for the Egyptian armies in hot pursuit to bring them back to slavery.

They were now free. Safe on the other side of the Red Sea, these several million people broke out in a song of thanks to God for their deliverance. Except for the hymn the pharaoh Akhenaton composed, this song is probably the oldest known written song in existence. They were to begin a new life, and centuries would pass as they worshiped and learned about their God.

SOME 500 YEARS AFTER THEY LEFT EGYPT, the Israelites wanted an anointed and crowned king to rule over their country. They wanted a king with the power to tell them exactly what to do, instead of a judge, who would determine if a certain act had been right or wrong.

The nations around them had kings instead of judges. They wanted their country to be governed like the nations who were idol worshipers. So, for roughly the next 500 years, until the kingdom of Judea fell to King Nebuchadnezzar of Babylon, the Israelites, chosen by God to carry on the lineage leading to Jesus Christ, experienced times of turmoil. They went through periods of apostasy when God was forgotten, followed by short periods of revival when they cried to God in Heaven for help.

One of the best-known revivals during this 500-year time period was during the reign of King Josiah. When the temple was being repaired, the books of the law, which would have been the writings of Moses, were found. God had told them to get these writings out once every seven years and read them to the people, but this had been neglected. These God-inspired books had been completely forgotten.

The yearly Passover celebration, which was God's way of the younger generation learning from the older, was also neglected.

Beginning with the king, who rent his clothes and wept when he realized how sinful the nation had become, a sincere repentance was made throughout the land. A Passover such as had not been held for hundreds of years was kept. The people again turned to God, and God's judgment upon the land was postponed (2 Kings, Chapters 22 and 23, and 2 Chronicles, Chapters 34 and 35).

But even this revival did not last, and as punishment, the land of Judea was devastated and many thousands of their young people were herded to Babylon as slaves.

The people in slavery in Babylonia turned to God again. Then God punished the Babylonians for their evil doings by permitting the Persians to take over their powerful empire. The Persians set the Hebrews free and permitted them to return to their homeland after being slaves in a foreign land for seventy years. In his proclamation permitting the Jews to return, the Persian king, Darius the Great, also released the temple valuables which had been in storage for seventy years. These were carried back to Jerusalem.

NOT ALL THE JEWS RETURNED to the country of their forefathers. Evidently some had established well paying businesses and become prosperous, so they chose to stay on under the Persian rule. Some of them, such as Mordecai (Esther 2:5) and Nehemiah (Nehemiah 1:1), had worked up to respected positions of importance in the Persian government. However, a vast throng of the Jews did return to Judea (Ezra, Chapter 2). They were encouraged to rebuild the temple, destroyed seventy years earlier. Everyone felt their first work was to have a house of worship and resume the morning and evening burnt offerings to the Lord on the altar that they had set up "upon his bases" (Ezra 3:3). This was evidently on the flat rock on the temple mount.

The work on the temple was started, but was soon to be frustrated by the enemies of the Jews, especially by the people of neighboring Samaria (Ezra, Chapter 4).

The interest in the project waned; the work slowed down and later stopped altogether. The temple remained unfinished for some time.

When the work was at a standstill for several years, God sent the prophets Haggai and Zechariah to encourage the Jews to take up the work again and finish it. In those days, as also in our times, the worship of God should come first. Through the urging of these prophets and the guiding hand of God, the work was taken up again.

King Darius the Great helped the returning exiles to rebuild their temple. He made sure that the golden and silver vessels stolen years before by the Babylonians were restored again to the Jews in Jerusalem, and he forbade anyone from again hindering the work (Ezra, Chapter 6). He also gave a large sum from the royal treasury to help the Jews build their temple.

When the rebuilding of the temple was completed, although the dedication of the new temple was a joyous event, many of the older people, who still remembered seeing the magnificence of the first temple, wept when the services started in the new temple. The temple built by their young people had so much less splendor than the first one built by Solomon (Ezra 3:12 and Haggai 2:3).

THERE WERE THREE KINGS NAMED DARIUS: King Darius the Mede, King Darius the Great, and King Darius the Third. We remember King Darius the Mede, who ruled before the other two kings, as the ruler who spent a restless night after Daniel was thrown into the den of lions (Daniel 6:18). The second Darius to rule was King Darius the Great, ruler of Persia (550?–486 B.C.). He is mentioned in the prophetic books of Haggai and Zechariah, and also in the book of Ezra. King Darius the Third was killed when fleeing before the approaching armies of Alexander the Great about two centuries after the time of Darius the Second.

This second King Darius—King Darius the Great—who was so helpful to the Israelites when they were working to rebuild their temple, had another side to his character that is recorded in different history annals.

The famous inscription at Behistun, telling of the exploits of Darius the Great, is one example. This 2,400-year-old carving can still be seen in our day along the road that was once a main trading route between Babylon and the city now called Hamadan. Carved 345 feet above the ground into the high stone face of a mountain overlooking a large plain, it includes a large portrait of King Darius the Great. The inscription proudly boasts that eight of his ancestors were kings and tells how he had taken over the throne after slaying a rival king "who had lied to the people." He proudly tells how he built the "city of Persepolis "secure and beautiful." Today the city is only a set of ruins.

It also records his victories in nineteen different battles and tells how he put down nine rebellions against him, and how he is now the king of twenty-three different lands. Like a large, modern billboard, it was best seen at a spring where traveling caravans always stopped on their way.

Darius wanted his victories and his might to be remembered by posterity. Worried that someone might later go up and deface the inscriptions on the limestone cliff, he evidently had the workmen cut away the access and destroy the stone ledge they had worked on. When they were finished, the accessibility to the carvings was shut off for over 23 centuries. Only in modern times, using steeplejack methods, were the carvings again seen close-up. At a great risk to their lives, several history scholars scaled the heights and made wet-paper impressions of the carvings so that they could be studied.

These inscriptions were carved in large letters in three different languages. Like the breaking of a code, this helped the history scholars of the 1800s to unravel the reading of many other inscriptions found in Persia and Babylonia. Till then, many carved inscriptions found were in an extinct language that could not be read.

King Darius the Great, whose far-flung empire extended eastward as far as India, also opened a canal between the Nile River and the Red Sea that greatly shortened a water route for the boats and shipping barges. This canal was the ancient forerunner of the modern-day Suez Canal that was opened up in 1868.

King Darius the Great is also credited with introducing the religion of the teacher Zoroaster as the state religion of Persia. These beliefs seemed to be somewhat of a mix of the one-God religion of the Jews with the pagan worship of the sun and the stars. This was the reason Abraham had left this same country 1,500 years earlier.

The well-known Magi, or the so-called wise men of the East, were probably priests of this religion of Zoroaster. What they knew of the prophecy of a newborn King of the Jews probably came from the Jews living in that land some 500 years earlier.

Even though it is doubtful that any scrolls of the books of Moses existed among the Jewish slaves, these Godly people, living in the land, could well have influenced the religious system of their neighbors. Even the king respected their beliefs.

King Darius the Great, Ruler of Persia, which is now the modern-day country of Iran, so often in today's news, also wrote an epitaph to be put on his own tomb. It is carved in three languages and is still readable in our days.

A part of it reads, "By the grace of my God, I am of such a sort that I am a friend to right and I am not a friend to wrong." He wanted his virtues to be remembered after he was gone.

DARIUS THE GREAT HAD A SON NAMED Ahasuerus, who ruled the empire of Persia after him. Also known to historians as Xerxes, he is believed to be the king who chose Esther as his queen after his first wife greatly displeased him by not immediately honoring a sudden idle whim of his.

This story is written in the Bible in the book of Esther, Chapter 2, and in the history of the Jews, written by Josephus, in chapter eleven.

The way it all came about that this Jewish orphan girl was given in marriage to a divorced pagan king would be repugnant to us in our days, but such morals were common among the heathen people of that time and among the Jews who had elected to stay in Persia.

This Esther was the queen who, at great peril to her own life, saved the Jewish race from a total extinction when all the Jews were under Persian rule. The hate for them came from a proud self-seeking man named Haman, who evidently was a survivor of the descendants of the Amalekites. These Amalekites were a people descended from Esau (Genesis 36:12), who all throughout the time from Moses to King David were continually doing their best to waylay and harass the children of Israel whenever they were at their weakest. They were a little like the enemy of the Christian Church who, always starting at their weak point, tries his best in every way he knows to weaken or destroy it.

Haman had hatched an evil plot to kill every Jew throughout all the provinces of Persia. When Esther was told of this, she risked her life to go before her husband the king, who might well have had her killed for daring to present herself to him without his permission. She used her abilities to save her people by exposing the hateful and corrupt Haman. If Haman had gotten his way, every one of the prophecies of a Savior of mankind being born into a Jewish family would have been made useless.

The courage of Queen Esther and the story of how the Jewish people were saved from massacre and extinction by God, who worked by giving King Ahasuerus a sleepless night, are still remembered every year by the Jewish people at the annual celebration of Purim.

SEVERAL DECADES AFTER THE TEMPLE had been rebuilt, the city of Jerusalem still did not have a wall around it. The enemies of the Jews living around Jerusalem could go in and out as they pleased. Then also, merchants who came in and sold their wares to the Jewish people profaned the Sabbath day. Clearly the city needed a wall with gates that could be closed at night and on the Sabbath.

This work was started by a man of prayer named Nehemiah, once a servant in the palace of the Persian king. His encouragement persuaded the ex-slaves to say, "Let us rise up and build" (Nehemiah, Chapter 2).

Guided by Nehemiah's genius, the people kept on working even though the foreigners living outside the city did their best to stop the work. They scoffed, mocked, and made threats on Nehemiah's life, but the work went on. They tried to put a fear into him so that he would shut himself up in the temple to save his life, but he did not let their concealed plots keep him from the work on the wall.

He knew there was a time to go to the temple to worship, but he also knew there was a time to rise up from his kneeling and go on with the work that needed to be done.

The people kept on working with a will. Some worked with one hand and held a weapon in the other. They took turns. Some worked on the walls while others kept watch.

Nehemiah had each family assigned to build a part of the wall, and because each family did their work well, the wall did not have any places for the enemies to get through. Even the women and the girls helped.

In only 52 days the wall was finished because "the people had a mind to work." The short time required to build the wall, even though a few of the people thought they were too "noble" to help (Nehemiah 3:5), was probably because they had no stone quarrying to do. They used the stones from the rubble of the previous wall.

Surely, there are lessons of every kind to be learned about how to build up a church community from reading the Bible accounts of the rebuilding of the walls and the temple at Jerusalem.

DURING THE SO-CALLED "400 SILENT YEARS" between the Old and New Testaments, the history of the land of Judea was anything but still and silent. Although the Jewish people were still hoping that a descendant of King David of 600 years earlier would reign on a Jewish throne in Jerusalem, no new prophecies came to the Jews from God during this time.

In this time when there were no prophecies, many people thought God had forgotten about the people who were worshiping Him.

One notable person living during this time who is not mentioned in the Bible, but who certainly had an influence on Bible history was Alexander the Great (356-323 B.C.). The Greek philosopher Aristotle (384-322 B.C.) tutored Alexander in his youth. The "Great Encyclopedia of Useful Knowledge" that this famous teacher compiled was for a long time considered the last word as far as knowledge was concerned.

Aristotle had been a student of Plato, a disciple of the well-known teacher, Socrates. To the educated Greeks and Romans, the study of philosophy had become almost like a religion in itself.

Alexander's father, Philip of Macedonia, mentioned in the apocryphal book of the First Maccabees, had defeated the Greek armies. Leading the battle had been his son, the young and fearless Alexander, then only eighteen years old. Two years later, Philip was assassinated at the wedding of one of his daughters. The curly-haired Alexander, scarcely out of his teens at the age of twenty, became the king.

In six years' time he had gained mastery of countries as far east as India. In the terror and destruction of his wars, it is estimated that 1,200,000 people lost their lives. By the time he was thirty-three years old, Alexander and his armies had conquered more of the known world than anyone before or since has done. In his 14,000-mile route of marching his armies, he won every battle he fought. He founded seventy cities and established an empire that covered around one million square miles. He pushed his conquests on so fast and with so much fury that his enemies did not have the courage to make a stand.

He fought right alongside his men and acted as if he did not know what fear was. At one time he kept on going after an arrow had been shot through one of his lungs. He ordered his men to shave their faces and heads so that an enemy intending to behead them could not grab them by their hair or beard.

It is said that he never asked any of his men to do something he himself wouldn't do. He knew the first names of hundreds of his men. Because he always quickly put down any revolts against him, few dared to oppose him. He had no pity for anyone who defied him. After the city of Troy was destroyed, he hung two thousand people on crosses. The shrieking and moaning and groaning of the people crucified in this massacre was enough to nip any other rebellion against him in the bud.

His conquests included overthrowing and becoming the absolute master of the Persian Empire, often mentioned in the Bible while Darius the Second was king. Because it was believed that Darius the Third had instigated the assassination of Philip, the father of Alexander, Darius was frightened and fled away from his armies when Alexander stormed through Persia. Of course, Alexander had an easy victory over an army without a commander.

After the great slaughter when he overthrew the Persian Empire, Alexander and his armies swept through the lands of the Bible, now called the "Holy Lands."

As he was making his way toward Jerusalem, the high priest asked the terrified people to join him in sacrifice and prayer to God. The high priest in his priestly robes was led to open the city gates and went forward to greet Alexander.

Such a welcome took Alexander by complete surprise. Entering the city without resistance, he ordered no blood to be shed. Shown the book of the prophet Daniel where the prophecy in Chapter 8, Verses 20 to 22, could be taken to mean that one of the Greeks should destroy the empire of the Persians, he was flattered to think that Jewish prophecy had mentioned him and that he himself was the mighty king written about in Daniel 8:2-4.

He did not put the city to spoil, as his soldiers were anxious to do, but permitted the Jews to keep their religious practices and their temple.

For the history of this happening, which occurred during the "400 silent years" period, we are indebted to the writings of the Jewish historian, Josephus, who was later to write an eyewitness account of the destruction of Jerusalem and its temple in A.D. 70.

Alexander's successes seemed to convince him of his own divinity and that he was something like a god who should proclaim himself a divine pharaoh. After becoming the master of the vast lands he had conquered, he lusted for still more fame, honor, and homage. He bribed the pagan priests to proclaim him as a god, the son of another god. Fearing his wrath, the priests did so.

Alexander's mother started circulating the story that she was a virgin when Alexander was born. Acting on this false tale, he required his subjects to worship him as a god. What a contrast several centuries later when the real Virgin Mary never proclaimed even what she knew was the truth, but kept all these things and pondered them in her heart (Luke 2:19 and 51).

Because of Alexander's swift conquests, even to this day, he is considered the greatest military leader in history. At one of his victories, his tactic was to start out toward the enemy camp every evening as though he were attacking, and then retreat. He did this every day for many days until the enemy no longer reacted. He then attacked and won. However, it is said he never used the same tactic twice.

His reputation as a world leader has captured the imaginations of many strong generals ever since, and much misery and killing has been the result. Napoleon

Bonaparte, the political dictator of France in the 1800s had a goal to become as powerful a hero as Alexander. He spent much time studying Alexander's military tactics while his French armies were sweeping across Europe over 2,000 years after Alexander was dead and gone.

However, Alexander had ambitions that were never to be satisfied. At the height of his power, when he was the absolute ruler of all the people and lands that he had conquered, he is said to have wept because he knew of no other lands left for him to conquer.

It is ironic that he never became strong enough to conquer his addiction to strong drink. At the young age of 33, the same age Jesus Christ was when He was crucified about 350 years later, Alexander the Great breathed his last from the effects of a drinking spree from which he did not recover.

Only shortly before his death, Alexander had conquered the great city of Babylon and was making it the capital for the government of his far-flung empire. A great prize, the city extended for about 60 miles out around, encompassing the strong inner wall of about eleven miles in circumference.

Alexander died while celebrating his victories at the palace built by King Nebuchadnezzar, who is often mentioned in the Bible. His body was carried to Alexandria, Egypt, a great city he had founded, nearly a thousand miles away from the place of his death. There he was interred in a grandiose mausoleum.

Soon after Alexander died, his small son, born shortly after Alexander's death, and his widow, Roxana, a Persian princess, were put to death to keep any of his heirs from later sitting on his throne.

For the next fifteen years his bodyguards and generals fought for power, each one trying to prove they were the strongest. The huge and far-flung empire of Alexander was broken up into a number of smaller kingdoms. Alexander's dream of one permanent government over the entire world became an utter failure.

The dramatic might and glory of Babylon, which had been fortified by the powerful King Nebuchadnezzar (Daniel 4:30) about 300 years before Alexander's time was also doomed. This great and mighty city, which was renewed in splendor by Alexander, was to later be utterly destroyed.

It became a site of grown-over mounds and a part of the city was eventually buried under the silt deposited from floods on a branch of the Euphrates River flowing close by. For a long time, until it was uncovered by archaeology, it was unknown that the greatest city of the East and the site of the Tower of Babel had been located in that area.

ALTHOUGH IT WAS SHORT-LIVED and fell apart after his death, the area that had been Alexander's extensive empire adopted the Greek tongue as its chief language. The cities he subdued became peopled with Greek settlers, so Greek became the language of international trade. It was spoken and understood almost everywhere. A large number of cities with the Greek culture and language were established in the lands Alexander had conquered. Most all of these would later be absorbed into the Roman Empire, the next world power.

The city of Alexandria, an important seaport city in Egypt founded by Alexander the Great, was to become the capital city of Egypt. For over 1,000 years this city would be the seat of government for Egypt. Here the Old Testament, with its writings of Moses and the prophets, would be translated from its original Hebrew into the Greek language. Because of Alexander's conquests, the writing of what is now our New Testament became written in Greek instead of the Hebrew.

The mighty empires of Babylonia, Persia, Greece, and Rome, now lying in the dust, unwittingly helped to pave the way for the rapid spread of the religion of the humble teacher, Jesus Christ, who came in the fullness of time.

Without using the arrow, sword, or spear, His kingdom will last forever.

A section of the Great Wall of China from the air. Photo credits—the Great Wall of China—Cheng Dalin.

Traces of badly deteriorated parts of the wall.

...Thou hast brought his strong holds to ruin. Ps. 89:40

Chapter 11

All Enemies, Keep Out!

WHEN WE THINK ABOUT LARGE MAN-MADE structures, we may think about the long, high bridges or great skyscrapers we have seen or read about. We may remember the tall Twin Towers of New York City that looked as solid as the Manhatten bedrock they were built upon, but which unbelievably were reduced to enormous piles of rubble in several hours' time.

However, the first prize for the largest man-made structure ever built in the world goes to the Great Wall of China, one of the incredible wonders of the ancient world.

The Great Wall was built with stones and bricks beyond counting. Sometimes called "The Wall of Tears" because of the toil, suffering, and death that occurred during the building of this wall, it has proved to be a colossal failure!

AFTER A RUTHLESS WAR in which hundreds of thousands of people were slaughtered, a Chinese ruler named Zheny brought together the provinces of China to live in peace. Not only did he then proclaim himself the sole ruler of this vast empire, he also made sweeping changes in the laws of the country.

Zheny adopted a standard system of writing and made it compulsory to use standard weights and measures. He required the axles of all carts built be uniform in width so the carts could use the same ruts in the roads.

His enemies, or so Zheny thought, were now dead. All rivals in the countries to the north were conquered. Yet he still had one big worry: How could he hold the hordes of fierce, galloping horsemen from the tribes outside China at bay? Suppose his enemies would rally and try to invade China again?

Zheny decided on the ambitious project of building a fortified wall to protect every inch of China's borders. He drafted 300,000 men—about one-third of all the able-bodied men in the country—and put them to work building a wall.

The work on the wall began about 287 B.C. and continued, off and on, for many hundreds of years.

Built of bricks and stone slabs, it twists and turns, snaking its way over and around the high and towering mountains of northern China. It protrudes for a distance into the sea before coming to an end.

Most of the wall was built from 20 to 50 feet high, 15 to 20 feet wide at the base and 12 feet wide at the top. This was wide enough for two chariots to pass each other with room to spare. At approximately every 200 feet there was a 40-foot-high guard tower.

It is estimated that the total volume of material used would build a wall three feet wide and fifteen feet high and stretching more than ten times around the world.

At some points, a series of four walls stood between China and an invading army fighting its way in. An old inscription bears the words "The Strongest Fortress under Heaven."

AT THE TIME JESUS WAS ON EARTH, the Chinese were busy working on this wall. Parts of the wall were by then already 300 years old.

Jesus may have been thinking about the work going on in the far-off land of China when He made the remark about building a tower without considering how much it would cost (Luke 14:28).

Jesus may also have been thinking about you and me, who so often fail because we are unwilling or unable to admit that the cost of the building up we are doing in our lives will take more than we have of ourselves. Didn't He say, "For which of you?"

Work on the wall continued for many hundreds of years and finally ceased around 1600 A.D. Chinese leaders by that time had come to accept the fact that building a wall around a country to keep out enemies was useless. The wall was never completed. Its only use today is an attraction for tourists.

Hundreds of miles of this wall remain standing today. Some parts are in good condition. Other parts are badly deteriorated, reduced to sand mounds or long rows of stone heaps. Looking like a winding serpent from a distance, this wall, well over 1,600 miles long (plus over 1,500 miles of unfinished parts), would stretch a good way across the United States.

THE MASSIVE AMOUNT OF LABOR NEEDED to do all this building is almost beyond anything we can imagine in our days. The many millions of bricks used were probably passed from hand to hand for many miles. Massive stones, some weighing over a half ton, are found on the tops of mountains. Using all the energy human muscle can create, men worked until they died, carrying these building supplies.

Many of the men drafted for this slave labor never saw their families again. Workers by the hundreds of thousands perished. The bodies of men dying from overwork and disease were thrown into the trench between the two walls before it was filled up and paved over with flat stones. Other workers got killed when the stones rolled backwards as ropes snapped or levers slipped.

Anyone convicted of a crime was sent to forced labor on the wall. The penalty for some of the serious crimes was "slavery forever," which meant that when the criminal died, his son would have to take his place, then his grandson, his great-grandson, and all future children of his line. It is known that work on the wall was done by boys as young as seven years old.

It is estimated that one worker died for every three feet of wall. Only God knows how many died, but in our times the wall is known as "the longest cemetery in the world."

Thousands of families, forced to resettle on farmlands near the wall, provided food for the multitudes of workers and those doing guard duty. In mountainous areas where farming was impossible, donkeys carrying grain traveled hundreds of miles. These lengthy trips took so much time that when the grain arrived, up to 90% was already used up.

A CHINESE PROVERB SAYS, "No barrier is more reliable than the men behind it." This was certainly true of the Great Wall of China. Death was the penalty for any watchman sounding a false alarm or failing to sound an alarm if an enemy was discovered trying to invade.

A system of torch and flag signals were set up between the watchtowers so that, should an invasion take place, help would see the signals and soon swarm to where they were needed. Bonfire signals were used at night and smoke signals by day.

Sentries and watchmen posted in the towers day and night regularly guarded and patrolled the wall. At important mountain passes, large beds of sand outside the wall were raked smooth each day and watched to reveal tracks of enemy scouts creeping in under cover of darkness.

The commanders ordered their soldiers to defend themselves when an enemy came, but warned, "Do not chase after them when they leave. You can't defeat the enemy anyway. Just keep them out of our country!"

The Chinese had it all figured out. The secure feeling of having a barrier against all foreign invaders once the wall was finished would be worth everything it had taken to build it.

But in spite of all the precautions, enemies did break through. Many times the enemy bribed betraying gatekeepers who opened the gates without sounding an alarm, giving rise to another Chinese proverb: "One false traitor inside will do more damage to a fort than a thousand angry enemies outside."

There is an interesting story found in the annals of Chinese history of an emperor who himself unwittingly helped an enemy break inside the wall. This emperor observed a young lady in his court who had a captivating smile, and was noticed by all. Enchanted by her smile, the emperor made her his queen.

As time passed, she became gloomy and seldom smiled. The emperor brought in the court jesters to tell jokes. But even the antics of court clowns failed to amuse her. The emperor, determined to see her smile again, thought of a plan. Perhaps he could find a way to amuse her. He arranged for a false alarm to be sent out from the wall, sending the signal that the enemies were attacking close by. Troops rushed to protect the emperor and his queen. Commanders shouted orders. The queen was so amused by the rushing troops and shouting commanders that she broke out into a hearty laugh.

The emperor's plan to cheer his queen worked, but the guards, troops, and commanders were not amused when they found out it was only a joke.

This prank cost the emperor his life. Some time after this event, an enemy force arrived at the outside of the wall. The emperor sounded an urgent and desperate call for immediate protection.

Not one soldier came to his aid. The emperor was killed, and his young queen with the pretty smile was carried away.

THE BUILDERS OF THE GREAT WALL expected it to keep them safe and secure from all enemies and to protect everything they had won in their battles. However, like the building of the Tower of Babel and the building of the pyramids of Egypt, the Great Wall of China is now just another reminder of the futility and uselessness of the works of men when done for glory, pride, defense, or honor. Sooner or later the great works of men here on earth are doomed to destruction and obliteration. "What goes up is sure to at some time come down," can be said of everything men have ever or will ever build.

Only the marvels of God continue and will endure—some as long as the world stands, some into eternity.

"Except the Lord build the house, they labor in vain that build it" (Psalm 127:1).

WORLD BOOK – 1970

The engraving above shows an early drawing of the ancient city of Athens, in Greece. This was where the unusual teacher, Socrates, was born and lived.

It is said the legendary Aesop (c. 620-560 B.C.) was born at and lived in Athens. Although he is believed to have been a very-much-deformed dwarf, he is remembered as a very interesting master story teller. He used his stories, which were mostly about animals, to illustrate the human virtues and faults which he saw all around him. It is said his wit and wisdom so impressed his slave master that he was given his freedom.

Athens had become the center of Greek culture. Because of the unusual form of government in the villages of Greece, there was no king over the land. Each city or village had its own elected officials.

This city-state of Athens was the same place that almost 450 years after the time of Socrates would stir the spirit of the Apostle Paul, who could see "the city wholly given to idolatry." Although many gods were worshiped in the city, some of the people must have felt that something of true worship was still missing, because an altar had been set up with the inscription, "To the Unknown God." And sacrifices were being offered upon it.

We can read the story in Acts 17, which goes on to tell how Paul used this worship of the unknown God to get started telling the people of Athens about the life hereafter and the resurrection of the dead.

Athens was the city from which Paul would write his two letters to the Christian Church at Thessalonica, also a city in Greece, about 200 miles to the north.

Athens was the city that in World War II would not be bombed by the Germans because its citizens declared it to be a neutral city that would not be fortified or defended from any enemy. Nevertheless, the German army soon occupied the city, and the town citizens, having put up no resistance, soon had very little to eat and nothing to heat their homes for a while. Due to this nonresistance, the city, unlike most other places, escaped becoming destroyed.

Chapter 12

Becoming Hated for Good Teaching

THE LAST OF THE PROPHETS in our Old Testament was Malachi, a name that means "a messenger." He prophesied of the coming of a man who would open up the way by announcing the arrival of a Deliverer, or Messiah, for the Jewish people. Not until 400 years later did his prophecy come to pass in the mission of John the Baptist.

However, the main point of Malachi's message seems to be that God wanted more than temple sacrifices and burnt offerings from the people with whom He had chosen to make a covenant of life and peace (Chapter 2, Verse 5).

God did not choose these people because they were better than other people, but because He needed them to continue true worship so that this Savior could be born to a people knowing the true God. Having the Savior born to a people not knowing God would be futile and of no avail.

God needed to see the priests in the temple and the people who worshiped there live holy lives. A people worshiping a holy God should be living holy lives. God had blessed them, but they kept too much of their blessings for themselves. He told them to bring their tithes into His storehouse "and prove me...if I will not open you the windows of Heaven, and pour you out a blessing, that there shall not be room enough to receive it" (3:10).

Blessings from Heaven! What else could be more important in their lives than to become a people to whom the Lord of Hosts could say, "and they shall be mine" (3:17).

For the next long four hundred years, no prophets were sent to the people of Judea and Israel. No one stood up or wrote to tell the God-fearing people about the Messiah, the anointed one who would deliver the people from bondage.

During these four hundred years, the countries in what are now called "the Holy Lands" were overrun and subjected to the rule of many different heathen nations. The God-fearing people awaiting the fulfilling of God's prophecies, made many hundreds of years before this, could well begin to wonder, "Has God forgotten us?"

THERE IS ONE VERSE IN THE prophecy of Malachi that foretells the coming of a Savior who will make the name of God from the east to the west "great among the Gentiles and great among the heathen" (1:11). This person was to be Jesus Christ, whose story we can read about in the four Gospels.

Throughout those years, did the Gentiles and heathen people of the other nations know anything at all about the true God? Did everybody except the Jewish people worship idols, or the sun, moon, or stars? Had the God of the very first verses of the Holy Scriptures become completely forgotten and unknown by the Gentiles (non-Jews) and the heathen?

Fortunately not everything good was lost. Undoubtedly, there were many Gentile people who lived better lives than God's chosen people ,who surely should have known better. There was a strand of good thread passing down through the generations since Creation and kept unbroken by God-fearing families.

One remarkable person who is not mentioned in our Bible is Socrates (circa 469 - 399 B.C.). To be sure, Socrates' knowledge of the true God was very imperfect, but what would our beliefs and religious practices be like if our parents had not instructed us and taken us along to a church that taught us about the true God?

Socrates, who lived during the same time as the prophet Malachi, was born in Athens, Greece, which in ancient times had become a center of Greek culture.

He lived in a pagan culture that did not know of the true God, and felt called to become a teacher. He learned and taught wise ideas and deep insights about good moral living. It is astonishing how much Socrates knew and taught his pupils about God and the life hereafter while he lived in a pagan society that worshiped anything but the true God. He is one good example that the people of many generations ago were capable of reasoning and thinking of the highest order.

The life of Socrates puts to rest one of the theories of evolution that the people of long ago were less intelligent than people are today.

It was not because of ignorance that the people of long ago felt a need to worship the true God. It was not, as some moderns would have us believe, that the need for a belief and religion was present in the hearts of ancient human beings because they were not educated or fully civilized.

The belief of atheistic communism that a religious faith is needed by unlearned people as an opiate, or deadening of the senses, has been proved to be a deception. The very opposite is true.

Really, it was those who had chosen to keep on living in ignorance and darkness who were to become such enemies to Socrates and his teachings, and then about 450 years later, to the teachings of Jesus Christ.

SOCRATES WAS VERY POOR. He lived and dressed very simply while walking around barefooted in a threadbare cloak. He had a stubby nose and was short in height. His personal appearance was often the object of ridicule, but it is said he disarmed ridicule by expecting it ahead of time. He would take all mockery unruffled and with self-control.

The young people in Athens came to respect him. His young friends appreciated his unusually keen sense of humor, and they held him in high admiration and developed a warm attachment to him. He was no show-off. Because he kept insisting to his pupils that he didn't know much, they accepted him as being one of them.

Socrates argued that the soul of man could never die. He defined the soul as the breath of life and the part of a person that is truly the self of a person. The soul is only temporarily using the body for a place to live. His lines of reasoning made people think, and inspired many lively discussions between Socrates and the idol-worshiping people of Athens.

The outspoken belief of Socrates in the immortality of the soul, a belief that gives meaning to human existence, came from thinking deeply about things that some people have tried to avoid, even down to our day.

We do not know how it came to be that Socrates was able to think so differently, and on a nobler and higher level than other philosophers of his time, who taught that life was empty and had no purpose or meaning. His way of teaching was not by telling his pupils what he knew, or by merely giving them a long list of facts to learn, but by getting them started thinking by asking them intelligent questions.

His response to their questions was often another question that got them thinking again. His questions made him more persuasive than any argument could be. By asking questions, his pupils were made aware why they themselves and others thought and acted as they did. Socrates did not argue with anybody. He asked pointed questions that helped his students see the error of their ways, and by putting their answers into questions, he often helped them to learn to better express their beliefs in their own words.

Because his way was listening more than talking, and questioning more than answering, his methods of teaching were very successful. His pupils learned to think for themselves, and would also often agree with him where they had earlier disgreed.

SOCRATES ENJOYED TALKING WITH PEOPLE at the marketplaces, "How many things are here that I do not even need!" he at one time exclaimed. As he looked over the many things that could be taken home by anyone who had enough coins to pay for them, he knew a disciplined lifestyle brings with it many rewards of its own, and was known for moderation in eating and drinking.

At one time the friends of Socrates wanted him to accept a public office, but he declined. Taking part in politics and having the power to tell other people what to do would be going against his principles.

He was sure many people ruined their lives by taking care of their possessions before they took care of their soul. "Contentment is natural wealth; luxury is artificial poverty," he would say. He taught that unlimited wealth and power is not good for the soul because it is too often wrongly used.

Although Socrates was a pagan because he had never heard of the true God of the Bible, he gave advice that is still excellent for our days. "To want as little as possible is to make a nearest approach to God," he said. It is said that his prayers to the God he believed in were short. "Give me only what you know is good for me," he would say.

The Golden Rule in its reverse form has been attributed to Socrates. "Whatever you do not want others to do to you, do not so to them," he would say. He also said, "We should injure no one, however much that person has injured us."

Socrates was a good-humored teacher and would say that it is better to be silent and be thought a fool than to speak up and remove all doubt! In his way of wise and effective persuading, he would also never bluntly tell a man he was wrong, even if it was very obvious that he was.

He taught his pupils to think out what the results of actions might be. In this way he helped them to think about their own conduct of living and better understand themselves instead of blindly accepting the beliefs of others as their own. Socrates' purpose in this was to teach the young to live wisely and be convinced that wisdom and honesty were more important than fame or riches. He was a master in teaching the young to think without telling them what to think.

He urged the young not to merely accept the beliefs of the government and that of their elders as sacred, but to study and think out their own beliefs. He thought in this way their beliefs and values would have better and deeper roots and would not merely be secondhand or handed-down traditional beliefs.

Socrates was sure if his students thought carefully, they would accept the virtues of the elders as their own, and more importantly, it would be rare that they would rebel against the values held dear by those with experience.

The men of influence in the city misunderstood such teachings. They began to resent these teachings about not blindly accepting all the laws they were making. Teaching the young to think for themselves could be dangerous to their authority, and would only invite more youthful rebellion and disobedience.

The presence of Socrates in public places in Athens asking questions that made people stop and consider things they had never thought of before became upsetting, and led these men of influence to contradict themselves. It sometimes exposed their hypocrisy of pretending to be better than they really were. As can be expected, some of the men in authority began to cultivate a deep anger against Socrates.

The politicians of the city also remembered that Socrates had spoken up in the behalf of several army generals who had been put to trial several years earlier. The court, full of false witnesses and reeking of corruption, refused to listen to the defense of the generals put forth by Socrates, showing that they were innocent. Justice or not, it seems the court had decided beforehand what the verdict would be.

The generals were executed and, of course, Socrates was branded as somewhat of a traitor just because he dared to speak well of the men who were falsely branded as "enemies of our society."

SOCRATES WAS PUT TO TRIAL. Now seventy years old, he was tried because he did not believe in the many gods worshiped in Athens. He was called "an atheist who failed to worship our gods." Another charge against him was that "he is corrupting our youth by teaching them to think for themselves."

Accused of teaching religion and political subversion, the court refused to explain what he had done wrong or what laws he had broken. He remained calm, which further angered the judges. He refused to promise to stop his way of teaching.

A jury of his fellow citizens of Athens sentenced him to be executed "because of his stubbornness." Socrates became a victim of hatred, and was sentenced to die for his ideas and thinking.

THE METHOD OF EXECUTION WAS BY POISON, a slow and painful way to die. Socrates' friends wanted to help him escape, which he easily could have done, but he did not want them to go to any bother about him.

Still showing his usual complete self-control, he bid farewell to his weeping friends and told them what he was feeling in his body as the poison was doing its terrible and deadly work. In his last words, Socrates quietly reminded a friend not to forget to pay a small debt that he remembered he owed.

As he was dying from the cupful of poison he had been given, Socrates, the thinker who never felt any anger against anyone, remained calm and said he cherished no ill will against those who had accused and condemned him. In his last hours, he said he believed his soul would depart to the place where he would "spend the rest of time with God."

Socrates taught that a good person doesn't need to fear either life or death. He said evil could never harm a good person.

Socrates felt that the nature of a person would cause him or her to act as they do. About 450 years later, Jesus Christ offered us a way to correct this flaw in man when He said we need the birth of a new nature within us to see the Kingdom of God (John 3:3).

SOCRATES DID NO WRITING HIMSELF, but his pupils later became writers. One of these was Plato (circa 428 to circa 348 B.C.), who had known Socrates from boyhood. Plato became a Greek philosopher, and was one of the most influential Greek thinkers of his time. He was also for better and more wholesome ways of living and was disgusted by the gross sensuality of living at the numerous places he visited.

Much of what we know of the life and teachings of Socrates has come down to us from the writings of Plato. He described the reality of things seen in this world as no more than like a shadow cast by an object in front of a fire in a cave. If a man were to be chained so that he could only see the shadows, he would have only an imperfect knowledge of the real object. To Plato, it was as if we were chained in this life and kept from seeing what is real.

The difference in the shadow and what is real is about the difference in what can be seen now and what will be seen in eternity. It is only "the evidence of things not seen" (Hebrews 11:1).

Even during the life of Socrates, when the citizens of Athens did not believe in the true God and many gods were worshiped, some people felt something of true worship was missing, because at some time an altar had been set up which bore the inscription "To the Unknown God," and sacrifices were offered upon it.

We also have a record of one of the ancient Athenian philosophers during that time of history making the remark that "if ever a man perfectly good were to be found, he would not be tolerated by society. They would hate him and would kill him." How prophetic!

About 450 years later, in the city-state of Athens, after the time of Socrates, the Apostle Paul would see "the city wholly given to idolatry." We can read about this in Acts, Chapter 17, which tells us how Paul used this worship of the Unknown God to start telling the people of Athens about the life hereafter and the resurrection of the dead.

Athens was the city from which Paul would write his two letters to the Christian Church at Thessalonica, also a city in Greece, about 200 miles to the north.

IN OUR DAY, HISTORIANS DO NOT ALWAYS interpret the story of Socrates as God's way of keeping a semblance of the true worship during a time of spiritual ignorance and darkness. Because of the unusual form of government in the country of Greece during the time of Socrates, there was no king over the land. Each city or village had its own elected officials. When Socrates was executed, many of his pupils fled Athens, fearing for their lives. This may have been God's way of spreading the unusual influence of Socrates. It is known that the life and teachings of Socrates undoubtedly helped to destroy the Greek belief in heathen gods. It helped to make the Greek world, under the Roman Empire, ready for the wide spread of Christianity several centuries later.

When the Apostle John opened his Gospel, he started it out in the majestic way we think Socrates might also have worded it had he lived several centuries later: "In the beginning was the Word, and the Word was with God, and the Word was God" (John 1:1).

Parashah 1: B'resheet

בראשית ברא אלהים את השמים ואת הארץ: והארץ
היתה תהו ובהו וחשך על־פני תהום ורוח אלהים
מרחפת על־פני המים: ויאמר אלהים יהי אור ויהי
אור: וירא אלהים את־האור כי־טוב ויבדל אלהים בין
האור ובין החשך: ויקרא אלהים ׀ לאור יום ולחשך
קרא לילה ויהי־ערב ויהי־בקר יום אחד:

1. The original Hebrew by Moses—Circa 1400-1500 B.C.

ΓΕΝΕΣΙΣ.

2 ἘΝ ἀρχῇ ἐποίησεν ὁ Θεὸς τὸν οὐρανὸν καὶ τὴν γῆν. Ἡ δὲ γῆ ἦν ἀόρατος καὶ ἀκατασκεύαστος, καὶ σκότος ἐπάνω τῆς 3 ἀβύσσου· καὶ πνεῦμα Θεοῦ ἐπεφέρετο ἐπάνω τοῦ ὕδατος. Καὶ 4 εἶπεν ὁ Θεὸς, γενηθήτω φῶς· καὶ ἐγένετο φῶς. Καὶ εἶδεν ὁ Θεὸς τὸ φῶς, ὅτι καλόν· καὶ διεχώρισεν ὁ Θεὸς ἀνὰ μέσον τοῦ 5 φωτὸς, καὶ ἀνὰ μέσον τοῦ σκότους. Καὶ ἐκάλεσεν ὁ Θεὸς τὸ φῶς ἡμέραν, καὶ τὸ σκότος ἐκάλεσε νύκτα. Καὶ ἐγένετο ἑσπέρα, καὶ ἐγένετο πρωΐ, ἡμέρα μία.

2. Greek Septuagint—Circa 250 B.C. The first translation of Scripture ever.

GENESIS

IN the beginning God made the heaven and the earth. [2]But the earth was unsightly and unfurnished, and darkness was over the deep, and the Spirit of God moved over the water. [3]And God said, Let there be light, and there was light. [4]And God saw the light that it was good, and God divided between the light [β]and the darkness. [5]And God called the light Day, and the darkness he called Night, and there was evening and there was morning, the first day.

3. Parallel English translation—1851

GENESIS

1 WHEN GOD BEGAN creating[a] the heavens and the earth, [2]the earth was at first[b] a shapeless, chaotic mass,[c] with the Spirit of God brooding over the dark vapors.[d]

[3]Then[b] God said, "Let there be light." And light appeared. [4,5]And God was pleased with it, and divided the light from the darkness. So he let it shine for awhile, and then there was darkness again. He called the light "daytime," and the darkness "nighttime." Together they formed the first day.[e]

6. Living Bible Paraphrased English—1971

Das erſte Buch Moſe.

Das 1. Kapitel.

Schöpfung der Welt. Der Menſch ein Bild Gottes. (Vgl. Pſ. 104.)

1. Am Anfang ſchuf Gott Himmel und Erde.
Apg. 17, 24; Offenb. 4, 11; Hebr. 11, 3; Joh. 1, 1—3.
2. Und die Erde war wüſt und leer, und es war finſter auf der Tiefe; und der Geiſt Gottes ſchwebte auf dem Waſſer.
3. Und Gott ſprach: Es werde Licht! und es ward Licht. Pſ. 33, 9; 2. Kor. 4, 6.
4. Und Gott ſah, daß das Licht gut war. Da ſchied Gott das Licht von der Finſternis
5. und nannte das Licht Tag und die Finſternis Nacht. Da ward aus Abend und Morgen der erſte Tag.

5. Martin Luther German—1534

Das erste Buch Mose (Genesis)

Gott erschafft die Welt

1 Am Anfang schuf Gott Himmel und Erde. [2]Noch war die Erde leer und ohne Leben, von Wassermassen bedeckt. Finsternis herrschte, aber über dem Wasser schwebte der Geist Gottes.

[3]Da sprach Gott: «Licht soll entstehen!», und es wurde hell. [4]Gott sah, daß es gut war. Er trennte das Licht von der Dunkelheit [5]und nannte das Licht «Tag» und die Dunkelheit «Nacht». Es wurde Abend und wieder Morgen: Der erste Tag war vergangen.

4. Hoffnung Für Alle German—1996

OUDE TESTAMENT BOEK 1

GENESIS 1

1 *Hemel en aarde worden geschapen*

[1]In het begin schiep God de hemel en de aarde.

[2]De aarde was onherbergzaam en verlaten. Een watervloed bedekte haar en er heerste diepe duisternis. De wind van God joeg over het water.

[3]Toen zei God: 'Er moet licht zijn!' En er [4]was licht. God zag hoe mooi het licht was en hij scheidde het licht van de duisternis. [5]God noemde het licht dag en de duisternis nacht. Het werd avond en het werd ochtend, één dag was voorbij.

9. Groot Neiuws Bijbel Holland Dutch—1975

DIE BIBEL

in heutigem Deutsch

DAS ERSTE BUCH MOSE – GENESIS

Die Erschaffung der Welt

1 Am Anfang schuf Gott Himmel und Erde, die ganze Welt. [2]Auf der Erde war es noch wüst und unheimlich; es war finster, und Wasserfluten bedeckten alles. Über dem Wasser schwebte der Geist Gottes.[a]

[3]Da befahl Gott: »Licht soll aufstrahlen!«, und es wurde hell. [4]Gott hatte Freude an dem Licht; denn es war gut. Er trennte das Licht von der Dunkelheit [5]und nannte das Licht Tag, die Dunkelheit Nacht. Es wurde Abend und wieder Morgen: der erste Tag.

7. Die Bibel in Heutigem Deutsch—1983

GENESIS

The Beginning of All Things

The Beginning of the World

1 In the beginning God created the sky and the earth. [2]The earth was empty and had no form. Darkness covered the ocean, and God's Spirit[d] was moving over the water.

[3]Then God said, "Let there be light," and there was light. [4]God saw that the light was good, so he divided the light from the darkness. [5]God named the light "day" and the darkness "night." Evening passed, and morning came. This was the first day.

8. The everyday Bible in English—1987

Genesis

I: THE PRIMEVAL HISTORY

First Story of Creation

1 [1*†]IN THE BEGINNING, when God created the heavens and the earth, [2*†]the earth was a formless wasteland, and darkness covered the abyss, while a mighty wind swept over the waters.

[3*]Then God said, "Let there be light," and there was light. [4]God saw how good the light was. God then separated the light from the darkness. [5†]God called the light "day," and the darkness he called "night." Thus evening came, and morning followed—the first day.

12. The New American Catholic Bible—1970

THE FIRST BOOK OF MOSES, CALLED

GENESIS

CHAPTER 1

1 *The creation of heaven and earth,* 3 *of the light,* 6 *of the firmament,* 9 *of the earth separated from the waters,* 11 *and made fruitful,* 14 *of the sun, moon, and stars,* 20 *of fish and fowl,* 24 *of beasts and cattle,* 26 *of man in the image of God.* 29 *Also the appointment of food.*

IN the [a]beginning [b]God created the heaven and the earth.

2 And the earth was without form, and void; and darkness *was* upon the face of the deep. [c]And the Spirit of God moved upon the face of the waters.

3 [d]And God said, [e]Let there be light: and there was light.

4 And God saw the light, that *it was* good: and God divided [2]the light from the darkness.

5 And God called the light [f]Day, and the darkness he called Night. [3]And the evening and the morning were the first day.

B.C. 4004.

a John 1. 1, 2. Heb. 1. 10
b Ps. 8. 3; 33. 6; 89. 11, 12; 102. 25; 136. 5; 146. 6. Is. 44. 24. Jer. 10. 12; 51. 15. Zech. 12. 1. Acts 14. 15; 17. 24. Col. 1. 16, 17. Heb. 11. 3. Rev. 4. 11.
c Ps. 33. 6. Is. 40. 13, 14.
d Ps. 33. 9.
e 2 Cor. 4. 6.
2 Heb. *between the light and between the darkness.*
f Ps. 74. 16; 104. 20.
3 Heb. *And the evening was, and the morning was.*

10. King James English—1611

Geneſis

das erſt bůch Moſe.

Das erſte Capitel.

Von erſchaffung der welt, underſcheydung und zierd der geſchöpffen, formierung und aufenthalt des menſchen, darumb alle ding geſchaffen, und das in ſechs tagen.

A 4.Eſd.6. b Eccli.18. a Jer.10. b Hebr.11.a Jſa.44. c

M anfang ſchuoff GOtt den himmel und die erden: und die erd was wüſt und lár, und es was finſter auff der tieffe, und der geyſt GOttes hielt auff dem waſſer.

Und GOtt ſprach: Es werde liecht. Und es ward liecht. Und GOtt ſahe das liecht für gůt an. Do ſchied GOtt das liecht von der finſternuß, und nennet das liecht, Tag: und die finſternuß, Nacht. Do ward auß abend und morgen der erſte tag.

11. Swiss German Froschauer—1536

13. Actual page size of the complete miniature Bible. Oxford University Press, Glasglow—1896. The 896-page, ½" thick Bible could be read with the magnifyer included.

How many of us could get anything out of the Bible if it were available only in its original Hebrew and Greek languages? Thank God for translators!

Chapter 13

The Very First Translation of the Holy Scriptures

AS MANY BIBLE READERS know, the Old Testament was originally written, not in the German or English with which we are familiar, but in Hebrew. This was one of the earliest languages to use alphabet letters that represented speech sounds, rather than the earlier picture writing that represented ideas.

The ancestors of the Jewish people we read about in the Bible—Abraham, Moses, and David, and on down for the next many hundreds of years—all spoke Hebrew. It is natural that practically all the writings gathered together in what we call the Old Testament were written in the Hebrew language.

The Jewish people used the Hebrew language almost exclusively for speaking and writing until that watershed time of Jewish history, the captivity in the land of Babylon, took place.

As we learn in the very first chapter in the New Testament, one of the points of reference in the Gospel of Matthew's account of the royal lineage leading to Jesus Christ was the seventy years the Jewish people were slaves in Babylon.

This period of captivity has become an important part of Jewish history, just as the account of their forefather Abraham, the establishment of the family of King David as having lawful claim to the line of Jewish kings, and later the birth of Jesus Christ as their Savior. The remembrance of this part of their history became as important to the first-century Jewish Christians, as shown by the way Matthew begins his Gospel, as was that of their history of 400 years of slavery in the land of Egypt.

MANY OF THE AGED MEN AND WOMEN still living and strong enough to return to their homeland after seventy years of slavery would vividly remember having made the unhappy and forced march to Babylon when they were only young teenagers.

They would remember looking over their shoulders at their burning homes and at the temple in the city of Jerusalem, all of which had been stripped of everything of value before being leveled to the ground. The walls that had been built to protect the city were reduced to piles of rubble.

They would remember the trauma of being deported from the scenes of their childhood. They would recall the foreboding and fear in their hearts as they were herded like a bunch of driven cattle. As long as they lived, they would never forget the long and weary trek with Nebuchadnezzar's soldiers on both sides prodding them on to a strange land of exile.

They would remember the heartbreak as they were forced away from their parents and older folks, who were left behind in their desolated homeland to die. Because the elderly were past their prime of life, they were not worth taking along as slaves. One of them, the prophet Jeremiah, would write the five chapters of the book of Lamentations found in our Old Testament. With his graphic description of the desolation around him, he still wrote of his hope in a loving God with His mercies new every morning (Lamentations 3:21-66).

Until their dying day, these elderly and infirm people living in their sunset years could do nothing for their young people except pray that God would stay with them, even in the faraway pagan land among heathen people. It seemed hopeless—would their young people continue to worship the true God in such foreign surroundings? This was more than their forefathers had done when they had lived in independence and prosperity.

It looked as if the nation of Abraham's descendants would become lost among the other nations of the world. What would then become of the many prophecies of a Savior?

In this parting of the young and the strong from their elders, families were separated, never to see each other on earth again. There was no going back and forth to visit, and, of course, there was no mail.

The land was emptied of young people. Although no one knows for sure how many people were forcibly enslaved, one account gives the number of only the first wave of returning people seventy years later as being fifty thousand people. Can we imagine how desolated by weeds, thorns, and brambles our land would soon become if all our young, strong working people were suddenly taken from us?

Can we also imagine what it was like for the young people taken into slavery? After a month or more of a long and tiresome journey on foot, this multitude of young people would take off their heavy packs laden with the valuables of their elders. After the exhausting tramp of perhaps 700 miles, they were now in a strange foreign country. They were slaves of a heathen people they did not know. What could they expect? Those who were put to death when Jerusalem was besieged may have been better off than these young people were now.

Their masters in this new land must have heard that the Jewish people were good singers, and they must have wished to hear their gloomy slaves sing while at work. They asked their young slaves to sing the songs of their homeland.

We can well understand that they would have rather wept than sang. "How shall we sing the Lord's song in a strange land?" they would reply (Psalm 137:4).

DURING THE TIME THIS GENERATION of Jewish people were slaves in this idol-worshiping country so far away from their homeland, it is doubtful they would have heard the old Hebrew writings of such as Moses and the prophet Samuel being read to them in a worship service.

In fact, they may never have held any formal gatherings to sing and pray to God in this country where they were held captive. The native people in this strange land worshiped statues of kings and images of other gods. The third chapter of Daniel gives us a good picture of how the Jewish people in Babylonia were compelled with a deadly threat to take part in idol worship.

Yet, after a number of years, many changes took place. The Babylonians tolerated the Jewish people's belief in the true God. Everyone from the king on down could see that here were young people with high morals.

Eventually, the Babylonians were destroyed. As is well known to Bible readers, this happened on the night the Babylonian king, Belshazzar, a successor of King Nebuchadnezzar, was making a great feast for a thousand of his royal lords and mistresses (Daniel, Chapter 5). Remembering the gold and silver utensils stolen from the Jewish temple some fifty years earlier, Belshazzar had them brought forth and filled with wine. A riotous and wild drinking party was soon going on.

Suddenly, all was hushed and still. The partying and merrymaking was abruptly stopped. A mysterious hand could be seen writing an inscription on the wall close to the candleholders lighting the huge palace room.

No one there could read the words that were written. With his knees shaking in fear, the terrified king brought in Daniel, one of the captive Jews. Daniel, by then an old man, read and interpreted the prophecy that was written against the king for his impious actions. In his power and wealth, Belshazzar had not glorified God "in whose hand thy breath is" (Verse 23).

The prophecy was fulfilled that very same night. Through other ancient histories, we learn that the armies of the Medes and Persians had been busy just outside the city walls while all this feasting, drinking, and wild entertainment was going on at the king's palace.

Under cover of darkness, the enemy armies had diverted some of the waters of the Euphrates River that ran in one opening of the city wall and out another. Wading in waist-deep water, the army stealthily entered the city through these passages. They thronged to the king's palace.

Before daylight broke, the proud king was among the slain. Little had he realized while "enjoying his drunken mirth" that his life, which was in the hand of his Maker, was so close to its end. As the divine hand doing the handwriting on the wall had foretold, the mighty Babylonian Empire was then no more. Its collapse was sudden, complete, and final.

The ruin of the mighty city of Babylon, specifically foretold at least 100 times in the writings of the Jewish prophets, came to pass. For a long time, the area was such a mass of grown-over heaps that no one was even sure where Babylon had even been located.

Babylonia would never again be numbered among the nations of the earth. Affluence and prosperity had decayed it from within. Stronger nations with better work ethics and moral standards would take its place; at least until they in turn would get on the downward slide to ruin.

The Jewish people in this land so far from their homeland, some of whom had worked themselves up into responsible government positions, were now under the rule of the kindly king of the Medes. This would later become part of Persia, a land located in what is now modern-day Iran.

AS THE JEWISH PROPHETS correctly foretold in Jeremiah 29:10 and Isaiah 44:26-28, the Jewish people were permitted to return to their homeland during the reign of the Persian king named Cyrus.

It is incredible and beyond any human explanation that Isaiah's prophecy, which was made many years before the Jewish people had even been led into the Babylonian captivity, could correctly foretell their homecoming and the rebuilding of their temple. Even more improbable to a nonbeliever, this divinely inspired prophecy revealed, long before his birth, even the name of the king who would permit the Jews to return to the land of Judea.

While the Jewish people were captives in Babylonia, many changes took place. A change in their way of speaking began to happen. A curious mixture of the Hebrew tongue of their forefathers and the Chaldees language of the Babylonians they lived among and worked for evolved into an altogether new language. This "soup of words," as this speech has been called, was later known as Aramaic.

After the return to their homeland, the Jews kept using the Old Hebrew in their worship services because their sacred Scriptures and their Psalm Book were in the Hebrew language. They had never been translated. However, by then Aramaic was the everyday speaking language of the Jewish people.

When Jesus was here on earth several hundred years later, Aramaic was the language the people of Judea and Galilee used. This was the language Jesus would use when He was teaching His disciples and the people with whom He would come into contact. This was the everyday language they were able to understand.

SEVENTY YEARS OF SLAVERY IN A STRANGE and pagan land changed the Jewish people, especially the young. God was preparing them to have the Savior of the world born to a family in their midst. God used the Babylonians to take away Jewish wealth to bring his people back to Him, and it worked.

While still enslaved, this revival in their hearts and way of living took hold. Young Daniel and his friends resolved in their hearts not to defile themselves with forbidden foods from the king's table. They also firmly refused to drink any of his wine (Daniel, Chapter 1).

They would not bow to idols built by the king, even though they knew the punishment for refusing was to be thrown alive into a fiery furnace (Chapter 3). They prayed to the true God three times daily, even though the penalty was to be cast into a den of man-eating lions (Chapter 6).

These young Jews, long before they were freed, became a people who were serious in what they believed. Things of the Spirit became important to them. Under slavery they became a God-fearing people who kept God's laws much better than their parents who had lived for many generations in freedom and plenty.

They had learned their lesson well. After they were freed, the young people did not fall back into the ways of the past, or follow the sinful examples of their forefathers who had turned away from the God whose hand had guided them out of the cruel oppression in Egypt and into a land of plenty.

AFTER HAVING LIVED IN AN IDOL-WORSHIPING COUNTRY for seventy years as a punishment for idol-worshiping in their homeland, the Jewish people after their return were never again to this day known to have become worshipers of idols.

After this, even in modern times, there would be no images or sculptures of any kind in Jewish homes and places of worship. All artwork depicting God or anything religious was strictly forbidden. Having images around would be too much like idolatry.

Other religions, even many Christian denominations of today, have religious artwork on display, but the Jews do not. Other nations had ensigns on the soldiers' shields, but not the Jews. Only the Star of David, made with two triangles interlaced to form a six-pointed star would be the universal symbol of the Jewish people. It appears now on the flag of the State of Israel and in their synagogues.

God answered the prayers of the Jewish people left behind when their young people were taken away to a life of slavery in a strange land. God was with them.

The great king himself saw the likeness of the Son of God (Daniel 3:25) among the group of steadfast young people he ordered thrown into a fiery furnace. Their prayers were answered when God protected Daniel's life when he spent a whole night in a locked cage with man-eating lions.

The prayers of parents in our days, as their children go out the door to school or to be with the young people, can be just as effective as they were in those days when the parents watched their young people leave for a land of slavery. We have the same God, and He will hear our prayers.

AFTER THE JEWISH PEOPLE RETURNED FROM THEIR EXILE, a new sect within the Jewish society was to originate. This was that of the well-known Pharisees. Many historians try to trace the beginnings of this sect to Ezra, the scribe who taught God's laws to the people when they returned to their homeland after seventy years of slavery.

Not only could Ezra read in Hebrew, but also he seems to have had the talent for reading these ancient books in a way that was interesting and understandable to the people (Nehemiah, Chapter 8). The time was getting ripe for the Jewish people to get themselves ready for the fulfilling of the prophecies that in "the fullness of time" would come to pass.

The very worthy aims and high ideals of these people, called "Hasidim" or "loyal to God" or "loved of God," were commendable, especially in the beginning. Their goal was to rigidly keep the ancient written laws, along with the oral and traditional laws that had grown out of many years of popular usage. This sect was also called "Pharisees," coming from the Hebrew words meaning "the separated ones."

They believed in a life after death. They probably quoted the verses in their Hebrew Scriptures such as "and I will dwell in the house of the Lord forever" (Psalm 23:6) and "For I know that my Redeemer liveth…in my flesh I shall see God" (Job 19:25 and 26). Like King David in 2 Samuel 12:23, they believed in a future reuniting of friends and loved ones.

In early days, the Pharisees related better to the common people than did the upper-class Jews of that time. They sought to keep themselves free from the influences of the unconcerned and irreligious people of their day. They were well versed in the writings of Moses and the prophets and helped to keep alive the hope of a Deliverer of the Jewish people during a time when there were probably only a few people who could read the very few existing copies of the Hebrew Scriptures of their forefathers.

The Pharisees were waiting for the time when God would send them a King who would lead them from one victory of war into another. This King, prophesied to come from the line of King David, was also prophesied to lead a kingdom that would have no end. Belonging to a people they believed would soon become a world power was something they thought was reason enough to be a little proud about!

THESE PHARISEES LATER ABUSED BEING GOOD BY THE STRICT observance of the letter, but not the spirit, of their religious laws. In the beginning of their time of leadership they seemed to be a Godly influence on all with whom they came into contact.

It is sad to read of this group becoming corrupt by pretending to be highly moral and virtuous, without being so. They became skilled at putting on a good front. They did good works only to be seen and praised by men. Without an inner change of heart, they had only the outward appearance of being good people.

In hypocrisy, they tried to be what they were not, and they looked down on the righteousness of other people as inferior to them and their righteousness.

It seems there is nothing more damaging to the cause of being righteous than hypocrisy. In the Gospels, we read of the Pharisees of several hundred years later, who seem to have abused and lost the original and noble intent of their beginnings. These were the people who were inflamed with hate against Jesus when He exposed their first-class hypocrisy. They feared their good reputation would be lost if Jesus were to be permitted to live.

A good cause corrupted is really what caused the crucifixion of Jesus when God's time was up for Him to be on to earth. Bible prophecy was fulfilled right in their midst, but being blinded by their feelings of self-importance, they knew Him not.

Zoroaster

ANY OF OUR READERS WHO find the study of different religions and beliefs of mankind fascinating may have read of the religious teacher called Zoroaster.

During the time that Darius the Great was king, the teachings of Zoroaster were introduced into Persia and become the state religion of that country.

Zoroaster believed in one God, a belief that virtually all the tribes and nations of that time, with the exception of the Hebrews, had lost. All the other nations had invented their own set of gods, and then credited them as helping to win wars over the gods in which their enemy nations believed.

In the religion of Zoroastrianism, the believers thought there was a continuous battle of good and evil, and that the good would ultimately prevail. They believed in a future resurrection of the dead and an afterlife.

It is interesting that this religion developed in the far-flung Persian Empire that extended eastward as far as India, right around the exact time that the Jews lived in this land as slaves. This religious system was to dominate Persia for hundreds of years until the country became converted to Islam, which occurred in the seventh century of the Christian era. Since then, up to our present time, nearly all of the people of Iran, which used to be called Persia, are believers in the Muslim religion.

Although this Persian religion emphasized a belief in one God, it remained mixed with paganism and with much magic and superstition. However, nearly all students of religious history will agree that the teachings of Zoroaster had a closer resemblance to the present-day Jewish and Christian beliefs than any other known ancient religion. It was a religion of the reforming of morals, truthfulness, trustworthiness, and honesty.

Because in many ways this religion was very much like the true beliefs taught in the Bible of the one true God, it has been suggested that this may explain the willingness of King Darius to help the Jewish people with the rebuilding of their temple (Ezra, Chapter 6).

It has also been suggested that the Jews borrowed some of their religious ideas from Zoroastrianism and from some of the other Eastern religions while they were slaves in Babylonia and Persia. However, it makes more sense to give the Jewish people the credit for believing in and living out their worthy religion in a way that was noticed by the people around them.

Like the little captive maid in the pagan country of Syria, which we read about in 2 Kings, Chapter 5, the captive Jewish people, who lived seventy years in the pagan country, were a good influence that rubbed off on the people around them. There is no other satisfactory explanation as to where this Persian one-God religion, even with its flaws, got started in Persia at this exact same time.

THE WELL-KNOWN MAGI, known in most German and English translations of Matthew, Chapter 2, Verse 1, as "the wise men", are believed to have been priests of the religion of Zoroaster. It is known that the priests of this religion lived lives of self-denial, and they were credited with having a profound religious knowledge. They were the night watchers of the skies above them and studied the movements of the stars and planets. They were the scientists of those days. Their knowledge kept them from falling into the first idolatry of mankind, the worshiping of the sun, moon, and stars.

About five centuries after the time of the Persian King Darius, a small group of these Magi discovered a new star and were led to the place where Jesus was born. Here they found the newborn King they had probably heard vague prophecies about—passed on down to them from 500 years earlier.

One reason God wanted this story to be included in the New Testament may be so we can conclude that the Jewish people who lived in the East 500 years earlier must have explained their beliefs to their pagan neighbors.

Perhaps God wants us all to know that even a small group of sincere Christians in any land will leave a vestige of influence that could last for a long time. Knowing this should motivate all of us to work at becoming better present-day disciples of Jesus Christ.

Then also, God may have placed that story of the wise men in the Bible as an example for anyone who searches for the truth. When they follow a light like the wise men did and find Jesus, they will take up another way and will not go on as they planned on going.

The first people on earth knew about the true God who created and controls Heaven and earth. The true belief in God and the living of hallowed lives has always had plenty of counterfeits. Truth can so easily become diluted and grossly corrupt.

It is a sobering thought that the true beliefs have, since Creation, always been only one generation away from being extinct.

The Ptolemy Kings and Their Contributions

A NUMBER OF YEARS LATER, the son of one of Alexander the Great's generals became king of Egypt; one of the five kingdoms of what had once been Alexander's extensive empire. Ptolemy I, as he was called, seemed to be a man more interested in books and learning than in war and in the conquering of more lands.

He started an ambitious plan to establish a large library. He planned and built this library in the city of Alexandria, Egypt, a large city built by Alexander the Great and named after him.

This was the city we read about in the *Martyrs Mirror* where the Gospel writer, Mark, would be martyred several hundred years later when he was introducing Christianity to the people living in Egypt. This city, still in existence to this day, is situated near the mouth of the Nile River.

The aim of King Ptolemy I was to have a copy of all the books ever written placed in one huge building. All the world's knowledge and wisdom would be gathered under one roof. Here would be the world's largest research institute, available for anyone to consult the texts of ancient writers. Many of these would not be available anywhere else.

It is known that the inscription "Medicine for the Soul" was often placed at the entrance to the libraries of sacred literature. Very probably the words were inscribed over one of the doorways of this library.

This was long before the days of printed books with pages, as we know them today. These were all handwritten scrolls, the tedious labor of scholars, scribes, and copyists.

These bulky rolls were made either with vellum, which is a thin leather sewed or pasted together, or were a heavy parchment handmade from the papyrus plant that grew in abundance along the banks of the Nile River.

It is not certain how many scrolls were on the shelves of this library. The means of getting accurate figures in those times did not exist as they do today. The various accounts of the size of the library and of its destruction later are often vague and are sometimes even contradictory. One account that tells us the library housed 700,000 manuscripts may be exaggerated, but it is known that the number was large. This library became to be called one of the wonders of the ancient world.

The work of classifying and indexing the collection itself is said to have taken up some 120 scrolls, each of which was a bulky roll many yards long.

King Ptolemy I, with a wide range of interests and a seeker after knowledge, placed books in the library from countries all over the known world. Expense didn't matter. To enlarge the collection, his soldiers were ordered to seize the books from any ships that docked in the large and busy Alexandrian harbor nearby.

Scribes appointed by the king copied these books. The originals were kept and placed in the library. The ships were sent away with only the handwritten copies of what they had before.

Scholars came from all over the known world to study and do research in every known branch of learning at this famous Royal Alexandrian Library.

THE NEXT KING IN THE LINE, Ptolemy II, like his father, was also interested in book learning. He developed a keen interest in the religions of the different peoples he heard and read about. He wanted the Alexandrian library to include the sacred writings of every one of these different religions, and he collected these books, written in the languages of their lands. He put his scholars to work translating these texts into the Greek language so that they could be read and understood by many more people.

By this time, most of what had been Alexander the Great's far-flung empire had adopted the Greek culture and its customs. People all over were using the Greek language as their second language to go along with the tongue they used in their homelands.

Even the Jewish people, the self-appointed guardians of the Hebrew language, started using Greek in the many Jewish settlements in far-off lands, and in different places than Jerusalem.

At that time, one of the largest groups of Jews living outside of Palestine was in the northern sector of the city of Alexandria. This influential and prosperous Jewish community, many thousands of people strong, has been estimated by some historians as being the home of more Jewish people than there were Jews living in Jerusalem at that time.

These Jews probably made the pilgrimage to the Jerusalem temple over the Passover or Pentecost feast at least several times in their lifetimes if they were able. The Jews at the religious celebration of Pentecost mentioned in Acts 2:10, as being from Egypt, may have been citizens of Alexandria. Like the pilgrims from the many other far-off lands, they were not accustomed to the Aramaic spoken by the Apostles. Their knowledge of Jewish history was limited to the stories their grandfathers related to them around the family table at the yearly Passover celebration.

Due to the widespread use of the Greek language, many of the Jews living in other lands became less and less familiar with the written Hebrew of their forefathers over the years. Some families were no longer able to read and understand any of it.

Instead of trying to understand what these Hebrew writings of Moses and the Prophets were saying, many of the younger Jews began to lose all interest in their sacred Scriptures still used by the educated teachers and ordained rabbis at their religious services.

Indeed, there were probably very few times in history that the writings God caused to be written about Creation, the Flood, and the coming of a world Savior came this close to being lost forever. There couldn't have been very many copies of the Hebrew Scriptures still existing from pre-captivity days. The few that were still around could be read and understood by only a few educated scribes.

Would enough of the younger generation learn the Old Hebrew as those of the older generations died off? What would happen to the prophecies that a Jewish King will come from the family of Abraham and

King David? The Bible stories of an all-powerful God creating the heavens and the earth were in danger of becoming replaced completely by pagan myths.

THEN SOMETHING TOTALLY UNEXPECTED HAPPENED. Something caused this King Ptolemy II to become more curious than ever to find out what the few old existing Hebrew writings were all about. The sacred writings that his Jewish subjects were using—writings that he could not read—interested this pagan king. He just had to know more about them. A Jewish tradition which cannot be verified for truth says that he was so eager for a copy of the Jewish Scriptures that he exchanged 100,000 captives of war for one set of scrolls.

Ptolemy felt that these ancient Hebrew writings of the Jewish people should be translated into a language that could be understood by more than just the few people around who were able to read in the Old Hebrew. At that time, Old Hebrew was a dying language because very few people were using it as their everyday speech anymore. The Jewish people who used Aramaic in their families and with each other, had by this time accepted the so-called worldly Greek. This was the language they used when writing to each other or in their visiting with their non-Jewish neighbors.

Translating God's sacred Word into another language was something that had never before been done. It was unheard of to write down God's sacred Word in another language, especially a secular or non-religious language like the Greek.

Up to this time the Jewish people had always considered their Old Hebrew language "too holy to be tampered with in this way." One ancient writer who protested against any translating being done said that what was expressed in the Hebrew language could never have the same force if it were ever to be translated into another language. He was adamant that the Scriptures should always be left to standing exactly as they were written.

It is evident that if everyone had been like him, all of us to this day would need to thoroughly learn the Hebrew language to read the Old Testament. We would need to spend many hundreds of hours taking college level courses to learn what God's Word really is saying to us.

Here a choice had to be made. If translating of the Scriptures were forbidden by religious law, everyone on up to our time would either need to learn the original languages of the Bible or be underprivileged and denied knowing what the Scriptures were saying.

Were it not for the translating done in the past, most of us would never find out about the great truths found in God's Word. At the best, only the highly educated would be able to explain it to us.

BY THE ORDER OF PTOLEMY II, HIS SCHOLARS TRANSLATED the Jewish Bible, which is now our Old Testament, into the Greek language. This work, called the Septuagint, was made about 250 years before Jesus was born on earth. This was the very first translation ever made of the sacred Scriptures from its original Hebrew into another language.

Before this, only those who knew Hebrew were able to read of the Creation and the Great Flood as written by Moses. The stories of Jewish history and the prophecies of a Savior were like a closed book to all people except the Jews who had earlier been well versed in the Hebrew language.

It is indeed ironic that a pagan Egyptian king should have commanded a work like this to be done. All we can say is that God surely knew what He was doing when He prompted such an unexpected urge into the thinking of a heathen king.

Most of the stories about translating these writings from Hebrew to Greek tell that Ptolemy brought in from Jerusalem, about 300 miles away, seventy-two learned Jews; six from each of the twelve tribes of Israel. These men did the work of translating in seventy-two days.

This Greek Septuagint translation of the Old Testament is often referred to by the Roman numerals for seventy, or as the LXX Version. In the Septuagint, the translators dropped many of the Hebrew names given to the books of the Old Testament and replaced them with names that had meaning in the Greek language.

Many of these names exist in our Bible to this day. The Hebrew names are all but forgotten. For example, the Hebrew name for the first book in the Bible, B'resheet, was given the Greek name of Genesis—"The Book of Beginnings." Many other books, such as Exodus, Leviticus, Numbers, and Deuteronomy, are names with Greek meanings that have stuck and are still being used in our times.

WHEN THE WORK WAS FINISHED, this collection of ancient Jewish writings on laws, hymns, and history gathered together as one book was read to the king. He was delighted and astonished at the depth of wisdom in the old Jewish writings.

The Septuagint was copied and recopied many, many times. The use of this translation of our Old Testament was to spread to the entire known world wherever the Jewish people established new colonies.

This new Greek version soon came to the attention of the orthodox Jews who had been bitterly opposed to any changes whatsoever being made in their religious practices and had resisted the work of translating their sacred writings. These Jews believed in using only the Old Hebrew in divine worship in their temple and synagogues.

They were sure the wrath of God would be vented upon those translators who dared to tamper with God's Holy Word. They were dead set against accepting any language except the Old Hebrew in their worship of God. Therefore, they kept the controversy raging against adopting the more commonly used Greek. No other language except what their forefathers had used would be good and holy enough.

Didn't God Himself speak the Hebrew language when He spoke to Adam and Eve in the Garden of Eden?

Nevertheless, all this opposition could not keep this Greek-language Jewish Bible from widespread use by Jewish people who had gradually lost all, or nearly all, of the use of the Old Hebrew as an everyday language in their homes. The Septuagint was welcomed by those Jewish families in which the decline in using the Old Hebrew had started when they had been slaves in Babylonia several generations earlier.

THIS TRANSLATION ALSO MADE the Jewish religious writings more easily available to non-Jewish people who were interested in the religious creed of their Jewish neighbors. These writings on how the world and the first human beings were created, the history of the Jewish people, and Bible stories that are so interesting and familiar to us, were read by thousands of people who weren't able to do so before this Greek translation became widely available.

It also appears that a number of Greeks, Egyptians, Romans, and people of other nations were impressed by the high moral standards of the Jews and their belief in one true God.

It seems many of these people were tired of the made-up myths and untrue legends that told of the many gods and goddesses warring with each other. These were deities of unpredictable actions, with sudden whims and impulses of anger. What could be divine in gods who overpowered and killed one another?

Here in the Jewish writings was something solid. Here was something with truth. Many people came to realize how stupid it was to bow down to man-made images of gods and to believe the myths were events that actually happened.

The Septuagint made it possible for non-Jews to read about the Jewish faith, which had the ring of truth. This was not myth and legend. Here were writings about the beliefs of the first humans created by God before the true faith was diluted and replaced by the false religions invented by tribes and families who had lost their belief in the true God.

Now they read about the blessings that God gives to all who live holy and upright lives. They learned of the curses God had for evil and wicked living.

The prophecies of a Savior of the world might never have been as widely known by Jews and many non-Jews if this easy-to-read Greek Septuagint had not existed.

This promise of a Savior coming to earth, then understood as being a powerful earthly King, was welcome news to many people living under oppressive governments. It gave them something good to long for. Sometime in the near future, a Messiah (the Greek word for a liberator of the downtrodden) would appear and the hopelessness of slavery would end.

He would bring freedom with Him. With His power He would set up a kingdom that would crush the might of all other nations. After having them punished for having oppressed God's people, all the earth would again live in a glorious peace.

An everlasting Jewish kingdom with all its enemies trodden underfoot! Wouldn't that be something to look forward to!

THE WIDESPREAD USE of this easy-to-read Greek Septuagint probably helped to pave the way for the rapid spread of Christianity throughout the world of the Roman Empire several hundred years later when the Apostles of Jesus, scattered by persecution, were to take the Good News of Jesus Christ with them.

What they were saying, and what they would write about the Prince of Peace was credible and believable. They had actually been there with Him when it had all happened.

It is not hard to understand why Christianity spread like wildfire, especially among the Gentiles, or the non-Jews, of the first century. This was so different from what they had learned in childhood of the gods of violence and war. Here was a religion reassuring to the mind and the spirit. Here was a creed and a faith they could accept. Here was a religion of both inward and outward peace.

Only after Christ lived on earth did they come to understand that the kingdom of Jesus Christ was not of the world, but of the Spirit. They realized then that the prophets of the Old Testament were not talking about the establishment of a permanent government here, in a world that before Christ had known nothing but the eventual decay of all the kingdoms that had ever existed. Enough is said when we note here that the prophets were talking about something much more eternal than the coming and going of kingdoms of the world!

The glories of every one of the ancient empires—Egypt, Assyria, Babylonia, Persia, and dozens of others had by that time all faded into oblivion.

The Great Library at Alexandria

THE HUGE LIBRARY ALONGSIDE THE MEDITERRANEAN SEA at Alexandria is no longer there at the present day.

It is a long story. During the time that the Roman Empire was rapidly expanding its borders from a small insignificant nation that had grown from a country village called Rome to an empire of two million square miles, the Roman emperors cast covetous eyes upon the rich land of Egypt.

In the last century before the birth of Christ, Cleopatra, a princess of the Ptolemy dynasty who had become a queen, ruled Egypt. She lived from 69 B.C. to 30 B.C. and was the last of the family of Ptolemy pharaohs that ruled Egypt for about 300 years.

A clever and ambitious politician, Cleopatra kept the Roman emperors and their armies at bay with her wiles and trickery until the time of the emperor Julius Caesar. He invaded Egypt, and doing better than his predecessors, reduced it to a province of the Roman Empire by becoming friendly with Cleopatra and making her his queen.

But wealth and power did not satisfy. Cleopatra is said to have ended her own life by holding an asp, a small, very poisonous snake, against her body until she received a deadly bite.

In the year 47 B.C., during one of the battles in this series of wars, the Roman soldiers were ordered to throw lighted torches soaked with pitch on the sixty enemy ships coming in to besiege the city of Alexandria. The windy night did not long remain dark. The night sky soon glowed red from the conflagration that followed. The destructive fire burned and sank many of the ships. The wind spread the catastrophic fire that then destroyed the naval yards and buildings on the shore.

It swept to the complex of buildings housing the Alexandrian library and destroyed most of it. Many of the ancient writings perished and were forever lost due to the folly of man's destruction in war.

This fire in this ancient library was one of the greatest setbacks suffered in the history of scholarship. It will never be known how much knowledge of the ancient world went up in flames and is now forever lost. This partial destruction of written records was a loss that cannot be measured, because no one can say what knowledge of the ancient world would still exist if all the books the library contained could still be read. However, the Septuagint had often enough been recopied, and thus it survived and escaped becoming extinct.

Later the library was partly rebuilt. It was again used for several hundred years afterward as a center for book study.

There are several conflicting accounts as to what happened at the Alexandrian library by the time history had moved several hundred years into the Christian era. It seems neither the Christians nor the Muslims wanted to take the blame for the demise of such an important historical legacy that had been passed down from antiquity.

Some of the historical accounts of the library are sure that many of the books were taken away and destroyed by a group of Alexandrian citizens converted to Christianity who were concerned about the influence of the works of some ancient pagan authors on the Christian church. They had come to the conclusion that all ancient knowledge was pagan and sinful. They set out to eliminate anything that was not Holy Scripture. In their ardent zeal, they are said to have destroyed especially the scrolls written in Egyptian hieroglyphs, which not a single person in those days could read anyway. They believed these books had some great secret knowledge of occult and satanic powers.

For the other side of the story, we will have to fast-forward to the time when an Arabian prophet named Mohammed (570 – 632 A.D.) founded the Islamic or Muslim religion. The Koran, containing the revelation they believe that Allah gave to Mohammed, is the Bible of the Muslim people.

The Arabian tribes, most of them being descendants of Ishmael and Esau, united in spreading their Muslim religion by the use of the sword. They conquered many lands, with the people being left to live only if they would accept the Islamic faith.

In 640 A.D., the Muslims captured the city of Alexandria in Egypt after having besieged it for fourteen months.

One account says that the question was put to the new Muslim ruler of the city as to what should be done with the no less than 400,000 scrolls still existing in the library of the captured city. He was begged not to destroy the valuable books. He said he needed time to think over the question.

When they came back for an answer, he said he came to the conclusion that any books in the library agreeing with their Muslim Bible, the Koran, would not be needed. They had their holy book, the Koran, and that was already more than sufficient. He gave orders that all such books should be destroyed.

As to the books that did not agree with the Koran, it was clear that they were harmful and should also not be kept, so he ruled that the whole library of books was to be destroyed. To comply with his wishes, every one of the scrolls, except for a few which were somehow salvaged, were distributed as fuel for heating the water in the hundreds of public baths throughout the city. Six months later, the great library was completely obliterated. The famous library of Alexandria was then no more.

Translating the Bible

THE SEPTUAGINT, RATHER THAN THE Jewish Hebrew Bible was the translation used by Jesus' disciples and the early Jewish Christians.

The God-inspired writers of the books of what is now our New Testament did not do their writing in the Old Hebrew of their religious services, nor in the Aramaic they used in everyday speech, but in the Greek language used in the universal commerce of those days.

In virtually every instance—over eighty in all—where the four Gospel writers, Matthew, Mark, Luke, and John wrote of the words of Jesus when He referred to the Scriptures, they would translate His quotes from the Greek Septuagint. When the writers of the Epistles, or letters to the young Christian churches, quoted a passage from what is now our Old Testament, they would lift the Greek words from the Septuagint.

When they were prayerfully writing what is now our beloved New Testament in its original Greek language, they may well have had a copy of the Greek language Septuagint by their side. Because Jesus and His disciples accepted a translated Bible, it can also be right for us to read and compare how different translators bring out Bible meanings.

Other Jewish religious writings from "the 400 silent years" were placed alongside of the Septuagint. The New Testament writers never quoted any of these books as Scripture. However, the so-called Early Church Fathers freely quoted from these books, now called the Apocrypha, and many Christian churches in our day include them in their Bibles.

The first complete Christian Holy Bible, a combination of the Old and New Testaments, came into being when the Greek Septuagint was joined with the four Gospels and the apostolic letters to the churches, also all written in Greek.

Thanks be to God that Bible translating did not end with the Greek language Bible. It has been estimated that only one out of every 2,000 people in the world know Greek, so the Bible would be a virtually unknown book.

IN BIBLE TRANSLATING done in many hundreds of other languages by Bible scholars down through the centuries, the Greek Septuagint, even more than the original Hebrew, was often the source of a large part of their work in translating the Old Testament. In other words, this work was proved accurate enough that they could use this translation to make other translations.

Martin Luther, who worked on the translation of the German Bible most plain people use in their homes and churches, knew the Hebrew language very well, but he relied heavily on the Greek Septuagint.

An English translation of the Septuagint used by serious students of the Bible text was published in the 1800s. Its writing closely follows the text as we know it in the King James Version. However, some of the chapter numbers, which were not included in the original version, written 2,250 years ago, do vary at some places. For one example, our well-known 23rd Psalm is Psalm XXII (22) in the Septuagint.

There are some interesting differences in the text. For example, the first verse in this Shepherd Psalm starts out, "The Lord tends me as a Shepherd, and I shall want nothing." The chapter ends with, "and my dwelling shall be in the houses of the Lord for a very long time."

Translating proves that the same thoughts can be expressed in different languages and even in different words in the same language. It seems that biased or careless translations made by those who were not really conscientious and responsible are never fully accepted. This may be God's method of sorting out the worthy from the unworthy. God is watching over what is being done with His Word. He never permits it to become extinct.

Anyone who translates must be careful not to change any meanings. Different translations often bring new insights and understanding to some of the Bible verses we know so well, but are no longer really thinking deeply about what they mean.

The fulfillment of prophecy in the Bible is written not only to tell us that all evil will be judged. It may be there to give all believers the sure hope that God and what is good will triumph in the end.

May God's Holy Spirit, which was the source of inspiration for the Bible writers, and which we believe has helped all conscientious Bible translators since then use good judgment, also help us as we strive to make what the Bible is teaching be part and parcel of our lives!

The only translation of the Bible ever read by many people may be what they see translated into the lives of the Christian people they know.

WINTERTHUR GARDENS

The teaching of Jesus made clear that thinking on the finery of our clothing is not all that important—"And why take ye thought for raiment? Consider the lilies of the field, how they grow; they toil not, neither do they spin. And yet I say unto you, that even Solomon in all his glory was not arrayed like one of these" (Matthew 6:28-29).

Chapter 14

Never Before or After a Life Lived Like This

THE BEGINNINGS OF THE HISTORY of our Christian churches go back to the story of a life lived here on earth about two thousand years ago.

We all know the story well. We hear it at our Communion services and often in between. In fact, we may hear it so often that we may sometimes feel it is no longer interesting; but nevertheless, the life of Jesus Christ, written in the Gospels of Matthew, Mark, Luke, and John, is the greatest story ever told.

If we use a three-generation per century average, it was only sixty generations ago that God used the greatest earthly power at that time, the Roman Empire, to unwittingly bring about the birth of Jesus in the little town of Bethlehem in Judea; at exactly where, 700 years earlier, it had been prophesied it would take place.

There was a short period of peace all over the world at the time Jesus, the Prince of Peace, was born. This is something very rare, because nearly always, before or since, people have been hatefully warring against each other somewhere in the world.

However, this was only a worldly peace. It was a peace due only to the fact that people all over feared the powerful Roman legions, the armies that overran virtually all of the world known of at that time. They kept peace by brute force, a peace that can never last.

This was not the true peace that Jesus brought when He came to earth, the peace that overflows into the inner recesses of the human heart. That is where true peace finds its home and there spreads from one person to another.

A ruling made by the Caesar of the Roman Empire who had been crowned "king of the world" in the year 27 B.C. indirectly brought about the birth of Jesus in a small Bethlehem stable. This man, at the pinnacle of worldly success, was named Caesar Augustus, a name meaning, "The King Majestic." Our eighth month, August, is named for this man.

Without realizing he was fulfilling divine prophecy, the man that the Roman citizens would always address as "The Divine Augustus" issued a decree that everyone in the world should be counted and taxed (Luke 2:1), then he would know exactly how many million people he was ruling. He thought the over two million square miles of his Roman Empire was the whole world. God knew it was not, and the Bible does not say it was. These were only the words of his proclamation.

In obeying the Caesar's decree, Joseph and Mary "happened to be" at Bethlehem instead of at their hometown of Nazareth when Jesus was born. We don't know if Joseph had registered their names and paid their tax as soon as they came to Bethlehem the day before, or if he did this later after Jesus was born. We have no way of knowing, therefore, whether or not the little baby Jesus was included in this count of all the citizens of the Roman Empire.

It would be interesting if these census books would be dug up at some time by archaeologists, to see if we would find the name of the little baby Jesus included. However, very few areas of the earth, except locations such as Egypt and the Dead Sea area, are dry enough the year round to preserve papyrus manuscripts for any length of time. Wars and wartime destruction of the records of antiquity left scholars with only here and there some stone tablets or pagan temple wall carvings to study.

The humble birth of Jesus came unnoticed by the Romans and by the Jewish religious authorities in Jerusalem. He was not born in the palace of a king, the way most everybody thought the promised Savior would enter the world. His humble place of birth was in a stable among the animals. He could have come fully formed and grown up, but He did not. Jesus was a descendant of Adam and Eve, and He wanted to be clothed in a human form during His time of ministry here on earth. If He bypassed the way of being born of a human mother, he would not have shared in our humanity. He could then not have been a human, born as a descendant of our first parents, as had been prophesied.

All humans have a father and a mother. The skeptics of our day say the virgin birth of Jesus is a "biological impossibility," but we know God was the Father of Jesus and Mary was His mother.

It is indeed amazing that God's way of sending His Son as the Savior into the world was through becoming a part of human flesh and blood; through a mother's love, in a human family.

A group of shepherds were watching over their sheep that night on a hillside outside of Bethlehem. Suddenly, a light as bright as day shone upon them. They were told of the birth of a Savior and they heard a host of heavenly angels praising God. The angels sang the well-known words we often hear and read about over the Christmas season. There could be no shorter, yet all-including, words to describe Christianity—"Glory to God in the highest, and on earth peace, good will toward men" (Luke 2:14).

Anything ever said or done on earth that meets the high standards of these words gives us an idea what the Christianity of Jesus Christ really is like.

JESUS GREW UP. THE CARPENTER BECAME A TEACHER who seemed to say and do the right thing at the right time. All humans at some time or other contradict themselves. But Jesus never did, and He was unworried about popularity. Most of us learn by making a mistake. Jesus didn't need to.

He grew up in a small town in Galilee called Nazareth, a town so unimportant that unlike many other cities and towns, it had no wall of defense built around it.

The evil enemy of God must have seen that he'd better set out some bait to bring around the downfall of the humanity of Jesus. About thirty years earlier he had failed in his evil plan to get the little baby Jesus murdered by King Herod's soldiers. This plan was foiled when Joseph, the legal father of Jesus, who has none of his spoken words recorded in the Scriptures, left just in the nick of time with the child and Mary the mother for safety in the land of Egypt.

What an inspiring thought that one man doing his duty as the head of a family saved God's plan of salvation for us from being defeated.

When the devil successfully tempted Eve to sin, he met her in the form of a serpent. To tempt Jesus he did not want or need a serpent representing him. He came in person.

He tried all three of the categories under which all sin, or the abuse of good, probably could be classified—appetite and desire, prestige and renown, and power and wealth.

If Jesus had yielded to the devil's temptations and sinned, He would be useless as the Savior for the sins of humanity. The devil's victory would make Jesus unfit to be the ruler of God's kingdom. In the same way, if we don't repent of the sins we have been led into, the devil wins and we are made unfit to claim an inheritance in God's kingdom.

Jesus walked the dusty roads of Galilee and Judea, teaching and doing miracles as He went. He wanted His work to be continued through other people, so He picked out twelve men as His disciples, no two of which had similar personalities.

He preached in houses, in synagogues, on the hillsides, and on the seashore. With the utter simplicity of His message, He was certainly not out for making a name of Himself. He spoke with His own authority. Moses and the Old Testament prophets would often say, "Thus saith the Lord." Jesus often said, "Verily, verily, I say unto you." He spoke such words of life as never had been spoken before.

He taught about the new birth. This is when something so totally different happens in a person's life in which God, not self, is the master. This life-changing experience does not mean that a person will be able to resist any and all temptations in the future, but we now know we have a source of divine help with a power far beyond what we ourselves have. It will not make an instant saint out of a sinner, but it is a brand new lease on life. It is the beginning of a new nature taking over and God, not self, is now in charge. God is now king over our actions. We will start thinking what is good for us in the long run instead of dwelling only in our own wants and desires.

The new birth does not bring instant maturity with it. It is the moment the cracking open of a hard and dry seed releases a growing sprout that, if nourished and taken care of, will increase and yield a harvest that God can use in His Kingdom. However, the birth of the Spirit of Jesus in a human heart is like the birth of Jesus at Bethlehem. There will always be an evil Herod who will want to kill it.

Jesus, in His Sermon on the Mount, brought a new and different message, which the people knew came from God. Although these three chapters in Matthew 5, 6, and 7 do not directly mention the new birth, this sermon tells us how to make a change for the better in any human relationship. It is a blueprint for following Christ.

Jesus also taught non revenge for the evil others do to us. If you get slapped on one cheek you are also to offer to be slapped on the other. This is a proven way to make respect increase and to make the sum total of hatred less.

His easily understood teachings impressed many of His hearers, especially the common people. He had no wealth, and was a man with no vice and sinful actions. He gently expressed, in simple language, the love of God for all men. He taught of goodwill among all relationships and practiced it Himself. No one before this had ever talked with such authority about both the Heaven or hell in the life after this.

Jesus taught forgiveness, no matter how much evil others do to you. He later demonstrated it while going through the intense suffering His enemies were putting Him through at His crucifixion.

He never demonstrated personal repentance, apology, and restitution for the simple reason He never needed to. But He taught us the importance of asking those we have wronged what we need to do to make things right before we make our offerings to God, so that God can accept them (Genesis 4:5 and Matthew 5:23 and 24). Jesus could have made a fortune with His miraculous power of healing sick and diseased people. Yet, unbelievably, only one place in the Gospels are we told that someone who was healed came back to thank Him for His merciful healing (Luke 17:11-19).

Jesus could also have been an able lawyer, but He wasn't interested (Luke 12:13 and 14). With His compelling arguments, He could have led the Jewish nation to independence and worldly glory, but He never had any ambitions to take over the government and rescue His fellow countrymen from the foreign power of Rome. The common people saw Jesus as a gifted teacher powerful enough to lead the Jewish people in throwing off the hated yoke of Rome.

It was hard for them to understand why He had a complete absence of the trait all humans have for ambition and power. At one time the people, probably thinking that a king keeping a free health clinic and giving out free lunches would be worth having, were ready to make Him their king by force, but He slipped away (John 6:15). They had yet to learn that Jesus was not a political Messiah, but a spiritual one.

It is also ironic that Jesus, about whom over 60,000 books have been written over the last hundred years, never wrote a single document or manuscript. In fact, the Library of Congress at Washington, D.C., the largest library in the world, has more books about Jesus in its index than about any other person.

This is the very opposite of what could be expected of Jesus' sayings as recorded in the four Gospels. By not going over any of it twice, it is said all the recorded words of Jesus can be read in eleven minutes.

One of Jesus' disciples closed his Gospel with the remark that if every one of the things that Jesus did should be written about, the world itself could not contain the books. He may have meant that the world would not receive and accept them anyway (John 21:25).

ALTHOUGH JESUS USED HIS miraculous power to heal the bodies of diseased people, His greatest miracles were the changing of people's minds—the changing of unsound thoughts and faulty thinking of sinful people. .

The prosperous, greedy Zacchaeus probably had a shady background of dishonest and illegal dealings. When Jesus came to his home, he became a changed man who gave half of his money to charity. He hadn't forgotten the cheating he had done, and gave back four times the monies he had taken by fraud (Luke 19:1-10). The woman caught in the act of adultery was forgiven when she was still too crushed in spirit to even ask for mercy, and given a chance to begin a new and cleansed life (John 8:1-11). Mary Magdalene, healed of the damage that seven of Satan's demons had done to her, experienced something that was nothing less than being born into a new life. She was a brand new person with a healed past (Mark 16:9 and Luke 8:2).

Jesus always forgave those who were sincerely repentant of their past sins. The contrite adulteress, who, in her shame, had not even been able yet to ask for pardon, is one example. We can be sure that when she felt Jesus was not condemning her, she made a resolve to go home and ask forgiveness of her husband and family. She would then be ready to make use of the unspoiled page she had been given. She now knew there was surely a better way to live than to continually be adding one sin upon another. Just because her life up to then had been wasted, did not mean that it was impossible to change and use what she had left of life for God's glory.

HOWEVER, NOT EVERYONE GLADLY HEARD the message of peace, love, forgiveness, and the new birth that Jesus brought.

One of the groups that started becoming hostile to Jesus was the joyless Pharisees. They were the professional holy men of that day who probably believed God would pick out a Messiah from their group. As is human nature, they thought that whenever sinners were mentioned, it always meant other people. They imagined they excelled all other people in their righteousness, and were quick to flash anger at anyone who did not think of them as being someone of importance. Floating on the praise they got from other people, they were pleased and impressed with themselves, never giving it a thought that they might be the ones on the wrong and sinful side.

The Pharisees wanted the people to think they always did more than their duty to God, and thus they considered themselves more in God's favor than were other people.

They were very inflexible and determined to keep Judaism and the keeping of Jewish traditions and customs in what, to their way of thinking, was the purest form possible. They were very strict with other people, and over the years they had added hundreds of extra rules to the Law of Moses until their code of regulations became a clutter that was ready to fall of its own weight. No one could keep track of all the standards they used to judge others.

Jesus did not spare words and was quite blunt and harsh on anyone who tried to put up a good front and was not inside what he pretended to be on the outside. He was not afraid to expose the hypocrisy of the Pharisees and tell them the truth about themselves.

In Matthew, Chapter 23, we read of a time when, after first speaking to a multitude of people on the love the Pharisees had for high positions and their false appearance of Godliness, Jesus dared to tell them the enormous amount of damage they were doing to God's cause of righteousness with their pretense of virtue.

This chapter is often misunderstood as a tirade of divine wrath and a harsh damnation of the Pharisees, but it was not. Jesus was using His temper instead of losing it. He was in total control of His indignation.

Many have taken it as the shouting of a very angry Jesus spitting hateful venom on the Jewish hypocrites. We know anger provokes and begets still more anger, and had Jesus done so, it could be reasoned that the anger of the Pharisees toward Jesus could be somewhat justified.

It is true, Jesus spared them not, and was quite blunt about the evils of false pretense, which is one of the greatest single reasons people strongly dislike and avoid a religious group in which they might otherwise feel at home. A false front put up by any of its members will make worshiping with them a negative experience, so we can understand why Jesus denounced them when they pretended to be what they were not.

People who say they are Christian, but are not living it out, and are not making efforts to make it a part and parcel of their lives, are doing more damage to the Kingdom of Christ than skeptics and atheists who are speaking against it.

If we look deeper into this chapter we can see that Jesus was exposing one of the most subtle of all sins—that of becoming self-righteous. This is the one bait that the enemy of our souls has left for those who think they are successfully resisting all temptations that are being dangled before them. This makes us, with our fallen inner natures, too proud and unwilling to admit we are far from perfect. This was keeping them and those around them from coming under the loving protection He was longing to give to them.

The Hebrew word "howy" and the Greek word "ousi," translated in our Bibles as "woe," never once means damning or condemnation. It means acute sorrow, feelings of sadness, and deep regret. It means to lament or grieve, very much as the exclamation of the word "alas." Jesus was feeling a deep grief for the self-righteousness and the blind and false ways that kept them from repentance. This thought is reinforced at the ending of the chapter when He wept and sorrowed over the unrepentant city of Jerusalem. Using the beautiful illustration of a mother hen desiring to care for her little chicks under her wings, He foretold the destruction coming upon them because they refused to come under the protection and safety only He could give.

Another group starting to sit up and take notice of Jesus were the temple priests and scribes, the religious authorities at the time of Jesus. They were angry when Jesus cleansed the temple of its commercialism. This kept them from making big money from the worshipers. To Jesus, God's temple was no place for profiteers to make money off the people.

When they saw His influence on the common people become too big to be ignored, it caused a widespread alarm among them. They did not like to see Him becoming a religious celebrity and hear of Him being liked by so many of the ordinary people. They started to seethe with the demons of envy at His simple genius that was touching the hearts of the multitudes; something they were not able to do.

It has been rightly said that envy, or being covetous, is the meanest feeling a person can have. It is the overwhelming desire to have everyone else as unsuccessful as you are. The jealousy, given a home in their hearts, became a raw hatred.

In their hostility to Him, they said the worst thing they could think up about Jesus: that He was possessed of the devil and that His power came from being in league with him. Trying to scandalize Jesus by smearing Him with a made-up bad reputation, His enemies said it was easy enough to explain His miracles; Jesus did them by the power of evil demons.

The teachings of Jesus polarized His listeners in one way or the other. When Jesus became angry, His words were not like those of a self-righteous preacher losing his temper because of an opinion clash. Even when He seemed harsh, Jesus was teaching and instructing men and women to behave in ways more pleasing to God.

Was Jesus a fascinating personality who had the answers to human problems, or was He one to be silenced, by fair means or foul? His threat to the authority that they believed was divinely given to them , and to them alone, made them decide He must be destroyed.

History of Judea around the Time of Jesus

THE POWERFUL ROMANS HAD CONQUERED the countries of Judea and Galilee nearly a hundred years before the time of Jesus. The Jewish people were not massacred or taken out of their homeland as slaves in the way that the Assyrians and Babylonians had done when they conquered a country. The Romans handled things differently. In the terms of the peace at the end of the war, it was understood and agreed that the Jews were to pay a heavy tax to the Romans, but the Romans were not to meddle with the Jewish practice of their religion as long as nothing interfered with the Roman law.

The executive power was taken from them and given to a Roman governor appointed by the Caesar. This governor at the time of Jesus was a man named Pontius Pilate.

Because for a long time no ancient Roman records of anyone being a governor of Judea with such a name had been found anywhere except in the Bible, many unbelievers were sure that the Scriptures were in error that a man with such a name had even existed.

To an unbeliever, it only helped prove that the stories about Jesus were made up by a bunch of fanatics wanting to start a new religion.

But in 1961, a stone was unearthed in Caesarea with three-inch lettering about Pontius Pilate, the governor of Judea. Later finds verified that Pilate was the Roman governor from about 26 to 36 A.D., not by election but by the appointment of the emperor in far-off Rome. Archaeology again helped to cinch and verify Bible truth.

The spade of the archaeologist has confirmed many other Bible passages formerly rejected by prejudiced critics. And many other carefully researched archaeological discoveries prove that the customs of that day were exactly as the Bible tells us they were. As far as is known, there has been no archaeological discovery made yet which upsets a statement made in the Bible.

The writings of the first-century Jewish historian, Flavius Josephus, also agree with the Bible that a man by the name of Caiaphas was the high priest in the Jewish temple at that time, having taken the place of his father-in-law, Annas, who was still a powerful figure behind the scenes.

The ruler of the country north of Judea, called Galilee, was King Herod, just as the Gospel writers say (Luke 3:1).

This Herod was not the same Herod who killed the innocents at Bethlehem (Matthew 2), but was the king who ordered the deaths of John the Baptist (Matthew 14 and Mark 6) and James, the first martyred apostle. This Herod died soon afterwards (Acts 12).

Although the small country of Judea was only like a back yard to the far-flung Roman Empire of thirty provinces and an area about three-fourths as large as the continental United States, the Jews living there proved to be a hard people for the Romans to handle.

The Jews hated these Roman foreigners who occupied and policed the land they felt they were entitled to by the blessings God had given to their forefather Abraham. Because the Jews were kept drained by excessive tax demands by the Romans who lived luxuriously, the Jewish people held a sullen anger at their oppressors, especially when they saw Roman soldiers marching throughout the land to show off their might and to make sure no one would forget who was in charge.

All this led to the forming of a radical Jewish group called the Zealots. They dedicated their lives to overthrowing the Romans by force and bloodshed if necessary. They were constantly starting riots against their conquerors, though they knew it often meant death to some of their numbers.

The Romans were constantly hunting down these rebels. Anybody found plotting an insurrection or revolt was taken care of and suppressed in a swift and ruthless way. Any rebellion breaking out against Rome was taken seriously and crushed without mercy.

What could settle down an unruly crowd more than crucifying several of their leaders along a well-traveled road just outside of the city gates? No public warning would strike an onlooker with more fear, or be more effective against planning rebellion than a display of the inhuman torture of crucifixion.

Crucifixion was one of the slowest and most brutal forms of execution ever invented. In some places, a sword or a blazing firebrand was used to execute criminals. Here, only a hammer and a few long nails were the instruments needed.

The excruciating muscle cramps, along with the body weight tearing at the gashes ripping through the hands and feet where the nails had been driven into a cross, made crucifixion one of the most torturous deaths known.

There was nothing left for a crucifixion victim to do until death came but to writhe in agony, shout hateful curses, or spit at his tormentors, none of which helped to ease the terrible pain he was suffering. The hapless Zealot victims were stripped of all their clothing except for a loincloth. The hardened Roman soldiers knew their victims would try to spit into their faces or do anything else to irritate and irk them while they were setting up the cross before plunking the lower end into a hole dug into the ground.

THE PRESENCE OF THE ROMANS IN JUDEA did not stop rebellion, and it did not keep the Jewish people from celebrating the yearly Passover. During the Passover week, the approximately 36 acres (985 ft. by 1,575 ft.) of courtyard surrounding the temple building was alive with people and the animals they brought to be sacrificed by the priests. Most of these animals were bought from livestock dealers right on the temple grounds. This was easier than bringing them along from the far-off countries many of them came from. To do all this dealing, they also needed to get their foreign coins, minted with the very objectionable likenesses of a their emperor, changed into Jewish coins. To them, these coins were nothing less than idols or graven images, not to be used at temple offerings.

Each family sacrificed one unblemished lamb as a symbol of the perfect sacrifice prophesied that would someday be offered as a pardon and release from their sins.

These sacrifices were made as a substitute death. They knew their God of justice could demand the life of anyone who had done something considered a sinful act since last year's Passover. They knew God's forgiveness would require the shedding of innocent lifeblood as a substitute for the death they themselves deserved.

During Passover week, the Jerusalem streets were choked with Jewish pilgrims pouring in from all over the known world. The city, with an estimated population of something like a hundred and fifty thousand people, was often thronged with at least three times that number. Jerusalem was especially heavy with Roman troops, whose watchful eyes were alert for any signs of trouble. They were the police, there to maintain order and to nip in the bud any revolt that might be brewing. A tight lid had to be kept on the Jews.

THE EVENTS THAT CLOSED the short 35 or 40 months of the earthly ministry of Jesus Christ happened quickly and defy a rational explanation.

It seems unbelievable that His own countrymen were the ones who came to hate Him fiercely enough to demand His execution. Although the heathen Romans, who worshiped all kinds of gods, were the ones who did the actual bloody work of crucifying Jesus, they were not the ones who instigated His death.

It was His own people, chosen by God to be a good example to other nations, who turned against Him. It was those to whom Jesus had taught God's message of love that hated Him enough to demand His death. The demons of first-degree envy and jealousy in the hearts of the self-righteous were to be the cause of the crucifixion of Jesus Christ. If the devil isn't able to tempt people into gross sins, he can always fall back into trying to get them to be righteous in their own eyes.

The temple priests and the Pharisees were blind to what they were about to do. Their forefathers had waited hundreds of years for the prophesied Savior, and now the generation to whom He came was to kill Him.

It is just as difficult to imagine how one of Jesus' own disciples betrayed Him to the authorities. For about the same amount of money he could have earned in a month's wages, he gave Jesus a false kiss that tied up and restrained the healing hands of his Lord and Master.

Several years before this, the disciple named Judas, along with eleven others, had been picked out as special helpers in the great cause of teaching people God's plan of healing and redemption, repentance and love. Judas had started out well enough. Now he was the traitor. The story would be more believable if a proud Pharisee, still licking his wounded ego, had betrayed Jesus.

JESUS AND HIS DISCIPLES ALSO came to Jerusalem at the beginning of the Passover week. As He came through the city gate riding on a young donkey that had never been ridden before, His disciples and a host of His friends strewed their garments and palm leaves on the road and shouted praises to Him and to God.

Their words were very similar to those which the angels sang above the Bethlehem hills at Jesus' birth, except for one serious thing missing: the disciples said nothing about goodwill to men.

The way Jesus reacted to this public acclaim and the desire to crown Him a king probably seemed very strange to the people around Him that day, and it surely is not the way most people on up to our day would react to such an honor.

The eyes of Jesus overflowed on His way into the city. The tears ran down His face as He wept over the unrepentant city of Jerusalem and saw in His mind the destruction and massacre He knew was coming.

ALL THIS PUBLIC APPLAUSE made the enemies of Jesus all the more determined to get rid of Him. From then on, they would be watching for a good opportunity to put Him out of the way before He left Jerusalem for His homeland in Galilee again.

But how would they go about it, and who would do it? How could Jesus be captured without making an uproar among what has been estimated to be almost a half million people in and around Jerusalem at Passover time?

This was a dangerous plan. If a mob of His supporters were roused to protect Jesus, their plans could backfire and they might well be the ones getting killed. They knew their history well enough to know that when a king or some other public figure got killed, he seemed to always have plenty of followers determined to avenge his death. That had often happened in the past. It might be healthier, they decided, for them to keep plotting behind the scenes.

At one of these scheming sessions, everything seemed to fall into place when, to their surprise, one of Jesus' own disciples opened the door and entered.

He would betray Jesus for them. If they were too afraid of the people to have Jesus captured in broad daylight, he knew Him well enough to point Him out to a squad of armed soldiers at nighttime, especially since there would be a full moon toward the end of the week. He could easily find out where Jesus was spending His nights while He was staying in Jerusalem.

What would be the amount of the reward money? A deal was made. Judas left the room with the moneybag he carried to pay the expenses for Jesus and His disciples. The moneybag was thirty pieces of silver heavier.

We don't know how many conspirators Judas met with, but if there were thirty, it cost each man only one coin. This was shrewd and clever planning by the enemies of Jesus—and easy money for Judas.

IF JUDAS HOPED JESUS WOULD ANNOUNCE to His twelve disciples the house where they would celebrate the Passover meal that evening, he was disappointed. The way Jesus planned the location, only two of His disciples knew where to set the table for the meal Jesus knew would be His last supper. Jesus must have wanted His last time with His disciples to be uninterrupted.

That evening Jesus changed the Jewish Passover to the Holy Communion, or Eucharist (Latin word for service of thankfulness). He gave it new meaning, which will last as long as the earth will endure. This first Communion service had some similarities to the first Passover. The first Passover had been held the evening before God freed the Israelites from a slavery that would have lasted until the day of their deaths. The first Christian Communion service was held the evening before God opened up a way out of a slavery that had eternal consequences.

Never before or since could anything be compared with the "Last Supper." This was the only Passover in which both the last of the old and the first of the new were celebrated.

Before the sun would set again, two of the men at the table would be dead.

What Jesus taught around the Passover table that evening completely reversed and overturned the roles of servant and master.

Of all times, and of all people, a heated discussion came up among the disciples about who among them was the greatest. Evidently the seating arrangement around the table was significant to them. Some must have felt slighted and envious; others, who felt their importance, must have made their demeaning manner quite evident to those not quite as close to Jesus. They all wanted to sit next to the Master, as if where they sat would indicate a higher or lower rank.

That evening Jesus demonstrated to His disciples a humility we all might think was beneath the dignity of the Savior of the world. He washed the dust of the road off the bare feet of His disciples.

In those days of dusty roads and bare feet, this was always done by the lowest of the servants in a household, and not one of the disciples was ready to offer to do this for the others. Jesus shamed them all by bending down and doing it Himself.

One of the glimpses we get of Heaven in the Bible is Jesus seated on a gilded throne judging all men and ruling the entire universe. Like the disciple Peter, we are not quite ready to accept the role of Jesus being a humble servant in the kingdom of Heaven, as He described it on the evening before His crucifixion. In God's kingdom, Jesus will be the servant of the people living there. Here Jesus will faithfully be a table waiter at the tables around which all the redeemed will be enjoying the food of Heaven. We will always think it should be the other way around.

In effect, Jesus told His disciples that a group of believers should not be ruled like a nation of the world, with the lordship of a great crowned king making and enforcing all the rules. "But ye shall not be so," He said (Luke 22:25 and 26).

A church is not like a construction crew that needs a foreman, or an office that needs a manager, or a large corporation honoring a chairman of the board. In a church family, all should be as servants to one another.

The meaning of leadership was now no longer to be considered to be what the world thinks it is. Over the years, since Jesus spoke these words, many splits in the Christian Church can be traced to the failure of the people to consider themselves servants of one another. Refusing to keep a Christian communication open has often led those who were considered inferior to find company elsewhere. Jesus' teachings about the power of love has been changed to the world's teachings of the love of power.

The disciples would now no longer be under a master as servants who don't know what their master is up to next. From now on, Jesus said, He would no longer call His disciples His servants. He would call them His friends (John 15:15).

The disciples did not find everything that Jesus said easy to understand. When He passed the cup and told them to "Drink ye all of it" (Matthew 26:27), He may have meant that all who were present were to take part. However, He may also have had the cup of suffering in mind (Matthew 26:42). He may have meant to drink it all until the bitter dregs at the bottom were emptied, so that He could refill their lives with meaning and joy. The Christianity that Jesus taught doesn't make life something to be constantly endured; He makes it worth living and full of little unexpected joys.

Jesus also made the shocking prediction that Peter, of all the disciples, would deny Him. What was even more incredible was that this would happen, not at some time in the years ahead, but this very night, only several hours later. Peter would deny Him three times before the rooster woke and crowed, which we all know is very early in the morning.

Jesus knew ahead of time about Peter's fall and prayed that Peter's faith would not fail him in the test that the devil was to put him through. Peter's pride would be sifted out. Jesus told Peter that not until he was truly converted would his life be a help to strengthening his brethren (Luke 22:31 and 32). Being converted in God's eyes is measured by how our examples of living help to strengthen the people around us.

Jesus also made a prediction that shocked them all except Judas, who was present with his heavier than usual moneybag. Jesus said that one of the twelve would betray Him.

It seemed none of the disciples believed a betrayer was among them, because they all said they would die with Him before they would do something like that. They were too sure of themselves to know how weak they really were.

Jesus knew Judas was so absorbed in the material things of this life that he was disappointed in His teaching that in the end the only things that really matter and are essential are things of the Spirit.

Jesus also knew Judas had already made up his mind on what he was going to do. He knew Judas was beyond reasoning with, so He didn't waste any of His time trying to talk Judas out of it. In effect, He told Judas to go and get his evil plans carried out. Judas left the room. Jesus then talked to the remaining eleven at length while they were still sitting as a family around the table. He talked about living in the world, but not becoming a part of it. He told them of the joy and peace possible in their hearts—a peace that no one on earth could ever take from them.

He talked about the importance of living at peace with each other. If only later Christians had taken this advice to heart, it would have prevented every one of the thousands of splits that have occurred within Christianity over the last two thousand years.

Before they rose to leave the table, Jesus prayed for His disciples. This prayer takes up the entire chapter of John 17, and has been an inspiration ever since to the many millions of Christians who have read it. They sang several psalms of praise to God, and left for the Garden of Gethsemane. This was a grove of olive trees outside of the city walls, perhaps like a small public park at the foot of the Mount of Olives.

Here, multiplied a thousand times and more, occurred the struggle such as we have in our lives between what our human nature wants to do and what our new nature knows it should do. Since then, no one can point his finger at God and say, "You just don't understand."

In the Garden of Eden, man's love for God was tested, and failed. Here in this garden, God's love for man was put to a supreme test, and it was triumphant.

Why was facing His death so bitter to Jesus if He knew all along that He would be rising from His tomb again? Why all this agony, and why was Jesus so hesitant to go through the portals of death when He surely knew His suffering in this world would then be ended?

Thousands upon thousands of martyrs in later years would joyfully go to their deaths for their faith. Why then did Jesus shrink so much from the thought of crucifixion, but when He later felt its pain, He did not waver?

There is probably only one reason for this. Jesus knew He would be dying like a sinner dies. He would be dying alone. He would be dying without God by His side, an awful way to leave the world. Believers in God since that time do not have to experience this, because they know the God of mercy and grace and have experienced the forgiveness of repented sins. With God's hand leading us through the valley of the shadow of death, we will need to fear no evil when our time comes for us to go (Psalm 23:4).

WITH HIS HANDS BOUND BEHIND HIS BACK, Jesus was led out of the Garden of Gethsemane. He was brought inside the city walls of Jerusalem through what was called the sheep gate. This was the same door through which the lambs for sacrificial slaughter would be brought into the city on the day just coming up. In the very early hours of the morning, before many of the people in the crowded city were awake, a mock trial was held. The temple high priest in charge of slaying the Passover lambs later in the day presided over the trial.

This high priest, the religious leader of the Jewish people, was the only human being permitted to go beyond the great veil, probably over sixty feet high, at the entrance to the Holy of Holies room in the temple.

He was the man considered as "the priest that is greater than his brethren." On the afternoon of the same day as the trial, this high priest would push the temple veil aside just far enough so that he could enter with his basin of the blood of the innocent slaughtered lambs. Behind this veil, woven to a thickness of about four inches, he would repeat the yearly ritual of the Passover. He did this before God as an atonement, or substitute death, for the sins of the people in the past year.

At this hasty nighttime trial, the high priest made it appear as if Jesus was a threat to the Jewish religion. Before beginning his religious duties of the day, he knew he had to come up with a convincing charge against Jesus worthy of a death sentence. He knew well enough he wouldn't be able to prove Jesus had taught false doctrine, or used evil sorcery to do His miracles, so he accused Jesus of blaspheming God, the most serious religious offense he could think of.

In the law of Moses which God had given to the Hebrews many centuries earlier, the crime of blaspheming God carried a sentence of death by stoning (Leviticus 24:16). In sentencing Jesus to death, the high priest unwittingly became the instrument in the slaying of the perfect Passover Lamb, the last one ever to be needed.

Although the opponents of Jesus had almost stoned Jesus several times before this, even going as far as having picked up the stones, His enemies now knew it would be best if they could somehow get the occupying Romans to do the executing for them. They knew that doing the killing themselves could get them into plenty of trouble with the Roman soldiers posted in the city to keep the peace.

Then also, many of the common people believed in Jesus because of the good works He had done. If the high priest would have given the order for everyone to help stone Jesus, the rain of stones might have come back in the priests' direction!

SO OFF TO PILATE, THE ROMAN GOVERNOR, they went with their shackled prisoner to make their proceedings legal. In Pilate's palace, not far from the temple, the chief priests and Pharisees asked Pilate to confirm and carry out the death sentence they had placed on Jesus.

In this Passover week, because of their belief that entering the house of a Gentile would make them too unclean and unworthy before God to keep the Passover in the right way, the Pharisees stayed in the courtyard in front of the palace. What they were not realizing is that they were breaking nearly every one of the Ten Commandments, which they knew were of such importance.

At this historic trial, the Judge of all Heaven and earth would be tried and judged. Because of this, Pilate is the most widely known of any Roman of olden times. The proceedings of this court trial are more widely studied by legal experts than any other in history.

Pilate, whose job was to keep law and order and administer justice for wrongdoing, reviewed the evidence and could find no fault with Jesus. His record was spotless. He sensed that Jesus was brought before him out of spite and knew Jesus was totally innocent of the charges made up against Him. The accusation that Jesus was a blasphemer of God meant nothing to this pagan Roman.

To Pilate, Jesus was no threat politically. He couldn't be dangerous. Even His followers had deserted Him. Why not let the harmless man go? In all, Pilate tried at least four times to acquit Jesus and release Him. He did everything he knew to evade the action of ordering the death of Jesus.

To satisfy the accusers of Jesus, Pilate suggested that the prisoner be soundly whipped and then released. The cruel flogging that was Roman punishment for disobedient or recaptured slaves who had run away was carried out. The lashes, administered while a prisoner was tied to a Roman whipping post, were not meant to be only a series of sharp stinging blows. The poor victim was lashed until the skin on his bare back was all cut up, and only a mass of swollen and bloody flesh was left.

After the lashing, when Jesus was again brought back, Pilate hoped to awaken pity and mercy in the hearts of the bloodthirsty mob. He himself "marveled greatly" at how Jesus did not speak up in His own defense and how bravely He carried Himself.

He placed Jesus before them and shouted, "Behold the Man!" and later, "Behold your King!" which only infuriated them all the more.

Because they were not able to accuse Jesus of a crime in Roman law upon which a sentence of death could be justly placed, Pilate again spoke up for the release of Jesus. Those pagan Romans of that time could be cruel, but they did have laws. Their laws did have a measure of justice for those who were mistreated and slandered. To keep false accusers out of their courts, the law provided that if someone brought charges against someone else, and then failed to prove it by two witnesses, the accuser was to suffer the punishment the other would have suffered had he been proven guilty.

In other words, a false accuser under Roman law would suffer the same punishment he tried to get sentenced on another.

Small wonder then that when Pilate was trying to get Jesus released, His accusers nearly went wild. They incited the crowd of people gathered to shout for His crucifixion, even though many of them did not even fully understand what was happening. They madly tried to put some blame on Jesus so that Pilate would change his mind, which made the howling of the mob for the crucifying of Jesus all the worse. In their crying of "Away with Him" they were shouting away from themselves the blessing of having Jesus with them.

These otherwise religious people didn't care anymore how false their charges were against Jesus, such as saying He was making Himself king and that He had spoken against paying the Roman tax, both of which were patently false—they were desperate that Jesus' trial was making no headway in their favor. If Jesus were released, every one of them could have been punished for being false witnesses and for starting a riot in the city.

They kept on raving for Jesus' blood until they convinced Pilate that if he released Jesus, he would be disgraced and discredited in the eyes of the Roman Caesar (John 19:12). Of course, Pilate did not want to lose the favor of this man who was his superior, because his lucrative office as the governor of Judea depended on staying on good terms with the Caesar, who had appointed him to his position of authority. Pilate also likely feared the danger of a riot with the Jews in crowded Jerusalem if he refused to do this. His soldiers would be greatly outnumbered, and he may have been afraid of losing his own life.

At His hearings, Jesus never once spoke up to correct the false accusations made against Him. He said very few words, and none to defend Himself. Jesus did ask one of the officers of the high priest who struck Him with the palm of his hand to tell Him what it was, if He had said anything evil; but if what He said was true, "Why did you smite me?" (John, Chapter 18). He got no answer.

One of His responses to Pilate's questioning only prompted Pilate to ask, "What is truth?" But to Herod, who was hoping to see Jesus do some spectacular miracle, Jesus was silent and didn't answer.

Fearful of the doom of his political success and not wanting to risk losing his high position, Pilate went against his conscience. He gave the fatal order and pronounced the ultimate penalty upon Jesus. As a victim of a gross miscarriage of justice, Jesus was to suffer the capital punishment of public crucifixion.

Although Pilate's wife, believed to be a granddaughter of the great Augustus Caesar, told her husband of a troubling dream she had that pointed to Jesus' innocence, Pilate didn't release Jesus. Politics came before justice. To make it appear as if this were not his doing, Pilate washed his hands in a basin of water before the mob of Jesus' accusers and declared himself innocent of shedding the lifeblood of Jesus.

What a way for a man in authority to administer justice! Pilate, in the greatest crime in history, though he had at least three times pronounced Jesus innocent, in the end still pronounced the death sentence on Him.

THE SENTENCE THEY WANTED was passed upon Jesus, who was still in the custody of the Roman soldiers. Why not have a little sport with Him before they crucified Him? His enemies spit into His face and plucked the hair from off His cheeks (Isaiah 50:6). They gave Him fist blows in His face and jeered and mocked Him, but Jesus silently submitted to all their cruel and rough treatment. He didn't spit back; He did not return their blows; He did not reply to their insults and taunts.

Someone then came up with a "clever" idea. If He were a king He should be wearing a crown, so a wreath woven from the branches of a thorn tree was mockingly placed on His head. They used sticks to whack the crown of thorns on His head and caused blood to run, matting His hair and streaking His face with blood.

They would have liked to see Jesus provoked to anger, but there was no such defect in His divine character. What they did not realize was that because the human Jesus had a divine nature, they could not provoke Him to anger with all their cruelties and attempts to anger Him. This silent submission to their cruelties was a sign of this divine nature. His character was unmistakable evidence. He could have immediately laid them all in the dust, but He made the choice to empty Himself of His divine nature and die defenseless. Jesus humbled Himself and became completely helpless when He could have used His divine power in an instant to save Himself.

JESUS WENT TO HIS DEATH AS A LAMB is taken for shearing or slaughtering. He did not flinch, but willingly let them do with Him what they wanted. "He saved others, but He cannot save Himself," they scoffed. Yet not one of Jesus' seven sayings on the cross shows a trace of anger or hate toward those who were causing Him such great agony and pain.

The Roman crucifixion victims were left to die in agony while the guards sat around and watched so that none of their sympathetic friends would venture to help them down and revive them before death occurred.

The Roman soldiers were permitted to divide the possessions they found on the person of their victims. Many people throughout history have died with a great wealth that proved how "successful" they were. But when Jesus, the owner of the universe died, the only assets He owned were the clothes on His back. They found no valuables and no moneybag; He had none.

Seeing that the seamless garment Jesus wore was woven as one piece, the soldiers decided to gamble for it, probably by casting dice to see which one could keep this for himself. This garment was probably the same one Jesus wore when a woman, sick for twelve years, touched it and was healed. Now it became the take-home prize for one of the burly Roman gamblers who cast their dice at the foot of the cross (Matthew, Chapter 27, Mark, Chapter 15 and John, Chapter 19).

It was the custom for the Romans to place an inscription on the top of a cross stating the crime of the victim. On the card placed on Jesus' cross, Pilate had written, "Jesus of Nazareth, the King of the Jews," in three languages: Hebrew, Greek, and Latin.

The chief priests did not like the wording. They asked Pilate to change it to "He said I am the King of the Jews." But by this time Pilate was provoked at them enough that he curtly replied, "What I have written, I have written."

It is known that whenever someone has lost a lot of blood, an insatiable thirst for water follows. He, who had made countless bubbling springs of fresh water, was thirsty in the hot sun.

To add insult to injury, instead of giving Jesus a refreshing drink of cold water, someone dipped a sponge in bitter vinegar and put it to His mouth to drink.

From twelve o'clock until Jesus died at three o'clock, a sign from Heaven that Jesus' enemies had asked of Him only a week or so before now came upon them. A strange and frightening darkness descended upon the earth. All that we have ever known is that light will pierce darkness. At this time the light that God called into existence at Creation failed as Jesus Christ was dying. Here an intense darkness pierced and extinguished the light of a bright day for three hours.

The angels who lit up the night sky when Jesus was born were absent in the dark day when He was dying.

The histories and legends of a number of heathen tribes of many lands tell of "a dark day long ago" when the land was darkened at noonday. One pagan astronomer in Egypt wrote of the strange darkness that, "Either the Deity is suffering or the mechanism of the world is tumbling into ruin." Some cried out in terror that their gods were dead.

We don't know if this darkness came over all the earth at the same time, or if it followed the noonday sun in its twenty-four-hour course around the earth. We do know this wasn't a total eclipse of the sun because none ever lasts more than several minutes, and a solar eclipse never happens at full moon, which always occurred in the week the Jewish Passover was held.

EVEN THE TERRIFYING ripping of the temple veil from top to bottom, and the fearful unexpected earthquake when Jesus died did not frighten or cause the enemies of Jesus to reflect on what they had done to Him. They saw only what they thought was important: they had finally silenced Him for good. The life of the man who had once said He was the light of the world (John 8:12) was now extinguished. The man who was so obnoxious to His enemies was now dead.

Before any of us condemn the inconsistent religion, or the hatred and envy of the Pharisees and the chief priests, and before we deplore the seeking of prestige of the worldly Pilate and the pagan Roman soldiers, we would do well to examine our own past actions. Our Creator had every right to strike us dead, but Jesus chose to die for our deliberate wrongdoings and sins, and He did not make an appeal to anyone for His unjust death. In the same way, He has the right to be silent, and always is, if we ask Him in our prayers to do something spectacular or showy for us. His mercy is everlasting!

EMMA STOLTZFUS

"...Joseph of Arimathaea...went unto Pilate and begged the body of Jesus. And he took it down and wrapped it in linen, and laid it in a sepulchre that was hewn in stone." (Luke 23).

Chapter 15

Billions of Crosses

TWO HEAVY TIMBERS ARE *hewn out of a log, probably by a sweating slave under the orders of the harsh Roman authorities occupying the land since Judea lost a war with Rome some ninety years earlier. The best way to stop crime and rebellion in the powerful Roman Empire, and in the countries it conquered, is to put to death by crucifixion anyone defying their authority. Invented several centuries earlier, crucifixion is a prolonged ordeal and the victim suffers extreme torture while dying a slow but sure death.*

SHORTLY AFTER THE SLAVE LAYS DOWN HIS ADZE, *an itinerant religious teacher of humble birth is nailed to the timbers. Early that morning at a mock trial, all justice was taken from Him. The court, rigged and fraudulently manipulated, sentenced Him to death, although false witnesses called to testify against Him didn't agree on what His crime was, and the judge repeatedly declared He had done nothing wrong.*

Ironically, the world that had no room in the inn thirty-three years earlier for the birth of Jesus now had room for Him on a brutal cross.

The hardened Roman soldiers assigned to this horrific execution by crucifixion usually worked in groups of four. They commonly got themselves half drunk, rendering themselves insensitive to feelings of sympathy or pity as they prepared to do this terrible inhumane thing to their fellow human beings.

These seasoned soldiers knew what to expect as they made the brief struggle to overpower the victim who had his hands tied behind his back. He was thrown backwards on the ground, the ropes that bound his hands were cut, and his hands and feet were positioned on the wooden cross.

The screaming, swearing victim was never a match for the three soldiers who held his flailing arms and kicking legs down while the fourth soldier hammered several blunt seven-inch-long spikes into the quivering flesh.

After the victim was securely fastened just like another framing timber and unable to do anything more than writhe in terrible pain, the soldiers heard the familiar curses shrieked at them. The victim would spit on the soldiers if they got too close, and scream the wrath of the pagan Roman gods upon their tormentors.

BUT WHAT HAPPENED AT THIS Friday morning crucifixion was different; something these unfeeling Roman soldiers would not at all be able to explain.

Strange indeed!

Not one ounce of resistance is made. There is no struggle. All is still and quiet until the hammer is heard pounding the spikes home, first through the flesh and then into the wood of the cross.

Then another sound broke the silence. They could hear the victim quietly saying something. They could hear He was praying! "Father, forgive them for they know not what they do!" Can you believe it? After what He is going through, He is asking His Father to forgive them. He is praying to His God for forgiveness for them and they didn't even realize they needed forgiveness!

Divine love—returning good for evil—leaving the revenge for an injustice up to God—blessing even those who are heaping persecution with suffering or shame upon you—forgiving those who hate you. These Roman soldiers had been brought up in a society where everyone first took care of himself. They were not used to something like this.

Jesus was doing what is always the hardest part for anybody to do, which is putting into Christian practice all that has ever been preached and written about Christianity. Only a heart with a complete absence of revenge and malice could return good for the evil that had been done to Him as this man was doing.

How different this was from what every one of us would want to do! We lose our goodwill to others at the slightest offense. The instant they do something to us that hurts a thousand times less than what they were doing to Jesus, we will bristle with anger.

Jesus must have had a divine nature that is still almost dormant in virtually every one of us! We may say we have that new divine nature born into our hearts, but like any newborn it will not last long if we don't nourish it and give it life-giving care.

THERE IS SOMETHING ELSE *here that is not right. The hands of Jesus are now restrained by the bloody nails from doing their healing touch, while the blood of Jesus flowing from His wounds to the now bloody hands of His executioners (Acts 2:23) will probably soon be washed clean again at the brook Kidron, only a short distance away.*

The last healing the hands of Jesus had done was only a few hours ago when He miraculously healed the bloody damage done by one of His sword-swinging disciples. Soon afterwards, as the knot was jerked tight to tie the healing hands of Jesus behind His back, He would feel the first of the physical pain He would endure to the end.

Something else 2,000 years later is not right. It is true you and I were not in the middle of the crowd clamoring for the death of Jesus, but for true justice to be done, it is not fair that the hands of Jesus, which had never reached out toward sin or greed, should have been shackled.

Our hands that have so often reached out in sinful doings and pulled things toward us that we would have by far been better off without, are the ones that should have been stayed and kept from moving by being nailed to a cross.

This should not have been done to the hands and feet of Jesus. Your feet and my feet should have been nailed down and restrained by our Creator who had a much more noble plan for our lives than going on our own way to places that we would have been better off not being there.

THE CROSS IS PLUNKED UPRIGHT IN A HOLE IN THE GROUND. *With His weight suspended on the nails driven through His hands and feet, Jesus will be left to die.*

Many of His followers believe He is divine, or, in other words, someone beyond human. If He is divine, surely divine and supernatural help is coming to rescue Him from death. If He is in God's favor, He will get God's help. Anybody God would send to save others would surely be able to do a miracle and save Himself.

However, what happened to Jesus was what happened to all criminals crucified by the Romans. After a time of intense agony and suffering, He died.

To make sure Jesus was dead, one of the soldiers stepped back a short ways and ran his spear into the side of Jesus. The lifeblood of Jesus, along with its clear fluid part called plasma, drained from His heart. The two streams flowed down His body and off His feet, soaking the ground around the cross.

***BY THIS TIME, MOST OF HIS DISAPPOINTED COMPANIONS** have fled the scene. Only His heartbroken mother and one of His grief-stricken disciples, who seemed to be especially close to the family, remain. The other disciples are nowhere to be seen. Filled with terror at the turn of events, they keep themselves at a great distance from the site of the crucifixion, in fear that they will be considered partners in crime. Anybody witnessing the brutality of a crucifixion would not want to be the next to get nailed up.*

Even if a man hanging on a Roman cross was your best friend, you would know enough to either join in the mockery to avoid being a suspect, or you would get out of sight as soon as you were able. By befriending or showing pity on anyone, a Roman court of law could condemn you for showing that you questioned their worldwide reputation for justice. No Roman authority would ever admit their system of justice was flawed or imperfect. Any plea for mercy would be hushed. It would fall only on deaf ears and stony hearts.

NICODEMUS AND JOSEPH OF ARIMATHAEA were men of uncommon courage. These two influential men did not concern themselves with possible danger to their reputations, or even to their lives, in doing an act of love for the Jesus they had only briefly known. They did the grisly job of taking the pierced and bloody body of Jesus down from the cross. We don't know if they first pried the nails out of the wooden cross or if they freed the hands and feet of Jesus by pulling them away from the cross, leaving the long spikes still in the wood.

At any rate, it would take all the strength of two men to do what they did. No one helped them; not even the disciples of Jesus were around. Evidently, even the disciple John and the mother of Jesus did not stay until the body of Jesus had been taken down from the cross (John 19:27).

There is no time for a funeral. In several minutes the sun would go down behind the hills between Jerusalem and the Great Sea. The sun, setting behind the western horizon, was the signal for the beginning of the Jewish Sabbath, when all manual labor would cease for 24 hours.

One of these two men, Joseph of Arimathaea, was wealthy enough to have previously bought a piece of rocky real estate just outside the city wall of Jerusalem. He had hired workmen to chisel a tomb out of the rock cliff that he expected to use for his interment. He wanted to be buried close to God's temple, not far from the city wall. He had planned that his mortal remains would lie at rest here until the day of God's Judgment. Instead, in this newly cut tomb, he placed the limp and lifeless body of Jesus.

A "very great stone" (Mark 16:4) that may have weighed at least two tons was rolled to cover the entrance. A Roman seal was placed upon the stone.

Roman law spelled out a quick death for anyone caught rifling a tomb. Anyone breaking the seal without official permission would soon wish he hadn't done it. Although it was unusual to place a Roman seal on the grave of a criminal, no chances were being taken that the followers of Jesus would come and steal His broken body, and then claim He had risen from the dead.

The Cross

THE CROSS MADE BY AN UNKNOWN SLAVE, stained with the lifeblood of Jesus, the Christ, has become the symbol of Christianity. Since that dark Friday, the cross has a unique and permanent place in the history of the world.

The slave could not have known that he was making an object that would be copied many billions of times in the ages of the future. There are more replicas, copies, paintings, icons, and illustrations made of the cross Jesus Christ died upon than any other single object in history.

The first Christians did not permit the illustrating of the cross in artwork. It would have been too inappropriate and not at all proper for them. The cross did not become common in religious sculpture, art, and jewelry until that generation of people who had seen the actual blood and gore of a real crucifixion had died.

The armies of the Crusaders who went out to take possession of the Holy Land and the city of Jerusalem had crosses painted or engraved on their shields. One of the first acts of a medieval explorer when he set foot on a newly discovered land was to plant a huge cross on the shore. This was to show to all that a country of state church Christianity claimed these lands.

The cross on which He suffered His agony and bowed His head in death has been depicted in anything from huge statues to the crosses on church steeples soaring to dizzying heights. It has been sculptured on fancy building decorations and on thousands upon thousands of tombstones.

Pictures of the cross illustrate millions of hand painted and printed books. It is portrayed on Easter greeting cards, and countless pieces of candy sold the world over during the Easter season are even formed into the shape of a cross.

It is seen on countless trinkets worn as ornaments—some made of costly jewels, gold, and gems—others made of cheap imitations. Some people wear a cross as a magic or good luck charm. Others wear a cross as a reminder to themselves and others that they are Christians, and to identify themselves as Christians.

The thousands of joyful songs sung at countless Christian worship services all over the world for nearly two thousand years also remember the suffering and excruciating death of our Lord and Savior on the cross. The redemption of mankind at the cruel cross has turned sorrow and grief into song!

However, not only the people of the plain Christian churches, but many others also do not believe that exalting and making a display of the cross, the symbol of the sufferings of Christ, is what Christianity is all about. We want to remember that it is Christ Himself, not the cross to which He was nailed, that we wish to exalt and glorify. The cross itself is not for a superstitious worship or honor.

Even though the cross is a symbol of hope, redemption, and new life, we believe that being obedient to the command of Jesus to "take up my cross and follow Me" is required of every faithful Christian. Taking up the cross means living a self-denying life. There is much more to life than trying to get for us everything we may desire, afford, and wish for.

Many of the songs about the cross have the theme of sometimes exchanging the cross of this life for a crown in the life after death. While the well-known Quaker, William Penn, was in prison for his faith he wrote an inspiring book in which he emphasized the blessings God will give to a life of self-denial and on setting our sights on things above. The title Penn gave to the book, "No Cross—No Crown," was inspired by the dying words of a friend he had once visited.

THERE IS AN OLD PARABLE about carrying the cross that has been going around for a long time in a number of different versions.

As the story goes, a traveler going heavenward is carrying a cross to show other pilgrims along the way that he is a Christian. The way is uphill and he gets tired, especially being burdened with the weight of the cross.

He gets a bright idea. Why not saw just a little off from each of the four ends? The load will be lighter, but he will still be carrying something looking like the required cross.

He does this once, then several times afterward. Every time he does so, his conscience bothers him less than it did before. The load is lightened enough to make his traveling easier than ever. The efforts to keep going uphill are no longer as hard, but others still see him carrying a cross.

At last he is almost there!

However, just at this side of the gate which he wants to enter, he comes upon a wide and dangerous chasm with steep sides and with wildly raging waters at the bottom.

Here he finds he is to use the cross he has been carrying as a bridge to get to the other side. There is no other way over!

Now it dawns on him that his abbreviated and shortened cross has been made too short to bridge the wide gorge. How he wishes he had faithfully carried the entire cross and not tampered with it. But it is too late.

Very few people committed to following the teachings of Christ throughout the last twenty centuries that have come and gone since the crucifixion of Jesus have had to die on a cross. We

may not need to die on a cross, but all Christians are expected by their Maker to live a cross-bearing life, and in this way help to carry the cross of their Lord and Master. Hearing or reading about the sufferings of Jesus Christ may not make much difference in our lives, but if any one of us were to experience hanging on a cross for only one minute, our lives would never again be the same.

A.D. 30

APRIL						
S	M	T	W	T	F	S
..	..	..	..	..	..	1
2	3	4	5	6	7	8
9	10	11	12	13	14	15
16	17	18	19	20	21	22
23	24	25	26	27	28	29
30	....	....	....	....	....	....

This illustration shows how the calendar page of April A.D. 30 would have appeared if the people of the first century A.D. would have had calendars with our system of beginning the year with the first of January.

It is not certain in which year Jesus was crucified. There are not enough reliable historical clues to verify the exact date and year when this happened. However, the only four possible years for Jesus' death are A.D. 27, 30, 33, or 34. Astronomers can calculate that only in these four years did a full moon occur on Friday or Saturday in the first month of the Hebrew year, during the time Pontius Pilate was the governor of Judea.

The Hebrew months always started on the evening when the new moon made its first appearance. The Hebrew year started on the first new moon after the spring equinox, which is when sunrise and sunset are due east and due west. This is also the first day of spring when day and night are equal all over the world. The Passover was held fourteen days later (Exodus 12:18), which would be the date of a full moon that evening. This method is still used every year to determine Easter Sunday.

Bible scholars believe King Herod, of the infamous Bethlehem massacre of the innocents, died several years before what is now considered the first year of the Christian Era. Due to a mistake in medieval calculations, our A.D. 1 may be several years off, by perhaps three or four years.

Dating forward from the year in which it is believed the death of King Herod occurred makes most Bible scholars believe that Jesus was crucified over the Passover season in the spring of A.D. 30.

Although some scholars over the years have tried to prove the crucifixion happened on Thursday of the Passion Week, nearly all now agree it happened on Friday. The name God's Friday, as it used to be called, became Good Friday.

We now have this day named Good Friday on our calendars and a day called Easter Sunday, but the day in between, the dark, dark day missing from history when evil and death had its short-lived triumph, never had a name.

Chapter 16

A Day Missing from History

THERE ARE MANY, MANY DAYS—even years—on the calendars of forever bygone times when very little or nothing was recorded for posterity. Even though in every single day and hour in history people were doing something somewhere, most of what happened in those days is lost and vanished in the mists of time.

What happened in those days that has not been retold or written about is forever buried out of our sight and is known only to God.

However, God has let us know a good bit about one week in the past history of the "Holy City" of Jerusalem in the vicinity of its Jewish temple. No other week in ancient times has been written down for us in greater detail than the week called "the Passion Week" or "the Holy Week." Even though the events happening in that week took place nearly two thousand years ago, they are well-known all over the world. The books written about this week alone, the week that changed the course of history, would fill long lines of bookshelves.

Though we live in days far removed from the happenings of this Holy Week, thanks to God and the four Gospel writers who went into detail, we have a record of much of what took place on the first six of those seven days.

One-third of Mark's Gospel is concentrated on this week in the life of Jesus, and we find that 24 of the 89 Gospel chapters focus on the crucifixion week.

BUT DO WE HAVE ANY RECORD of what happened on the quiet Jewish Sabbath on the seventh and last day of that week? Unfortunately, we don't. Unlike the earlier part of the week, this is one day that no written record has come down to us.

However, we find that all four Gospel writers indirectly make mention of that day, which was the Sabbath day for the Jews. Matthew writes "at the end of the Sabbath" (Matthew 28:1). Mark makes mention of "when the Sabbath was past" (Mark 16:1), Luke tells us "they rested the Sabbath day according to the commandment" (Luke 23:56), and John writes of the Jews' preparation day (for the Sabbath) in John 19:31 and 42.

Other than these several very indirect Gospel references and the five verses that Matthew writes (62 to 66 in chapter 27), there is no record in all of recorded history of what went on during that dark seventh day of the week when Jesus lay silent and dead in a borrowed tomb.

WE DO KNOW THAT when the seventh day of the week came around, the Jewish people rested and kept quiet so that the holiness of their Sabbath would not be violated. The Pharisees had made a number of extra Jewish laws on the proper observance of the Sabbath. These rulings, made with very good intentions, had undoubtedly helped to make God's Sabbath holy and sacred in the minds of the Jewish people. As long as these Sabbath day guidelines were practiced with conscience and common sense, they did not cause hostility and division, but helped keep the Jewish people separated from the sinful nations around them.

One of these Jewish laws forbade them to travel more than a short distance on the Sabbath; the distance of which was called a Sabbath day's journey. This was the distance which some sources give as 3,000 feet and some as 3,500 feet. Whatever the exact length of it was, it was roughly two-third mile in today's measurements.

The chief priests and Pharisees found out about the burial of Jesus in the tomb of Joseph of Arimathaea just before sundown, which marked the beginning of the Jewish Sabbath. Breaking the Jewish laws of keeping completely quiet during those twenty-four hours from the sunset of the sixth day to the sunset of the seventh day, they went to the Roman governor and asked him to set a group of guards around the sepulchre of Jesus for several days. They talked Pilate into placing an armed guard around the tomb to keep a round-the-clock watch so that the disciples would not steal away the body of their Master.

They were concerned about what would happen if the disciples were to remove the body of Jesus and put out a report that He arose from the dead. They remembered that Jesus had predicted He would arise from the dead in three days—but it seems everyone else, even the disciples of Jesus who had repeatedly heard Him saying so, had completely forgotten all about this prophecy. The enemies of Jesus had better memories of what He had foretold about His resurrection than His disciples.

EXCEPT FOR THIS WRITTEN RECORD of the visit of the chief priests and the Pharisees to Pilate, and the guards armed with swords and spears surrounding the tomb with a lifeless Jesus inside, we know practically nothing as to what happened on this dark day of history.

We can imagine that when the guards came to the tomb to guard it, they took a good look inside before sealing it to make sure the body of Jesus was still lying there undisturbed.

The Sabbath Day After Christ Was Crucified

On this Sabbath day, lost to history, let us imagine what may have been going on in Jerusalem, and how the disciples of the now dead Jesus felt.

The pilgrims who had come to celebrate the yearly Passover were making sacrifices in the temple only the day before. Many woke up that Sabbath day in their makeshift tents, set up in the narrow Jerusalem streets. Others had stayed with friends or relatives.

The next morning, on the first day of the week, most of these pilgrims would start out again for their homelands. Some would be going to Emmaus, only six or seven miles away. Some would start out for Galilee, some ninety miles to the north. That trip, walking alongside a donkey bearing their baggage, might take the best part of four or five days.

Others would be going to their homelands still further off, such as Alexandria in Egypt, and would be traveling for several weeks or more.

WHEN SOMETHING UNUSUAL HAPPENS in a neighborhood, the people will think about it. When they get together they will try to analyze the happenings and talk about what could come out of the event.

The crucifixions of the three men just outside of the city wall and the foreboding and frightening darkness of yesterday afternoon, along with the earthquake and the unexplained ripping of the heavy veil, which let light into the darkness of the Holy of Holies room in the temple at the time the lambs were being sacrificed, would certainly be no exception.

Something out of the ordinary had happened. The whole city knew about it, but nobody could explain what it was all about.

If there had been any local Jerusalem newspapers at that time, the headlines would have told about the crucifixion and the strange darkness over the land.

But even if newspapers had told the story, the archives of back issues would have been destroyed when Jerusalem became desolated after the Roman army leveled it some forty years later.

The Roman records of the trial of Jesus, if there were any, and without any doubt there were, would have been destroyed along with Jerusalem. If the Creator who watches over and gently guides history according to His plan hadn't done something about it, the knowledge of everything that happened in the capital city of the Roman province of Judea during Passion Week would have become lost.

But we have the four Gospel writers. Like four newspaper reporters at the scene of a happening, the four Gospel writers didn't use the exact same words. Every detail of the story in their reports isn't exactly the same. As the writers at any happening of today make sure that the story is told accurately when it gets put in print for the next morning's paper, because it may be read by a number of people who were also there, we can rest assured that what the four Gospel writers tell of the story of Passion Week can be trusted to be truthful and honest.

All four Gospel writers, converts to Christianity, had either been there as eyewitnesses or had in later years written as a secretary to a disciple who had been an eyewitness. Mark may have done the writing for Peter. The Gospel writer Luke, who may have been something like a family doctor, shows by his writings that he was well acquainted with the disciples and with Mary, the mother of Jesus.

It is a miracle of the Almighty God that our New Testament containing these four Gospels has survived for nearly two thousand years. This often-forbidden book has survived fire, sword, and persecution. This is a miracle and is far more important than digging up an artifact or finding an ancient scrap of information on an undecayed newspaper.

The persecution of the Christian Church in Jerusalem several years later would prove to be an indirect blessing. Because of it the Christians were all out of Jerusalem when it fell and not one got killed in the massacre that followed. Not only would the story of Christ be spread to every corner of the vast Roman Empire by the fleeing Christians, it would also keep a committee of Gospel writers from being formed. Such a group would probably have kept some things out of the Gospels, deciding as a group what the public would not need to know, like Peter's cursing and swearing that he did not know Jesus (Matthew 26:74). Such a committee would probably have decided not to tell the story about the disciples who wanted to call fire down from Heaven to burn up a village of Samaritans (Luke 9:51-56).

None of the disciples would have thought it necessary to tell the whole world how they all had simply forgotten about the Resurrection concerning which Jesus often spoke so plainly. But then, they were like we also are if we fail to prepare for the eternity that we will be resurrected to after this life is over; something that has also often enough been made plainly known to us. We have been told eternity is coming closer all the time, and if we wake up on the wrong side on Resurrection Morning, we can't say we didn' know.

WHAT WERE THE SURVIVING DISCIPLES of Jesus thinking and doing on that quiet Sabbath day of the 30 A.D. Passover season? In sorrow they would go back to their homeland in Galilee as soon as they could slip out of the city without being noticed. They knew it was the Roman way to round up all fellow partners of an executed criminal and give them the same treatment as the crucified criminal. In great fear, they probably imagined the authorities were out looking high and low for them.

Going back over the same roads they had gone over when they had come to Jerusalem with Jesus only a week or so before would overwhelm them with memories. The bruised body of the Master they had followed for three years now lay dead in a stone-cold tomb.

What the surviving disciples of Jesus did on the dark Sabbath day after the crucifixion of Jesus is not recorded. Their tears of grief were not to be stopped, because we read that they were still mourning and weeping (Mark 16:10) at least 45 hours after Jesus had been nailed to the cross.

At that time it would seem nothing was left for the surviving eleven disciples to do but to go back to their home country and start all over again. They would have the rest of their lives to think over the folly of their three lost years.

We can't blame them one bit if they were sure their walk with Jesus was now over. To them, His influence was now crushed and His defeat was final. How could this man really have been such an impostor, a deceiver and a fraud? They weren't ready for this.

For three years they believed Jesus was on the way to becoming a king. They had every reason to believe that here was the Messiah who would throw off Rome. What about the kingdom—that promised kingdom such as had never before been seen on earth—that they thought Jesus had the power to establish? How could they ever have been brainwashed into all this?

THE HOPES OF THE NOW LEADERLESS DISCIPLES were dashed to pieces. The changes had come so suddenly. Only a few days ago they had felt they were God's favored people, and they were sure God would do miracles for them as He had done for their forefathers in Egypt. They knew Jewish history, and up to now God had shown other nations that in the long run it was not healthy for them to oppose the people that God had blessed.

Jesus had healed the hopelessly sick. He had made the blind able to see; even one who had been born blind, a miracle such as had never been heard of before (John 9:32). The disciples had been present when, with a miracle they could not explain, Jesus had increased a small amount of food until it was more than enough to feed thousands of people.

Jesus had resurrected one of their friends after he had been dead for several days. Their thinking of the power of Jesus at that time could have been that if He had not cried out the name of Lazarus, all the dead in the graveyard would have come forth! Just this miracle alone had given them high hopes that Jesus was truly the Messiah, the anointed Deliverer promised to the Jewish people, the descendants of Abraham who had lived under God's blessings. In the Jewish Scriptures, the prophets wrote that the Messiah, when He came, would abide forever and would not die (references alongside John 12:34). The disciples could well have believed that Jesus conquered death itself when He brought at least two other dead bodies back to life.

It would be great to serve under a king with such power. Such a king would easily win the loyalty of multitudes of people!

The great promise they had hoped in had failed. To the saddened followers of Jesus, the final tragedy had taken place the day before. Their Master's life had ended in a horrible and shameful way. The distraught and depressed men and women, who had once been willing servants of Jesus, were now overwhelmed with disappointment and sorrow.

Should they now dismiss Jesus as just another one of the false prophets who had proclaimed themselves the deliverers of the land of Judea? There had been several dozen such men in the last hundred years or so whose claims had been proved a fake and had ended in humiliation.

But Jesus had been a friend who had done so much for them. He should at least have been given a decent burial. The interment last evening had been too hurried before sundown to get everything together.

Several women would meet at the sepulchre early tomorrow morning to complete the funeral. It would be best for the men to stay in hiding for a while longer.

THE DISCIPLES WELL REMEMBERED how proud they had felt to be a part of the selected twelve only six days ago, when Jesus had entered the gates of Jerusalem.

The immense crowd of people, made up of Jerusalem citizens and the early-arriving Passover pilgrims, had been cheering for their Master. They had imagined their future then as having a part with Jesus in royal glory and power.

THE WHOLE CITY had felt like a tinderbox ready to burst into flames when their Master had ridden a small donkey through the city gates earlier in the week, with the cautious Roman soldiers and seething Pharisees watching from a distance. Ironically, one of the Roman soldiers keeping the peace would only five days later be the owner of the seamless robe Jesus was now wearing.

If military action were necessary, the disciples had believed, their Master would have risen to the occasion. The history of their nation from that time on would have pages written of the mighty military leader who, with His flaming sword, had kept the peace. They just knew He had some kind of divine power that no one would dare to oppose. Had Jesus given the word, the mob of people would easily have taken over both the temple and the palace of Pilate.

Hadn't the Jewish prophets of old said that God's chosen people, the Jews, would shortly be ruling all the nations of the earth? The longing for a happy, peaceful, and prosperous kingdom ruled by God's promised Messiah had at the beginning of the week seemed to be on the verge of being fulfilled.

NEXT TO JESUS, THE KING of this newly established Jewish realm, would be the twelve disciples. Such were their excited thoughts and their self-important dreams! They were really congratulating themselves. They were the hand-picked disciples of such a popular hero. This could all be a shortcut to wealth and high position and fame!

Jesus would soon drive those hateful Romans, who loved to show authority, right out of the land. All those rich, greedy, and cheating fellow Jewish tax collectors who were keeping the people poor by the extra money they kept would be swept right out with the Romans upon whom their jobs depended.

And they, the loyal twelve disciples of their miracle-working Master would be of the select few to share in this fame, honor, and success. They would be of the elite few who would help Jesus rule the land God would give to His favored people.

Perhaps the whole world would be brought under Jewish rule. Wouldn't that be something great to be a part of!

When the group was going into Jerusalem on the first day of this week the proud disciples, basking in the limelight, could probably feel deep in their inner beings what they sensed was the envy of the people watching them. It felt good to think that because the Master had selected them, they were more worthy than anyone else. The prestige and renown of being a disciple of Jesus fired up their self-esteem. It felt good to be admired by so many people.

Of course, not one of them would want to admit it, but every one of them always felt a twinge of envy in his heart when he saw any one of the others edging closer to Jesus than he had been able to do. Every one of them kept watching the others to make sure there was no slight effort to seek for positions of favor. But, of course, that would cause no problems as long as Jesus would keep treating them all alike and would not start playing favorites.

They probably thought they had kept this jockeying for position and recognition in the background subtle enough that the Master hadn't taken notice. That little talk He had given at the Passover supper table about only those who serve being the greatest were His instructions to the household servants and slaves and, of course, not to them, the chosen twelve.

They could remember when several small arguments had taken place in the past as to which ones of Jesus' followers would be chosen to be the Top Two; those who would be asked to be His chief advisors and to sit on the left and to the right of His throne. These two would have more authority and honor among the people, and more favor with the Master than the others who would be placed on seats of lesser levels of honor.

The one incident that had really been the most upsetting to the others was when the mother of two of the disciples, the wife of Zebedee—just like any parents who want their children to be respected—had the nerve to ask Jesus to give her two sons the most exalted official places in His coming kingdom (Matthew 20:20-24). The other ten were relieved when Jesus didn't promise.

Of course, they were aware that Jesus had a few enemies. They knew the strict Pharisees were provoked with the demons of envy and anger within, and could not stand having Jesus around. They could sense that the Pharisees had chosen to reject and hate Jesus, but what did that matter? Jesus would put them in their place once His kingdom was set up. His wisdom always put them to silence whenever they had confronted Him. And as far as the disciples knew, Jesus had no enemies among the Romans. With His divine power, what if He did? Those who didn't like Him could not long hinder their Master from becoming a king such as the world had never seen before.

Jesus was a direct descendant of the great King David of about a thousand years earlier, and the Jewish Scriptures had prophesied that David's dynasty, or succession of rulers, would reign forever. The disciples believed these prophecies, taught to them as children, would come to pass exactly as they had been foretold.

IT SEEMED LIKE AGES AGO when they had all been together only the evening before last to eat the traditional Passover Supper with the Master. How dark and foreboding everything had sounded when their Master followed the meal with a ceremony that seemed very unusual and strange to them all. An atmosphere of gloom surrounded them all when Jesus talked about His shed blood and broken body. He talked about "going away" and about suffering and death. What Jesus was talking about sounded like a farewell to them, but that did not make any sense either.

At that time they were preoccupied with the thinking that Jesus would still be crowned an earthly king of their nation, and they had not understood His talk of returning to be their Comforter in their coming trials.

BUT WAS JESUS REALLY A WEAKLING, after all, that He was arrested and then crucified on a Roman cross? Why had He let Himself be taken into custody with His hands bound behind His back? Why had there been no struggle and no display of the power the disciples always thought He had. He had even set one of His disciples straight when he, with a swinging sword, had done his best to keep Jesus' enemies at bay.

Making no resistance to having a person's hands tied up had never been heard of before, but Jesus was practicing the nonresistance He had preached about.

When Jesus was standing before the judgment seat of Pilate and before the throne of the important King Herod, there would still have been time to exercise His power. If Jesus would have done some spectacular or showy miracle before Herod, He probably would have been set free right there. Herod had been hearing from time to time of the miracle-working teacher in his kingdom, but this was the first time he met Him face to face.

Then also, with the force of His words such as when He stilled the storm, Jesus could have demanded both Pilate and Herod to step down and He would have taken their seats and judged them.

Jesus could also have taken the seat of the unworthy high priest who was the first to declare a formal sentence of death upon Him. The abuse of authority in the hierarchy of the Jewish religion would be taken care of if only Jesus would have stood on the rights that the law of Moses provided for those unjustly judged and oppressed. Jesus could have taken over and made religion what God had intended it to be.

It surely must have irked all three of these men in authority when they sensed how unimportant their prisoner had considered the "worldly" power of the high positions they thought they possessed. Jesus hadn't shown them more honor than He did to the lowly servants who surrounded them to instantly carry out their wishes.

What a chance Jesus had missed to unseat these tyrants who thought more of political power than of rightful justice. How easily He could have placed Himself in a position to pass sentence upon all three of them.

He had done greater miracles than that in His day. Nature had obeyed Him instantly when the wind and waves braked to a sudden stop when He told them to. Driving out the devils that then crazed a large herd of swine was also a miracle, but a greater miracle was the great change in the man who could not be tamed, even when they had bound him down with chains. Jesus had completely healed him; he was in his right mind; he was content and was found peacefully sitting at the feet of Jesus.

There was no reason why Jesus could not also have made the bonds on His hands fall off and made Himself a master of Pilate or Herod or the high priest.

That action would have triggered the start of a new and glorious kingdom, free from all political and religious oppressors. Starting with the fall of the Roman Empire, Jesus could have made Jerusalem the capital of a kingdom that could easily have conquered the whole wide world!

WHERE WERE THE SHOUTING crowds who had followed Jesus through the city gates of Jerusalem earlier in the week? Little did anyone in the multitude of cheering people realize when they were passing the exact spot where Jesus would be crucified only five days later how short-lived their emotional fervor for Him would last.

If that number of people would have dared to make an attempt to rescue Jesus from the Roman soldiers when He was being led to His crucifixion yesterday morning, His life could probably have been saved. The Roman soldiers assigned to the duty of crucifying Jesus would have been outnumbered and could easily have been overpowered.

How could the tide of public opinion change in such a short time? On the first day of the week it seemed as if Jesus had no enemies; yesterday it looked as if He had no friends. How could the opinions of the people about Jesus make such a clean reversal in less than a week?

The cheering crowds following Him into the city on the first day of the week changed into jeering crowds following Him out of the city only five days later. The same road and the same highly excited people changed from for to against in such a short time.

Will human nature never change? Will people always cheer for the winning side of the moment? Will they always be too embarrassed and ashamed to put in a good word for the underdog? Will the losing and underprivileged minority and oppressed always have to go on without public support and sympathy?

BUT THE TERRIBLE TRUTH was that Jesus seemed to have lost all His friends. He was now dead.

In fact, another one of the men present at the Last Supper only the evening before the last was no longer living; this was the turncoat disciple who had betrayed Jesus to those who hated Him; he had become his own executioner.

The other disciples may have wondered at the strange and unexplained actions of Judas, their fellow disciple, during the last week of Jesus' earthly life. Later it all started to make sense, when, after his death by his own hand, they found out he had secretly bargained to betray Jesus for thirty pieces of silver, paid for ahead of time.

At Gethsemane, the money in the pockets of Judas was thirty coins heavier. These coins had paid for the false kiss that was fatal to Jesus. This greeting had made the rest of the disciples think Judas was still a friend and may have kept Peter from striking Judas dead with his sword.

It is indeed ironic that these betrayal coins, the amount an average laborer would be able to earn in thirty days (Matthew 20), would never be spent by Judas. They would be used for the buying of a burial ground for the poverty-stricken, friendless. or almost unknown persons—exactly the kind of people to whom Jesus had liked to be a friend.

It is also ironic that this Judas, who had illicitly associated with the highest leaders of the Jewish religion to betray his Master, was dead before Jesus was.

How could it be possible that one of the men who was one of Jesus' helpers and had baptized others (John 4:2) in the name of Jesus became untrue to his Lord. Here he had been one of the twelve disciples, the only people in the whole history of mankind who had enjoyed the privilege and special favor of walking the roads of Judea and Galilee with Jesus for three years as an eyewitness to all His teachings and miracles.

How could it have been possible for one of the disciples who had helped the Master do miracles and drive out devils in others to later permit the devil to enter his own heart? (Luke 22:3).

According to the Gospel, the last two times Jesus was called Master, a title of honor, before his death was not by His true friends, but by the false betrayer at the supper table (Matthew 26:25) and at his treachery and deceit just before Jesus' hands were bound behind His back (Matthew 26:49).

Was the faith in the money he carried in his bag the only faith Judas had? Had money, and what he could buy with money, become his god?

How could he have made such a muddle and mess of his life? Why, oh why did he utterly despair when the living Jesus was still close enough to him that he could have gone to Him with his confession and to implore His forgiveness? He did confess that he had sinned (Matthew 27:3-10) to the temple priests, but they were of no help to him. He should have gone to true and understanding friends with his confession. They could have pointed him to Jesus for total forgiveness and for a lasting peace and a new lease on life.

If Judas would have permitted God to resurrect a drastic change in his life, he would probably have become an apostle like the others who suffered a martyr's death later on. The Apostle Paul, who had done his best to destroy the Christian Church, became one of its most loyal supporters. The Apostle Peter, who had cursed and sworn he did not know Jesus, would later in his life write of being born again into a living hope (I Peter 1:3).

Judas missed the life-giving power of God that could have come into his life. He sacrificed the peace of God for the thirty pieces of silver that he would have been able to earn in a much better way.

Peter's Sorrow

IN THAT DAY LOST TO HISTORY, Peter had a lot to think about. Did he remember how Jesus severely reprimanded him when he told his Master that he didn't like His talk of suffering and death (Matthew 16:21-23)? Peter could still feel the sting of being called a satan for suggesting that Jesus should save Himself from having to suffer and die.

Many things had happened in Peter's life since his brother Andrew first introduced him to Jesus (John 1:40-42) some three years earlier, and since Jesus healed his mother-in- law who had at one time been bedfast (Mark 1:29-31; Luke 4:38-39).

It is very unlikely that in these three years Peter ever came really close to understanding Jesus.

The closest Peter ever came to expressing that awareness was one day in Caesarea Philippi. Jesus asked His disciples who they would say that He was, and Peter promptly made a statement very similar to one made by all who are about to be baptized: "Thou art the Christ, the Son of the living God" (Matthew 16:16).

Peter, the former fisherman, well remembered the Passover meal in the Upper Room. At that time Peter so confidently asserted he would stay with Jesus whatever would happen, and would die with Him if it would come to that.

Did Peter now cringe in shame when he remembered through his tears how things had gone that early morning? He had cursed and sworn to the bystanders at Jesus' trial that he did not know the Man (Mark 14:71). How could he have been so scared and such a coward?

A young girl had "earnestly looked upon" Peter (Luke 22:56) when she recognized him as one of the disciples of Jesus. It appears she may have been one of the household servants who wanted to know more about Jesus. She may have had a sympathetic heart when she saw what was happening to Him. She could have been ready to weep tears of grief with Peter if only he had been in a different frame of mind.

Then also, no one in our day and age will know more details about this other girl (Mark 14:69) who seemed to have recognized Peter as one of the disciples. What was she doing, still away from home at this early hour of the morning, so close to the barracks where the pagan Roman soldiers were stationed in Jerusalem? Had she at one time heard of this Jesus who loved sinners but hated the sin? Was she ready for peace in her heart instead of the remorse and regret that follows sinful living?

Did Peter realize that if he were a "helper of people" instead of afraid to reach out because of his cowardice, he could have made a difference in her life by pointing her to the forgiveness and soul-cleansing power of Jesus and to the birth of a new nature?

How his own resolve had failed him! Why didn't he stay awake and go to his Master's side to pray with Him the night before the last at Gethsemane?

He must have remembered hearing some of the words Jesus was praying, "O my Father, if it be possible, let this cup pass from me," but not until later would Peter begin to grasp the significance of what Jesus added to His prayer. "Nevertheless, not as I will, but as Thou wilt!"

If Peter thought back to that same night, he would remember himself as very self-sure and courageous. He was fully confident of his own strength when the armed soldiers had come to arrest Jesus. Then Peter had been fully awake. Yes, he had later been a cowardly deserter at the trial of Jesus, but earlier that same evening, the loud and self-sure Peter still couldn't understand why Jesus did not permit him to keep up a fight. He felt able to protect Jesus and keep Him safe by striking His enemies to the ground. He had grabbed the sword by his side when the soldiers were roughly tightening the ropes that handcuffed his Master.

He had lunged forward and started hacking right and left. Slashing his sword toward the servant of the high priest, Peter had hit his head, but the only damage done was an ear sliced off.

Jesus didn't have to die! If only He would have accepted help. All other kings had bodyguards who would fight to their deaths to protect them if it became necessary to do so.

But Jesus had told Peter to put his sword away. His last act of healing in this life was to make right the damage Peter had done in uncontrolled zeal to protect Him. The hands of Jesus performed this miracle of healing just before they were tied. Why hadn't Peter's Master done just one more miracle to keep His freedom?

Peter had no way of seeing into the future years of his life, but we now know that was the last time Peter ever used the sword. He had learned his lesson. Jesus would not need any of the sword-wielding protection of His followers to enlarge His kingdom.

Peter would be glad in times to come that Jesus healed the ear and corrected the damage that he had done. How could Christian historians of future years explain a nonresistant Prince of Peace to the world if He had permitted His disciples to kill or maim other human beings for the sake of protecting Him, even though such an action could be called righteous anger or be excused as thoughtless courage?

On this sad day, the bold, outspoken, and sword-swinging Peter was now defeated, dejected, and humiliated. He had suddenly become a big coward, afraid to admit to these young girls who wanted someone to tell them more about Jesus that he had ever known Him. He deserted and failed His Master at a time when Jesus, who had a longing for human company, needed him most. His Master, who had saved him from drowning when he was beginning to plummet to the depth of the Sea of Galilee (Matthew 14:24-32), was now dead. The mockery of the crowds yesterday, "He saved others; Himself He cannot save" (Matthew 27:42 and Mark 15:31) may have been true after all.

We don't know how long Peter wept bitter tears of remorse and sorrow (Luke 22:62), but when the first day of the next week was dawning, which was Easter Sunday, the disciples were still weeping and mourning for their fallen King (Mark 16:10).

Mary, the Mother of Jesus

THE CHIEF PRIESTS AND PHARISEES WHO INSTIGATED Jesus' arrest, and the Romans who yesterday crucified Jesus, surely had hard hearts if they were not affected by seeing Mary, the mother of Jesus, at the foot of the cross. The mother love in Mary's breaking heart prevailed over her fear of death. She would stay close to the cross and die with her son if that were the way it was to be.

In her great sorrow, and with a love only a mother can know, she probably wept with swollen eyes until she could weep no more. Mary probably often wondered about the prophecy 33 years earlier about the sword that would pierce through her, into her own soul. But now she knew.

Yesterday had been a terrible ordeal for Mary. Of course, her thoughts may also have gone back to earlier days in her little hometown of Nazareth shortly before the birth of her firstborn.

She could remember when tongues wagged and fingers pointed at her as if she were nothing more than a harlot. If Mary had told her neighbors of her wonderful experience of the angel visit, the unbelievers among them would not only have doubted her chastity but would have been sure she was also a little mentally unbalanced.

The Christians in future ages would call Mary blessed, but not one of them would really know the ordeal Mary went through in her life—being ordained to be the mother of the Messiah.

An unmarried girl in her condition under Jewish law could be stoned to death for her sin. But the loyal and faithful Joseph, whose spoken words are nowhere recorded in the Bible, stood by her. He believed she was a chaste virgin, even though it appeared she was not. He believed what she told him of being visited by an angel and being overshadowed by the Holy Spirit.

We know Joseph was poor, for he offered two young pigeons as a temple sacrifice because he could not afford to buy a lamb. Soon after the birth of Jesus He protected the baby and His mother Mary from the evil King Herod by fleeing into the land of Egypt.

The ordeal of that flight into Egypt may have gone through the mind of Mary on this dark day, along with the memories of many other unexplainable happenings, such as the visit of the shepherds and wise men, that Mary had pondered in her heart over the years (Luke 2:19 and 51).

MARY WAS THE ONE CLOSEST TO the cross when her son Jesus was suffering and dying. She may have been the only person close enough to the three crosses to hear the exchange of words between Jesus and the two thieves who were paying for their crimes to society.

Not even the disciples of Jesus at this time recognized Jesus as being a King, but one of these men did. "Lord, remember me when Thou comest into Thy kingdom," he sobbed.

As he saw a Roman soldier approach him with a heavy club, and before he fell into the unconsciousness before death, that thief heard the assurance of Jesus: "Verily I say unto thee, today shalt thou be with me in Paradise." This was not the final end after all!

The dying thief found one who could open a door to the future. As his eyes closed forever on the earthly scene of the city of Jerusalem before him, he had the promise from Jesus Himself of opening his eyes on the other side to something much better. He would find himself in Paradise, the Heavenly Jerusalem where God lives, a place of no more weeping, suffering, and pain.

This incident and the other incidents of Jesus' birth and boyhood that are written only by Luke could have been passed on to Luke by Mary, because Luke could have been the family doctor of the "Holy Family." Luke is also the only Gospel writer who accurately describes some of the diseases Jesus healed, just like a doctor would, along with some details of Jesus' birth which only Mary would know about.

Matthew

IT WOULD BE INTERESTING to us if Matthew, with his careful record-keeping background as a tax collector for the Romans, had left a daily journal of his doings and thoughts as a disciple of Jesus. The entry of his thoughts and what he was doing on this quiet Jewish Sabbath day after the crucifixion would be especially interesting. How we would be thrilled to read the notes he jotted down on April 8, A.D. 30. However, if Matthew kept a daily journal, he probably would not write it on that dark and gloomy Sabbath day when Jesus was lying lifeless in a borrowed tomb. He would have been too stunned. The last things in Matthew's thoughts that day were that he would, in his later years, write about the life of this man, Jesus.

Matthew, the careful and accurate record keeper in his years as a publican, probably often wished Jesus had preserved some of His life-changing teachings in writing. It was not that Jesus was illiterate, but now He was gone and not a single word of His divine teachings was preserved on paper.

Probably the only time His disciples could remember seeing Jesus writing anything was on that day when He wrote on the ground (John 8:3-11). Why didn't someone remember what Jesus wrote before it was soon tramped over and obliterated?

Now Jesus' words were probably lost forever. One of the last thoughts in the mind of Matthew on this day after the death of Jesus was that he would someday write a Gospel that would be translated into many languages and read all over the world hundreds and hundreds of years later.

Matthew had followed and walked with Jesus since that day when Jesus had called his name. His Gospel would become a part of the Scripture recording the words of Jesus—words more permanent than the heavens and the earth (Matthew 5:18 and 24:35).

About three years earlier Jesus had interrupted Matthew's well-paying tax collecting business for the Roman masters of Judea. Matthew's station at the border of the country, along a well-traveled trade route, had been a place where revenue was collected from everybody passing through—something like a toll road. Matthew also would have kept track of and taxed all merchandise that passed into and out of the country.

For taking on this hated work, the tax collectors were permitted to keep a big slice of what they collected. The rest that they sent to Rome was enough to keep the upper class of Roman society living in idleness and luxury.

The tax collectors were a thorn in the sides of the hardworking masses of common people in the Roman Empire. While the working poor made tax collectors rich, they themselves could never look forward to a better lot in life than staying poor.

The tax collectors got their jobs by putting in bids for the collecting from a certain region in a Roman province. The one making a promise to send in the largest amount to Rome from that district got the job. He made his bid high enough to outbid anyone else, and as high as he thought he could squeeze the money out of the people in that area. Of course, he didn't make his bid too high, because he was responsible for the amount he had promised to send in.

If he couldn't collect enough, he would have to scratch up the amount from somewhere else or make it up from his own bank account. After he was signed up, he would go easy on the rate he charged friends, but if there was someone rich he felt like getting even with, he had the authority to tell him how much he would have to pay. There was no appeal. If the tax collector wanted the money, it was to be paid. No one wanted to be known as a rebel against the Roman way of doing things, or he just might get crucified as an enemy of the Roman Empire. It was best to do as you were told and not ask any questions.

THIS MATTHEW, OF THE HATED CLASS of tax gatherers, was an outcast the Pharisees would never associate with or eat with at the same table.

If ever Matthew regretted that he left what he was doing to follow Jesus, it was probably on this day now lost to history. Several years earlier, when Jesus appointed one of the twelve to take care of the money donated to His cause, Matthew probably thought Jesus would recognize his experience in handling money and ask him to be the treasurer.

But Judas was chosen for that important work. Didn't Jesus know the money-managing abilities of Matthew? Why was he bypassed in favor of Judas? Did Matthew wonder if Jesus was a little ignorant at seeing the talents hidden within men? Was Matthew slighted? On this day following the day of crucifixion, Matthew may have regretted ever getting involved with the penniless traveling teacher. Matthew's hopes were now buried with Jesus, lifeless in His tomb.

However, those of us living 2,000 years later know that Matthew had a talent. He must have carefully studied the prophecies written in the Jewish Scriptures. Fulfillment of exacting prophecy in so many events of Jesus' life before Jesus was crucified must have convinced the bright and scholarly Matthew that Jesus was the promised Messiah for the Jewish people. We do know by his writings that Matthew was quite well acquainted with the ancient Jewish prophecies that foretold the coming of the Messiah, which in the Hebrew language meant "the anointed One." (The word "Christ" means the same thing in Greek.)

One instance of the exact fulfilling of prophecy was that Jesus was born in Bethlehem, the city of David. The birth took place where the prophet Micah foretold it over 700 years earlier (Micah 5:2). If the great Roman Emperor Caesar Augustus had not made a decree right at that time that each family was to be counted and taxed in the hometown of their forefathers, Joseph and Mary surely wouldn't have traveled far away from their home in Nazareth at this time.

Isaiah prophesied some 750 years earlier that Jesus would be born of a virgin and that was also fulfilled (Isaiah 7:14, Matthew 1:23, Luke 1:31 and 34), even though Jesus' enemies probably would not admit that His mother was chaste.

Many other prophecies, including that of Christ being a Nazarene and of being called out of Egypt, were so far fulfilled to the letter. Up until now the divine predictions of the Messiah and what happened in Jesus' life were matched perfectly.

Yes, the Scriptures may even have hinted that the Messiah would have to suffer and die for the Jewish people. The high priest had said not long ago that it would be better for the Jewish nation if Jesus were put to death than that the whole nation should perish (John 11:47-51). What the high priest had in mind, however, was not the fulfillment of the prophecy of a Redeemer. The high priest did not want a bloody riot or war with Rome started by a multitude following a man he thought was a false messiah. He could endorse the crucifixion of Jesus rather than have a riot started in Jerusalem's streets, which could have left thousands of Jewish people dead.

And Jesus was now dead. The man Matthew followed, convinced He was the Messiah, was dead before becoming a king like the Jewish Scriptures promised. The Jesus in whom Matthew had faith the last three years, dreaming of the day he would see Him wear a golden crown, had mockingly been only yesterday given a crown of thorns. Gathered from a prickly bush that grew as an unwelcome weed in Jewish gardens, it reminded Jewish people of the story of thorns and thistles, a part of God's curse on the ground Adam would be tilling after he disobeyed his Creator (Genesis 3:18).

Jesus had not looked like a king yesterday morning, blood streaming down His face as the sharp two-inch-long thorns from the fake crown dug into His skin. Some sight His bloody face had been. Wet with slimy spit, black and blue marks from the cruel blows made in an attempt to anger Him into striking back, blood ran down from the cuts inflicted by His crown.

On this day lost in history, Matthew would remember the crowd of ruffians belly laughing as they mocked and taunted the handcuffed prisoner. Why didn't Jesus try to somehow get even?

THERE COULD HAVE BEEN a thousand unanswered questions going through Matthew's mind on that dark Jewish Sabbath day after the crucifixion of Jesus. In his sorrow and bewilderment, Matthew felt Jesus' cause was now lost. Being a follower of Jesus was over.

He would now need to make another start somewhere else, but where? If only the fog would lift and he would find out it had all been one bad dream.

By now someone else would have his well-paying job at the border of the country. He couldn't go there and demand his job back again. But what else would be left for him to do? Never had the outlook for the future been so bleak and gloomy.

Where was the power of the Jesus who had stilled the storm and angry waves the night they nearly lost their lives when crossing the Sea of Galilee? Where was the power He had over sickness and disease when He restored to health people with all kinds of ailments? Had it not come from a divine source after all?

No longer sure, his hopes were dashed to pieces. Only yesterday the disciples had seen Him die, watching from a place far enough away for safety. His broken body now lying in a cold tomb would return to the dust of the earth from whence it had come.

IF MATTHEW WERE THINKING BACK over his days of following Jesus as His disciple, he may have thought about his relationship with another one of the disciples, Simon the Zealot. Matthew had worked as a government official for Rome, while Simon belonged to a group that hated Rome, a bad combination in a team of disciples.

The Zealots had never accepted any foreign control of their nation and hated any Gentile power. As fanatic patriots, they had never resigned themselves to living under Roman rule. They were fighters for freedom, a little like armed guerrillas, ready and waiting for a signal from someone with authority, so that they could strike the first blows of a revolution to destroy Roman influence.

They especially hated the tax collectors, who were actually made prosperous by the hated Roman occupiers of their land.

It had been a miracle of grace that these two disciples, with their different backgrounds, each with an altogether different and clashing philosophy, should have such a strangely warm feeling between them. Simon the tax hater and Matthew the tax collector, who were now brothers in Christ, had put away their differences and became loyal to the kingdom of Christ.

Simon the Zealot learned from Jesus to love his enemies; Matthew learned to do unto others as he would have them do to him.

Did all this come about when they started to practice the Godly love that Jesus talked so much about? If all followers of Christ since those days became such disciples (learners of Christ with a true Christian love for each other), there would never have been splits and divisions within the Christian Church. The power struggles in families, in churches, and in communities, and even between nations, would be absent if all power and authority, instead of being abused, would be given over to God. Christian love begins deep within our hearts. An attitude of searching the Bible for direction and guidance, along with welcoming insights from each other, never fails to preserve unity in the Church built by Jesus Christ. Jesus used strong language to make His point: "The gates of hell shall not prevail against it!"

The Lost Day in History

THIS DARK DAY IN HISTORY marks the beginning of a new system in the order of the seven-day week as it appears on our calendars. This would be the last seventh day in most of Christian history to be considered a Sabbath, the day of the week when mankind is to rest and be refreshed (Exodus 31:17).

This would be the last Old Testament Sabbath. Nearly all of the future Christian Church would celebrate the first day of the week as the Christian Sabbath or the Lord's Day.

The first day of the week, which was the day of the beginning of Creation, and the day on which the firstfruits of the fields were offered in Old Testament days (Leviticus 23:10 and 11), was to become a special day for future followers of Christ. It was the third day after Christ's crucifixion. This first day of the week, the Lord's Day, would, in the future, be the day of the outpouring of the Holy Spirit at Pentecost.

The Jewish Old Testament Sabbath, transferred one day ahead, would become the Christian New Testament Sabbath. Just because the pagan sun worshipers also happened to have the first day of the week off, and called that day Sunday in honor of the sun god, does not tell us that the Sabbath change had its roots in the culture of the heathens.

To make this change, which was done shortly after the first Christians started to assemble for worship, and still keep the sequence of observing one day out of seven days, one full day has to be blacked out.

The blackest day in history, the final day of Christ's final week in Jerusalem accounts for that missing day. That day when God, the Son, was dead in His tomb, was that missing day of history. It was the day of the devil's short-lived triumph.

Most Christians since have fully accepted this change of keeping the first day of the week as their Sabbath as being perfectly Scriptural. To them, that one dark day was like the deep darkness that comes just before the breaking of a new day. By erasing that day from the calendar of history the cycle of one holy day out of every seven is still beautifully kept up. Beginning the week with worshiping our Creator is in harmony with everything else that Jesus taught while He was here on earth.

THERE ARE YET TWO OTHER MEN WHO HAD A REASON to be thinking special thoughts on that sorrowful day after the crucifixion of Christ.

The first one was Simon of Cyrene. This was the man compelled by the Roman soldiers to carry the cross of Jesus to the place of execution. Jesus, human as He was, was worn down from His sleepless night and the flogging and rough treatment. He could no longer get one foot in front of the other while the disorderly crowd was going out of the city gates.

The weight of the cross He was carrying caused Him to collapse. He tottered and fell. Where were His frightened and scattered disciples who could have used their strength to carry His cross for Him?

Did Simon from Cyrene, a far-off city in North Africa, get to Jerusalem a little too late for the Passover celebration of the afternoon before? How did he feel carrying the cross of Jesus? It was considered a great humiliation and very undignified and very shameful to carry the cross of a condemned criminal.

Simon probably remembered as long as he lived the day when he could lay down the cross and did not have to die on it.

THE OTHER MAN WHO HAD SOMETHING TO THINK ABOUT was Barabbas. The story of Barabbas, unlike the stories of many other people living in Jesus' time, is mentioned in all four Gospels.

Barabbas had been caught and put behind bars for disturbing the peace. In stirring up rebellion, he had committed robbery and murder. The Roman punishment for that crime was death with torture. If the trial of Jesus hadn't been held yesterday, Barabbas would have been the one hanging on the center cross as the leader of the other two criminals crucified with Jesus.

What would have followed the death of Barabbas on a cross would have been just as debasing. As was the custom, the bodies of the crucified Roman criminals were usually thrown in a pit and buried with the refuse of the city after being removed from their crosses.

Only the day before, Barabbas was in his prison cell not far away from where Jesus was standing before Pilate's judgment seat. He could well have been close enough to hear the shouts of the angry and uncontrollable mob: "Away with this man!" and "Release unto us Barabbas!"

In sickening horror he could have heard in still louder shouts, "Crucify him! Crucify him!"

When Barabbas heard the key turn in the lock of his prison cell door a short time later, we can believe that one frightened man fully expected his time to be crucified had come. What did he have to look forward to except excruciating pain and torment?

But the totally unexpected happened! He was released. Free! Someone else was to die instead of him!

Barabbas, the former terrorist, now had a new and unexpected chance to either go back to his old way of robbing, killing, and plundering, or to start all over again with a new and better way of life. As interesting as it would be to know what Barabbas did with his new lease on life and his sudden unexpected freedom, the Bible is silent.

THE QUESTION THAT COMES CLOSER TO HOME IS: What are you and I going to do with the freedom that is given to us because Someone Else has gone to death in our place?

EMMA STOLTZFUS

As human beings, we are creatures who can think and question—and wonder.

One of the first questions that came to the minds of all of us soon after we started doing serious thinking in our lives was, "How did it all begin?"

We learn of the Almighty God of Creation.

As we approach the sunset and autumn of our lives we are still questioning, "What is on the other side?"

As friends and loved ones leave us for that unknown land from which they will never return, we become aware more than ever that we are not here to stay. As we keep on working and waiting we realize that the sands of our time is also running out and the day is approaching in which we will move on. Our lifetime warranty will run out and we will never again be given an opportunity for another pilgrimage through this world.

Every day that dawns is one day closer to our appointment with our Maker, to whom we are responsible for the time we lived here on earth.

We may try to avoid thinking about that day, but the young know it *could* come. The elderly know it *will* be soon. We all know we have one less day today than we had yesterday. No one will live on earth forever.

Our hope is the Resurrection of Jesus Christ. If we can believe in the infinite power of the God of Creation, it is easier to believe in the unending mercy and love of the God of the Resurrection.

Chapter 17

God's Greatest Miracle since Creation

AN UNBELIEVABLE EVENT HAPPENED. The tomb of Jesus was found empty on the third day after He had died on a Roman cross.

The Bible verses telling about the early hours of Resurrection morning are not many—the quaking of the earth—the angel from heaven looking like a flash of lightning, rolling the stone away—the guards at the tomb shaking and falling down as dead men—the unbelief of the disciples at the first evidence of Jesus being alive again—Thomas, still an unbeliever and a skeptic until he was shown convincing proof about a week later.

But these and the multitude of other verses found in the rest of the New Testament about the Resurrection of Jesus Christ are the foundation stones on which the Christian faith is solidly built.

If Jesus was seen alive only when His disciples were gathered together, the Resurrection story could have been reported by the enemies of Jesus as nothing more than a tale made up by these remaining eleven disciples of Jesus.

However, before He ascended into Heaven, Jesus was seen alive on numerous occasions. Some of His appearances came to only one or two persons, while at one time He was seen by one group of over 500 believers (I Corinthians 15:6).

Not one single person of this group ever later refuted the fact that they had seen Jesus alive. Many later joyfully went to their deaths after suffering unspeakable tortures. This alone would prove to any court of law that the evidence was truthful and was not made up.

After He was seen ascending into Heaven, Jesus appeared to one of the deacons of the early church just before his death from stoning (Acts 7:55 and 56). Jesus appeared to Saul (later called Paul), who then made one of the most dramatic conversions ever known in the life of a human being, and to John on the lonely island of Patmos before he wrote the last book in the Bible.

All of these appearances were totally unexpected, because after Jesus died, His disciples had completely forgotten His prophecies that He would arise again on the third day. In Mark 9:10 they had even questioned among themselves what rising from the dead should mean. If His disciples had remembered and really believed His prophecies, they would have waited outside the tomb entrance to greet Him. All their grief and anxiety was unnecessary. They went through all this because they failed to remember and believe in the plain promises of their Master of His Resurrection.

The belief in a just and merciful God, and His promise of the Resurrection of the dead has brought joy, meaning, and fulfillment to the lives of thousands upon thousands of people who were martyred for their faith.

The belief or disbelief in the resurrection of both the just and the unjust has, ever since the time of Jesus Christ, had a powerful impact on which direction a person's life is lived here on earth—including your life and mine.

THE RESURRECTION OF JESUS was not a deception. It is understandable that at first not all of Jesus' disciples believed they were seeing the actual same person who was crucified only several days earlier.

This would have been a good opportunity for a false impostor to pretend to be the resurrected Jesus, but when Jesus showed them the evidence of the scars of His death—the healed nail wounds on His hands and the deep scar from the spear wound in His side—they all believed (John 20:20-29). No other living man on earth would be able to show such scars on his body.

He was known by His scars. The scars from the wounds that caused His death were still there. The disciples who had abandoned all hope now knew Jesus was alive. They could start to hope again, and they went beyond believing in the Resurrection—they *knew* that Jesus lived! Satan's victory had been short-lived.

Most of the people who had seen Jesus alive before He ascended into Heaven were to suffer torture and martyrdom later in their lives, rather than deny a divine Master they knew to have risen from the dead. They became such strong believers that they would die for their beliefs, and nearly every one of them did. Nobody would die a martyr's death for what they would know to be a lie and a fraud.

There is no way to explain away the story of the Resurrection. Even the chief priests who had instigated the death of Jesus indirectly admitted that the tomb was empty or they would not have bribed the guards for a cover-up. They had shouted they would believe in Him if He would come down from the cross. Why didn't they believe when He arose from the dead?

They paid the soldiers who had been watching the tomb "large money" (Matthew 28:12) to put out the clearly untrue and absurd report that the disciples had stolen the body while the guards were sleeping.

That story cannot be believed, because people who sleep cannot give true evidence of what went on while they were not awake! The made-up story of the disciples stealing the body while the Roman soldiers slept also contradicts what we know of the Roman law of those days. Any Roman soldier falling asleep while on duty was executed without further ado for such a lapse in upholding the stern standards of Roman military practice.

Roman law also provided a death sentence on anyone known to have been rifling a grave or tomb. Had the disciples stolen the body, the enemies of Jesus would have seen to it that they were all executed. The disciples did not steal the body of Jesus. In fact, in their distraught and mentally confused condition, they could hardly believe the first reports that Jesus was alive again.

There is no other explanation than that the empty tomb was a supernatural event. Unbelievers since that time may have tried as much as they could, but the evidence that Jesus arose from the dead cannot be explained away.

Because of His Resurrection from the dead, the Gospel accounts of Jesus are a world apart from the stories of the hundreds of other influential religious teachers who have lived and died throughout history, no matter how great their reputations.

No other religious leader since the world began would have dared to make the astonishing statement that he would be killed and then arise again on the third day after his death, and, when the time came, would arise and correctly prove his own prophecy. Only someone divine who could see into the future could do so; a mere man could not.

We have a religion founded not by a dead prophet, but by our Master who is still living. Jesus did one thing that no one else would ever be able to counterfeit. His Resurrection verified Him to be the true Messiah.

Jesus was the first and only religious leader who

could speak with a ring of authority about Heaven. He knew the celestial place; He had come from there. By rising from the dead, Jesus proved to mankind that death is a foe that can be defeated. By His resurrection, Jesus established the fact that the bonds of death are not permanent; they will be broken by the birth of a new existence.

Resurrection is a release from the grip of death and is a journey from a world of passing and changing where nothing lasts to the eternal world where everything lasts.

The Resurrection is like the hatching of an egg or the sprouting of a hard-shelled seed. Something will stir and waken the breath of life within. The shell will be broken and a new life will come forth.

BECAUSE JESUS WAS HUMAN, He had to die as all humans do. If Jesus were divine only, we would not have the story of His temptations, or the story of His distress of soul at the Garden of Gethsemane just before He was crucified. He got hungry and thirsty and He got tired. His death proved He was human as we also are.

However, without His divine nature, we wouldn't have His Resurrection on Easter morning. His Resurrection proved once and for all that He was also divine. Because Jesus was divine and was one of the three forms of the one Almighty God, He was destined to live on forever. That is why He arose.

We can also only marvel at the timing of His Resurrection. He could have returned to life as He was being taken down from the cross, but He would then not have arisen from His tomb. He could have waited until a hundred years later, but then the people who had known Him would no longer have been around and His Resurrection would not have had the meaning it now has.

The Resurrection of Jesus was also different from that of Lazarus who was suddenly awakened from a four-day-old grave by the majestic command of the Son of God. Lazarus was released from the throes of death, but his friends had to release him from his grave clothes (John, Chapter 11).

It is evident that Lazarus died again at some later time. Jesus, who will not die again, did not disturb the linen cloth wrapped around His body (John 20:4-9), but slipped through them as something like a beam of intense light.

UNLIKE THE OTHER GOOD teachers in history who die and are never seen again, Jesus returned from the grave with a message of hope and comfort for all mankind. The empty grave of Jesus is the birthplace of the Christian belief in immortality, or the endless existence of human beings.

In eternity there will be no dying that will ever again cut off our existence. We will wake up either at home in Heaven with God or in the terrible place God has prepared for the devil and his angels. In the time we are living, which has been called the gestation period of eternity, there is death all around us. Eternity will be endless.

The Resurrection of Jesus proved that death is not the end. Because of His Resurrection we can believe that the grave is not an eternal prison for us when we die. It is just a quiet resting place to wait for Jesus' Second Coming on the Judgment Day (Daniel 12:13 and Acts 10:42). It is a sleep from which we will be awakened (I Corinthians 15:52 and I Thessalonians 4:13-18) from what may not seem longer than a short nap. We will know eternity is now here!

A fuller understanding of eternal life and the Resurrection had to await the coming of Jesus Christ and His death and rising from His tomb. We now have what the people of the Old Testament times were not able to clearly grasp.

That they had an assurance of a life after death, even though sometimes somewhat vague and indistinct, can be gathered from some of the Old Testament verses such as, "I have waited for thy salvation, O Lord" (Genesis 49:18); "For I know that my Redeemer liveth…in my flesh shall I see God, whom I shall see for myself (Job 19:25, 26 and 27); "Thy dead men shall live; together with my dead body shall they arise" (Isaiah 26:19); and "many of them that sleep in the dust of the earth shall awake, some to everlasting life, and some to shame and everlasting contempt" (Daniel 12:2).

The verses telling of the deaths of Abraham and the other patriarchs tell us that God's people, even in the Old Testament, did have a hope of a life after death. King David, at the death of his favorite son, wrote, "I shall go to him, but he shall not return to me (II Sam. 12:23).

It is well-known that unbelievers hostile to Christianity do not admit to a belief in the Resurrection. "An unlikely story," they say.

However, just because no one in our day has ever seen a person who had been really proved to be dead come alive again, does not in any way discredit the divine Resurrection of Jesus. We read many stories about incredible and true *near-death* experiences people had and were then revived again. However, coming back and telling about an *after-death* experience after the point of no return has been crossed would be something else.

Jesus and His Resurrection and the future Resurrection of the dead at the Judgment Day is about an *after-death* experience, something in a category all its own.

We Christians believe that Jesus endured death and returned from it. His ordeal of coming to earth was over. He survived death and so will we. There is a life beyond the grave. Knowing about the Resurrection of Jesus, we do not need to dread death or the grave; we do not need to have dark forebodings of evil for the future. We can have a living hope in the Lord.

Christianity is a religion of joy. We do not need to mourn and grieve over a dead and fallen leader, but we can rejoice that He still lives. "Because I live, ye shall live also" (John 14:19), are the words of Christ, the Son of the living God.

The miraculous empty tomb on the first Easter morning makes sure every grave will be emptied on Resurrection Morning.

When Christians fall asleep in Jesus they do not perish. God will not return humans to the nothingness from whence they came. We will not be snuffed out like a lighted lamp into extinction and annihilation. When the flame of life here on earth is extinguished, it will be like a light we turn off as the morning dawns, because we do not need it when the sun is now shining.

In the same way, we no longer need a lamp in that land of much brighter eternal day. Christians can view death as a release from the cares and trials of their life here on earth. God has provided the comfort of a living hope of going through a door to something eternally better.

The only thing in Heaven made by man will be the healed nail and spear scars on the body of Jesus. Toil and tears, suffering and sorrow will then be over. Heaven will be a home at last in a perfect and everlasting future. We will be finished forever with the earth here, which we know to be only a temporary home for Christian pilgrims.

When we close our eyes here for the last time, we will never ever again see any of the earthly things we were used to seeing. Then will we know how miserable were our little treasures cherished here on earth. In the meantime, God wants us to keep on working, hoping, and praying. It will not do for us to continually watch the heavens for His Second Coming.

IT COULD NOT HAVE BEEN CLEAR after our first parents sinned how anything could be done to redeem the fallen race of man. God may have made the prophecies of the first coming of Jesus Christ unclear and not easily understood to conceal His plans from the devil. But God had it all planned, and in spite of the designs and schemes of evil men, His plans were carried out.

Even the devil must not have understood God's plan or he would not have sowed hate in the hearts of men, who then cultivated it and plotted the death of Jesus to keep Him from becoming a king.

Through the Resurrection, the scheming of the devil brought about an unexpected result, and redemption for repentant humans is now possible. Little did the murderers of Jesus ever suspect that in crucifying Him they were glorifying His name.

The great evil which men were able to do to Jesus was not enough to foil and frustrate God's plan. This all goes to show that sooner or later evil is always overcome by God's power. Hate and evil crucified Jesus, but God was triumphant when Jesus arose from the dead.

The whole of Christianity is supported by belief in the Resurrection. Without it, all of Jesus' teachings would fall into worthless ruin. Christian truth would be reduced to a gigantic lie. "If Christ be not risen, then is our preaching vain, and your faith is also vain" (I Corinthians 15:14), wrote the Apostle Paul. The scriptural teachings of the forgiveness of our past sins would make no sense at all if Jesus had not arisen from

His tomb. None of us would rest in the assurance of living in a better world after we depart from this one.

CHRISTIANITY IS THE INVINCIBLE CHURCH founded by Christ, on the Rock, which is the belief that He is the Son of God. The enduring religion that Jesus inspired is outlasting its enemies who vowed to destroy it, including the mighty Roman Empire, under whose shadow it was brought to birth. The first-century attempts to stamp out Christianity, on down to Karl Marx's atheistic and Godless Communism which threatened to put an end to all Christianity in our time, have all failed.

When Jesus predicted that His Gospel would be preached throughout the whole world (Matthew 24:14), it was probably the most unlikely statement that any prophet could ever make; but in our time it has come to pass.

This revolutionary new idea of Christianity, starting from such a hopeless beginning of the crucified Jesus, with all His disciples forsaking Him, has brought a colossal impact on the history of the world. The three-year ministry of Jesus has radically altered the course of history. The tiny band of Jesus' followers, after His Resurrection, took on the powerful Roman Empire and rallied on while the Roman Empire has ceased to exist. It defies human reasoning that there is now no corner of the globe that has not in some measure been influenced by those people who worship One who suffered capital punishment two thousand years ago.

The world is evil, and many of the things in our times and in church history such as the Crusades, promoted by so-called Christians, were not good. However, only God knows how much more evil the world would be today if we did not have the teachings of Jesus to help us resist the wickedness and evil that is threatening to take over the whole earth.

It is beyond dispute that the life of Jesus has influenced more good being done during these twenty centuries than anyone else who lived on this planet. His influence on moral conduct and His patterns of virtue, along with His lofty religious thinking is just what the world needs.

Jesus did it all without leaving any manuscripts or documents that He personally wrote. Despite the many histories written which refuse to admit that Jesus ever existed except as a legend or a myth, it is certain that something happened from which a new faith was born. Even unbelievers know Christianity is good for the betterment of mankind.

Many religious writers admit they "cannot prove or disprove" the miraculous events of the first Easter Day as recorded in the four Gospels, but it is clear to all that the changes made in the lives of millions of people following the precepts of the teachings of the four Gospels are nothing short of a miracle.

EVEN THOUGH THE WORLD LARGELY IGNORES OR REFUSES to accept and live out the teachings of Jesus, the approximate year of His humble birth has made a worldwide impact in that it has been accepted universally as a pivotal point in history.

The reckoning of the passing years on our calendars are numbered either "before Christ" (B.C.) or "in the year of our Lord" (A.D.). Even though B.C. and A.D. are being changed to B.C.E. and C.E. (before common era and common era) to avoid any reference to Jesus Christ, He is still right in the center of history. The numbers of the years in history books and on our calendars still indicate what has been figured out by historians as His birth year a number of centuries ago.

The world is still using the method of olden days where the elapsed time was reckoned in each country by the number of years the present king had ruled in that country. An example is found in I Kings 6:1 that reads "in the fourth year of Solomon's reign over Israel." With our system the world still unwittingly recognizes the reign of the resurrected Christ as King over the world.

Even an atheist who writes a book refuting the life and Resurrection of Jesus Christ is indirectly paying homage to the birth of Jesus Christ by dating it on the calendar system based on the King of the universe.

The worldwide celebration of Easter and Christmas every year, even though sadly too much for merrymaking and commercial reasons, is a result of the brief life of the humble Nazarene here on earth.

Even industry and commerce grind down nearly to

a halt the world over on the Sunday of every week. This is directly the result of the Christian Church keeping the first day of the week as the Sabbath in order to celebrate the Resurrection of Christ from the dead on that day.

Although the world largely celebrates the day printed in red on millions of calendars as a fun day instead of a day of holiness and rest, the origin of the Sunday Sabbath came from Christianity.

SURELY ISAIAH was right when he prophesied over 700 years before it happened that a child would be born who would be called, "Wonderful, Counselor, The Mighty God, The Everlasting Father, The Prince of Peace" (Isaiah 9:6).

He has been called "the King of kings and Lord of lords" and rightly so, because Jesus is more influential than all the kings, presidents, emperors, pharaohs, kaisers, prime ministers, dictators, monarchs, potentates, and governors put together in all of history.

THERE WERE SEVERAL HUNDRED prophecies in the Old Testament about a Messiah coming to earth, and this all came to pass. There are several hundred prophecies in the New Testament that He will come again.

This will also surely come to pass. All mankind will see something like they have never seen before. All the dead will be resurrected in time to see Jesus coming in the skies. Lazarus opened his eyes and the first he saw was the Jesus who had called him forth. So will everyone else who will be awakened from the sleep of death on Resurrection Day (Acts 1:11 and Revelation 1:7).

The clock that God wound up at Creation will stop. Time will be no more.

The first eternal Resurrection was when Jesus arose from the dead on the third day. Those humans, whose day of dying will happen only three days before Jesus comes again, will also arise on their third day. Everyone else who ever lived will also experience Resurrection and be judged by their Maker for what they made out of their God-given responsibility of their God-given life here on earth.

NOW LET'S SUPPOSE JESUS would come, and seeing we are not ready for Him yet, would agree to give mankind yet another chance before He makes His final ascension to His home in Heaven. What do you think He would tell us?

He would tell us of His longing to help, guide, and comfort us, preparing us so that we would be ready to go with Him when He would come again. In His divine form of the Good Spirit, there will be no place in Heaven or earth beyond the reach of His grace to those who feel they need it.

Friends, that is exactly what He has already done about 2,000 years ago! He came to tell humanity to prepare for His next coming. The closing verses of the Holy Scriptures fit exactly for us to think on while we are gladly expecting and looking forward to the Second Coming of Jesus Christ.

Even so, come, Lord Jesus.

The grace of our Lord Jesus Christ be with you all. Amen (Revelation 22:20 and 21).